The Complete American Fantasies

The Complete
American Fantasies

by James Schevill

SWALLOW PRESS
OHIO UNIVERSITY PRESS
ATHENS

Ohio University Press, Athens, Ohio 45701
© 1996 by James Schevill
Printed in the United States of America
All rights reserved

02 01 00 99 98 97 96   5 4 3 2 1

Swallow Press/Ohio University Press books
are printed on acid-free paper ∞

Library of Congress Cataloging-in-Publication Data

Schevill, James Erwin, 1920-
    The complete American fantasies / James Schevill.
        p.   cm.
    ISBN 0-8040-0989-9 (alk. paper). — ISBN 0-8040-0990-2 (pbk. : alk. paper)
    I. Title.
PS3537.C3278A17   1996
811'.54—dc20   95-36124
                                                                        CIP

Designed by Laury A. Egan

FOR MARGOT

Contents

Preface   xix

Introductory Poem   xxi

1920s
THE OPTIMISTIC FRONTIER

Berkeley Wildfire   3

White Woman with the Navajos   4

The Shining Dust of Scholarship   6

The Great Rock Quarry of Youth   8

Learning How To Read   9

Edmund Wilson in the 1920s   10

Marsden Hartley: From Maine To Europe and Back Again   10

Jazz-Drift   12

Listening in a Greenwich Village Bar, Joe Gould Scribbles Notes for his "Oral History."   13

The Country Fair of Childhood   14

Home Life of the Circus Dancers   14

Windowshade Vision   15

Fra Elbertus or the Inspector General   16

Hats and Ears for Charles Ives   17

Willa Cather in Red Cloud, Nebraska   19

Ma Rainey's Boilin' Rhythm   21

1930s
VOICES IN THE DEPRESSION SPARKING THE NEW DEAL

Wallace Stevens At Ease with Marble Cake   25

Hershey's Chocolate Kiss   25

The Artist of Escape: Houdini   26

Hank Snow, the Evangelist, Prays for the President   28

A Funeral for Hinky Dink   29

Jazz Drift II   31
  (1) Bird   31
  (2) The Risk of Improvising   31

American Gigantism: Gutzon Borglum at Mt. Rushmore   32

The Corn Palace in Mitchell, South Dakota   33

Trailer Dweller in Miracle Valley   34

Off the Sea into the Merchant's Life or the Search for Quality   35

Indian Summer   36

The Exterminator   36

The Connoisseur's History of the Bathroom   37

Old Salesman Planning the Fit of his Death   39

Parade at the Live Stock Show   40

Mr. Castle's Vacation Drive   41

Neighbors in a Coastal Town   43

Boy Watching a Light-bulb Death in a Country Town   44

The Old Woman and the Cat   45

Frontier Photographer: Summer W. Matteson   46

Frank Lloyd Wright Desperately Designing a Chair   47

The Big Room   48

My Father, the Scholar   49

Death of my Brother   52

A Dream of High School   53

High School Football Coach   55

Fantasies of Europe   56

1940s
WARS WITHIN WAR

Perhaps a Prayer   63

The Refugee and his Library   63

A Fantasia for Harvard   64

History Flowing around Harvard

At Plymouth Rock   71

How to Create Music by William Billings   71

The Peaceable Kingdom of Edward Hicks   72

In the Peaceable Kingdom a Man Sings of Love   73

Jefferson Dreaming about the Declaration of Independence   73

Ralph Waldo Emerson Receives a Visit from the Sane Man
and Rejects Him   76

Whitman Stock-taking, Cataloguing   77

Mr. and Mrs. Herman Melville, at Home, Isolated in Their Rooms   78

Horatio Greenough Writes of Reason   79

James Gates Percival Pleads for a Unity of Vision   80

In Nervous Motion: Charles Willson Peale   80

Emily Dickinson in the Asylum of Poetry   82

The Glorious Devil at the Dovecot:
Edgar Allan Poe and Sarah Helen Whitman   83

Out of History into the Army, 1940s

Limited Service, 1942   88

Marriage in Wartime   91

Song of Misgiving: Officers' Candidate School   91

In the Arena of Ants: German Prisoners of War   92

One-Eye and the German Prisoners of War in Colorado   95

My Wife's Dream in the Midst of War   97

Shanghai Stories   98

The Saga of Walter Schoenstedt and the Re-Education
of German Prisoners of War   101

ix

1950s
LIVING BLINDLY IN THE DREAM OF VICTORY

Family Fantasies after the War

A Guilty Father to his Daughter	113
The Momentary Glimpses of Women through Windows	113
The Shape of the Poem	114
Flesh of the Fawn	114
Death of a Cat	115
Girl Covered with Pigeons	116
The Watch of the Live Oaks	116
City Funeral	117
The Japanese Tea Garden in San Francisco	118
The Washing Machine Cycle	118
The Dream of Fathers	119
Youth and the Abyss	120
First London Press Conference in the American Campaign to Bring the Yo-Yo to England	120
Confessions of an American Viewer of the Large Screen	121
The Corporation Lady in Bughouse Square, Chicago	122
New York Subway Rush Hour	122
Mr. Martin in his Advertising Agency	123
An Astonished Listener Hears the Radio Announcer Bat Out the Long Balls of Verbs, Nouns, and Adjectives	124
The White Writing of Mark Tobey	124
The Painter Studying Trees Without Leaves	125
A Drip Poem for Jackson Pollock	125
The Abstract Expressionist Searching for the Angel Track	126
Graveyard Aesthetics	127
Jazz-Drift 1950s	127
Blues from a Thunderhead	128
All Day Driving Across Kansas	129

The Fury of a Midwestern Thunderstorm   129

Oklahoma Farming Song   130

Clown at Crafts Fair   130

The Alcoholic's Imaginary Dinner   131

The Confidence Man as Soap Opera Salesman   131

Co-Pilot to God   132

The Immigrant Tailor Stitches the Singer's Concert Dress 132

At the Mexican Border   133

A Tongan in a Tree in Utah   134

Buffalo Man at the Cocktail Party   135

The Newsboy Enters the Bar   135

The Traveler of Lavishness   136

Confidential Data on the Loyalty Investigation of
Herbert Ashenfoot   137

In the Blind Years   137

Wrecking for the Freeway   138

1 9 6 0 s
CHAOTIC CHANGES

Bashir Was My Name   145

The Executive and the Giveaway List   146

Old Barry, The Balloon Seller   147

The Buddhist Car   147

Huck Finn at Ninety, Dying in a Chicago Boarding House Room   154

Joyrider   155

The Images of Execution   156

A Woman Staring Through a Telescope at Alcatraz   157

The Graffiti Fingers of the Theology Student   161

A Fame for Marilyn Monroe   162

Specialty Barber in Beast-Heads   164

The Violence and Glory of the American Spirit   164

And: A Funeral Hymn for Ernest Hemingway 169

Last Words for Count No 'Count 170

The Scientist Surveys the Protozoa 171

What Are the Most Unusual Things You Find in Garbage Cans? 172

On the Burning of Mingus's Bass 175

Meditation on the New Space Languge 175

The City Planner: Catherine Bauer Wurster 178

Mississippi Sheriff at the Klan Initiation 180

The "Vulgarians" 181

In the Ginsberg Supermarket 182

The Dance of Theodore Roethke 182

Chaotic Changes 184

Passion and Divorce 187

Kristallnacht 189

Place 190

The Shapes Our Searching Arms 194

Green Frog at Roadstead, Wisconsin 195

At Frank Lloyd Wright's Taliesin, Wisconsin 195

At Packer Lake 196

Alone, In Another Lost Room 196

Love, Do Not Shun the Dark Gargoyle 196

Where We Were 197

1970s
VIETNAM AND
THE SPLINTERED AFTERMATH

On the Photographs of Torture in Vietnam 203

The Game-Master Explains the Rules of the Game for Bombings 204

The Terrorist 205

In the Theater of the Absurd 206

In 1970 in Madrid, President Nixon Presents General Franco
with a Red, White, and Blue Golf Bag, Clubs, and
Twelve Autographed Golf Balls   206

At the White House, Washington, D.C., 1973   207

The Money Man   208

Purchasing New Bicentennial Stamps, 1975   209

Song of the Little Official of Maybe   209

In Praise of a Diane Arbus Photograph: "A Jewish Giant
at Home with is Parents in the Bronz, 1970"   210

Illumination: Martha Graham   211

The Commuter in Car Tunnels   211

The Jovial Mortician   212

Apple, the Family Love and Asshole   212

The Broken-Field Runner Through Age   213

The No-Name Woman in San Francisco   214

Dumb Love   215

The Motorcycle Gang Honors the Newsboy's Seventieth Birthday   215

A Screamer Discusses Methods of Screaming   216

Gambling in Las Vegas   216

The T-Shirt Phenomenon in Minnesota on the Fourth of July   217

The Quiet Man of Simplicity: Robert Francis   218

The Flower-Washer in New York   219

Looking at Wealth in Newport   220

If God Does Not See You   220

At Whitman's House in Camden   221

Dog-Pack   221

The Mathematician Thinking of Ghost Numbers   222

The Mailman and *Das Ewig Weibliche*   223

Living in a Boxcar in San Francisco   223

Song of Aeterna 27 Over Los Angeles   224

Hog's Elegy to the Butchers   224

The Columnist Listening to "You Know" in the Park   226

William Carlos Williams and T.S. Eliot Dancing Over London Bridge
in the Arizona Desert at Lake Havasu   227

The Suicide Runner   228

Report to the Moving Company   230

At the Sin and Flesh Pond   231

Theatre in Providence and Washington   232

Taped Watergate Dreams of Success   235

Death of a Teacher   237

Obsessive American Sight   239

The Last New England Transcendentalist   239

The Boilerman   241

The Forgotten Wall   242

Fabulous Debris   244

On the Beach Watched by a Seagull   245

The Duck Watcher   246

1980s
THEORY OF AMERICAN GROTESQUE

Theory of American Grotesque   251

At Frost's Farm in Derry, New Hampshire   254

A Game Against Age   255

Remedial   256

Sitting on the Porch at Dawn   256

The Search and Discovery of Rodin's Nude   257

The Moon and the Beautiful Woman   257

Bouncing Vision of the Commuter   258

The Elizabethan Fool Applies for a Corporate Position   258

The Real Parader   259

Lookin' for Gas at the Youth Guidance Center   260

The Listener to Rock Above the Pain Level   261

Street Corner Signals   261

The Search for a Subject   262

The Strange Names of America   262

Uncertain Messages across the Country   263

The American Dream on Superbowl Sunday   263

Driving through Clyde, Ohio, 1985   264

The Gold Salvation of Oral Roberts in Tulsa, Oklahoma   265

Out of the City into Miracle Valley   266

Singing Madly   267

Wander   267

Island Time of Animal Sensibilities   268

The Muscle Memories of Ancestral Houses   269

Winter Peace   269

Madness   271

Indian Dawn in Gallup   271

Pasadena Museum   272

Reading Creeley's Collected Poems   272

Donkey at the Door   272

The Maestro Pickpockets in New York   273

In a Bar at Las Vegas, New Mexico   274

How Language Spells Us: A Sequence for Josephine Miles   274

The Sound Magician   277

The Hippie Shack under the Redwood Tree   278

Ronald Reagan and the American Soul   280

They Call Me "Football"   280

The New England Island Handyman   281

The Dynamite Artist   282

Postmodern Mixed Media   283

The Refugee Jewish Grocer and the Vegetable Forest   284

Looking at Old Tombstones in a New England Graveyard   285

At Writer's End: for William Goyen 285

Love as a Cubist Landscape 286

Love Song in Summer's Furnace Heat 286

Masks in 1980 for Age 60 287

1990s
TOWARD THE MILLENIUM

Naked 293

Professional Lover 298

Colleagues 299

Song of Old Age in the Driftwood Landscape 299

Ghost Translations 300

Invisible Wrappings 300

Iona Brown Rehearsing Vivaldi's *Four Seasons* 301

The Kitsch Market of Desperation 301

The Test-Pilot Speaks of Pushing the Envelope 302

The Horror and Joy of American Saturated Life 302

Creating a Beautiful Place 303

Old Aging 303

The HIV Positive Dancer 304

In the World of Sunsets 305

Last Urban Cowboy 306

The Actor of Covert Action 307

In the Culture of Cruelty 307

The Creator of Corporation Culture 308

A Woman Cutting on the Killing Floor 309

Homeless in the Gourmet Ghetto

Life of a Panhandler 311

Stork Lady Confronting the Demon of Dignity 312

Death of the Plastic Man 312

Singular Museum Woman   313

Street Corner Counterpoint of Homeless Voices   313

Sitting in a Bar in Election Time   314

Master of the Colloquial   315

The Distance of Aids   316

The Spirit of Mark Twain in 1993 Thinking about
the Mississippi Flood   316

Arguments in the Coffee House   320

Listening in a Raging Rain   320

Sanctuary of the Blue Heron   321

The Song that Floats   322

The Fragrant White Blossoms of Spring   322

A Final Fantasy at 75   323

Acknowledgments   325

Index of titles   327

Preface

In my sequence of American Fantasies, I have attempted to catch the *tone* of the country as I witnessed it during the major part of the twentieth-century. An impossible task, of course, better to stick to one's restricted environment. But, through circumstances of war, theatre, poetry readings, and teaching, I have wandered and lived widely throughout my country, traveling frequently east, south, and north from my western upbringing.

The sequence begins in the 1920s with the narrator's subjective voice. While these experiences are mainly my own, I hope that the narrator is enlarged beyond reality to give a mythical scope to the poem's structure. Throughout the sequence, his first-person experiences are contrasted with a variety of dramatic, objective voices who have shaped, or are shaping for better or worse, American cultural history. These voices have set the standards from which our particular democratic principles rise or fall. Sometimes, as indicated in the poem's title, the objective character assumes a persona, speaking in the first person across time. Sometimes the character is portrayed in a third-person form I think of as a poem-biography.

Fantasies to me, as I wrote in an earlier 1983 edition of *American Fantasies*, are the active, visionary links between reality and imagination as my characters pursue their destinies. Although we pretend to be a pragmatic, materialistic country, our fantasies, once suppressed by tradition, peer increasingly through the media into our private and public behavior. In this sense fantasies are not daydreams—they are the invisible and visible strands of our lives, the dramatic, often incredible images that dominate us, whose actions we pursue. As a playwright, too, I have struggled to restore dramatic characters to poetry, people who have largely disappeared as fiction, nonfiction and drama have usurped from poetry its narrative function. To fit the wide-ranging subjects of this sequence, I have employed a variety of traditional and experimental forms. If the sequence is the major narrative form of our time, it requires an unusual range of forms to project the special rhythms and unique quality of the characters' lives.

In the United States, as our fantasies move to condition us, we must move to separate the creative from the destructive fantasies, and I hope this book will help to focus that necessity in these critical times.

Always We Walk through Unknown People

Always we walk through unknown people
Guessing them; the click of meeting
Steps lightly into passing; our guess
Rides through curious air in a glance
Or grimace, an elusive grin;
To walk through faces, eyes, legs,
Arms, nodding necks, similar veins.
A peculiar pulse plods through flesh,
Pounding a rage of recognition:
That person I guess is somewhere me,
Somehow I walk in his difference;
This meeting sometime is our parting . . .
To guess him is our only greeting.

1920s
THE OPTIMISTIC FRONTIER

Berkeley Wildfire

At the age of three, wildfire baptized me, the Berkeley wildfire of 1923, Hildegarde Flanner called it. Wildfire baptism, strange, frenzied ceremony of removal and loss. No one believed smoke drifting over dry brown hills in pleasant noonday sunlight. Smell of burning eucalyptus trees caressed puzzled nostrils. Jagged flames began leaping, soaring into blue sky.

I never saw the firestorm gather, hellish center of eclipse. With my older brothers, my mother removed us from our hill-home to a safe haven south of the university campus. Alone in a canyon surrounded by blazing hills, our house was spared. Why? My father, founder of the university's Spanish department, built a large, redwood-shingled house on Codornices Creek (Spanish-named after the scurrying quail along the creekbed) in a canyon on Tamalpais Road in the Berkeley hills. Exultantly above the front door, my mother, artist and poet enamored of animal mythology, carved a frieze of lions inviting majestic entrance.

On the seventeenth of September, 1923, an abnormal, hot, dry wind blew westward over parched hills and high grass, negating the usual northeastern wind, clearing the daily fogbank cooling San Francisco bay. Ominous wind caused deceptive lassitude in brilliant air, seductive peace; bold wind fostering fire in a bone-dry land. Houses burst like paper flowers into ashes. From two to four on a tranquil afternoon, wildfire consumed sixty city blocks, six hundred homes. Only blackened brick fireplaces with scarred, startled chimneys loomed as misshapen, ironic symbols of destroyed fire-shelters. Twisted pipes protruded from burnt soil like grotesque sculptures. The city turned into a desert of ashes. Ashen-faced people staggered around searching through burnt-out memories for lost possessions.

Smoldering clear of the burning world, our house survived. The university dismissed students to serve as firefighters. My father and his courageous students patrolled the roof, wetting it down with buckets of water after the fire hydrants failed, warding off wind-blown embers as wildfire burned down the canyonsides, our fragile wood-house surviving like a puzzling oasis between two burning hills. That year the university joke was the large number of students my father gave quick Ph.Ds. My childhood years were permeated by wild-words, wildfire-stories, haunting wildfire-doom.

3

The survivor's triumphant guilt remains. Edmond Jabès says God's truth is silence. Is God's truth also fire? Burnt-out knowledge, poetry, and laws, a city-wide bookburning of private and public libraries. Yet my father's library remained, enabling him to complete his lifelong editing of Cervantes' complete work in the original Spanish. Threat and haphazard blessing of fire. Corneille wrote: "Fire that seems out, oft sleeps beneath the ashes." In that sleeping darklight, language often blossoms as fire, burning wildfire.

Fire of brain, body, eyes. Fire of growth. Garden fire of colors. Red goddess of death and resurrection.

Fire in the eyes creates vision, makes solitude endurable. Relaxed fire pulling us to the hearth for family unity. Intimate fire, lovely, every Berkeley home built around a comforting fireplace. The great Berkeley architects, Bernard Maybeck and Julia Morgan, loved to design challenging, imposing fireplaces.Watching fire soothes or kills. Amazing mercy: no one burnt to death in this consuming wildfire. Fire heralds spring growth, sacrificial fire bearing the ashes of redemption, slash and burn for fertile growth the way ancient civilizations heralded possibilities of new planting. Every time I witness fire even from afar I cry with wonder, wonder of wildfire.

White Woman with the Navajos

(1)
Many mothers rule us and they are not real.
They shine above the mountains in Venus stars.
They brighten the lucid sky with meteors,
Create the legends of mercy and justice,
Give us the myths of love by which we live.

(2)
In 1920, after persuading the conductor
To slow the train at Canyon Diablo
In Northern Arizona
Where it crawled on a trestle,
My mother jumped off with the mail pouch.

4

She was entering "the trail of song,"
Seeking the rituals of Navajo life.

(3)
In the Navajo world unity is based on doubleness;
Light and dark come together to make a union.
Animals are divided into day and night animals,
Possessions are called soft goods and hard goods,
Not our white concept of military hardware.

(4)
Sitting around a campfire with Lorenzo Hubbell,
My mother saw Navajos dance and sing their myths,
Emerging exultantly from the "lake of the soul."
She saw the waters recede; a dark, barren landscape
Emerged inhabited only by insects. Slowly,
Animals appeared as people, people as animals.
In the lower world, people transformed slowly
Into masks of men and women in the upper world.
As the barren landscape burgeoned in time with
Water and plants, the masked figures became
Gods, winds, and stars in the high world of sky.
Space was the floating center of the earth.
Gradually, as she watched, the spirits emerged,
The Hero, the Holy Twins, the Earth Mother
And the Sky Father, the Witch Woman,
The Wise Old Man, the Hermaphrodite, the Shadow,
The Monsters, the Guardians of the Doors,
The Spiritual Guide, the Friendly Animals,
Coyote, the Trickster, who keeps things changing.

(5)
She began her journey learning the difficult spirit
Who must start as a beggar to break the taboos
Of his people and become the medicine man.
Descending into the underworld, he must find
The treasure of knowledge, then climb
In humility into the light of the upperworld.
After learning the ceremonies and chants, he must
Pass them on in wisdom to a younger brother.
Death then frees him from life to live with the gods
In another world of eternal knowledge.

It is the double way of relativity,
To be radiantly divine and endearingly human.
She writes: "If there is a master symbol
For the Navajos, it would have to be
A perfect piece of turquoise, the brilliant
Light blue color of the desert sky at noon."

(6)
It is forbidden to represent the Turquoise Goddess.
Sometimes she hides in the center of a sand painting,
But when she enters the holy space the gods bow
Their heads, do not look up as she seats herself.
The invisible power of holiness must be respected.

(7)
If we enter the magic circle, perhaps
We can find ourselves at the center.
Entering the Navajos' holy space, my mother
Is transformed by touch of the Turquoise Goddess.
Her new Navajo friends teach her how
To make "an everlasting and a peaceful world."

This she cannot pass on to her children
Sentenced to death and the white man's wars.
Her knowledge of this Indian world
Cannot even bring her final peace,
Since as an artist she must battle the
Commercial world that will not honor her search
Into feminine mysteries, communal visions.

Yet as fire dancers circled the central flame,
She turned eastward to breathe in the dawn,
As myths of an old civilization tuned to
The wisdom of time, danced fervently
The promise of eternal renewal in the sunrise.

The Shining Dust of Scholarship

As a boy, I stared into my father's study
With awe and impatience:
"Would he ever come out to play?"

An immense long table for a desk
Piled high with books and papers,
Black, yellow-eyed cat who
Preferred my father to me,
Purring as paperweight
On top of father's page proofs.

Peering in, all I could see were
High-stacked bookcases everywhere,
Foreign language books with musty odors
Like a shining, diseased orchard.
"Why do you have so many dull books, Dad?"

> I am that man sentenced to study dullness,
> define historical time, and to discover
> in that process the real masters of imagination.

A couch more for reading and contemplation
Than for sleeping. Myself entering timidly,
Asking, "Father, what are you doing in here?
Are you playing with ghosts?" Small boy
Searching for a father, not a spectre of books,
Finding a gentle presence, ghostly eyelids
Flickering through historical distance:

> Beware, son. Ghosts are real beings,
> Books the white speeches they make.

(2)
What is the unseen, I learned, but that realm
Where ghosts gather in time for haunting,
Where white speech measures fame,
    And the scholar translates white speech.

A boy suspects the ghosts' triumphant knowledge;
He cannot hear their legendary white speech,
Languages of magical, archaic diction,
    Ghost revels in ancient penmanship.

I stare at your handwriting now, father,
To reach you I cross many continents
Through mysteriously inscribed gates of time,
    Embrace finally where ghost-languages unite.

7

The Great Rock Quarry of Youth

The great rock quarry
Of my childhood is filled,
And I know it is true
Time is forgotten, killed.

I ponder an idle fact
Over years filled with dirt:
The quarry produced
A crushed, red chert.

The chert formed streets,
My western city boomed
With houses around the quarry
Lost in time, doomed.

A high fence was built
To guard children's innocence
Lured by spectacular cliffs
Away from common sense.

But sometimes I remember
How we sweated in hot sun,
Afraid on the steep cliffs
In age-climbing we'd begun.

Up, up in the dangerous climb
With white, joyous faces,
Handing out friendly praise
And joking disgraces.

Slowly, the great rock quarry
Of youth fills with birth,
And age walks wildly
Over the rim of earth.

Learning How to Read

If reading is the art of sharing,
How does one learn to share
The trauma of changing, battling words?
All those romance languages my father spoke
Awed me so that I could only croak.

Schoolkid I sat silently in the back row
Neutral in the shared conquest of knowledge.
Teachers' pets all shined supreme in language;
Parrot words I heard sounded conforming cute,
Subservient to convention, grammatically neat.

An inward rebel, I sat stiffnecked, absurd,
Spurting occasional intelligence to get by.
Slowly, spurred by friends, I began to share
Outlaw books, adventure, and sexual search,
Words as emotions seemed more mysterious than church.

Wise enough to encourage and let me alone,
My parents floated words around me for shelter;
Slowly I began to hear language with wonder;
The art of comparison taught me metaphor and rhyme,
Poised me for passionate leaps into eternal time.

When my parents told me work, learn structure,
Before I ran wild, I knew they counseled wisely,
But most school structures were too boring;
One teacher wrote blackboard poems with a formal grip
In strict metres like an aggravating water-drip.

Reading, sharing, grew like a confused bonanza.
In 1929 at age of nine, language startled me
Through the stock market's boom and sudden crash.
I knew no rich men jumping out of windows in Depression,
But money-lure seemed the failed national mission.

9

Edmund Wilson in the 1920s

In a bright time, rent felt like spare change.
With everything cheap as sunlit flowers,
Money was not the defining factor.
All my friends talked eagerly about art
And walked around with an erection;
Since Freud had proved life was sex-driven,
At night women glowed like fireflies with desire.

Scott Fitzgerald thought that somewhere
Things were "glimmering," and the future
Burned like huge, blazing logs celebrating
A radiant campfire company; enclosure was
Not a word we liked. Over drinks, hot conversation,
We volleyed ideas at each other like tennis balls,
Enjoying life through an alcoholic glaze.

Behind us World War I was a bear-trap we'd escaped.
If a God forgiving sin seemed like an impossible idea,
Rational wit could provide its own social salvation,
And the spectre of military corpses lay covered forever
By a frenzied ocean of possibilities; we hugged
And penetrated each other with joyous desire
Like dancing bears escaping from years of oblivion.

Marsden Hartley: From Maine to Europe and Back Again

My blazing blue eyes. I saw, painted, wrote poems
As if specialization was not a cancer in the country;
Art and poetry, one blaze of rhythm and color.
In the 1920s we all cut out for Europe,
Hemingway, Pound, Eliot, and myself singing:
"B is for Bach, and all his noble sons,"
Only a few orphans left in the American wasteland.

Is the sense of an American artist to live, move,
And have one's entire being in the strictly

American atmosphere? Has not Europe always been
More friendly, more sympathetic to culture?
What makes the work of Eakins, Homer, and Ryder
So American is the style of truth they express,
Essential truth bursting out of confined experience.

Only unembellished and unadorned experience
Without all-too-familiar influences can create
A national style. The critics searched for pure
American masters, but all we felt was the flow
Of European energy. In reality I felt feeble-minded
With New York surrounding, confronting me.
How could I paint my American nature there?

Our American problem is excessive adornment,
Surface layers of sentimental exuberance
Carrying the false promises of easy democracy.
Maine, that powerful landscape and bitter magnet
Always drawing me back like an aging crab,
Loomed as a geography of challenging forms
Struggling against being confined to canvas.

Maine, my bitter birthplace, my mother's death
When I was eight ruined my sense of order and place,
Condemned me forever to ceaseless wandering;
Maine to which I was always forced to return,
Compelled by mountain and coastal stone grandeur.
I've been a summer refugee in green New England
For sea-calm and a renewal of artistic intuition.

But in Maine there was no community of ideas.
I wavered constantly between people and rocks,
Searching for the perfect solitude to paint,
Yet knowing solitary one cannot create,
The artist is made for phantom pursuits,
So all my sixty years, I hurried from country
To city without a home, hotels and apartments my curse.

Alfred Stieglitz was my passion and my peril.
Using his camera like an imagistic painter,
He helped me, featured me at his New York gallery,
But wanted to classify me as an American artist
Like his wife, Georgia O'Keeffe. Perhaps he was

Wiser than I thought; I wished only as Cezanne said,
"To paint that thing between me and the object."

Through the perverse belief that I could be a
New realist, I sought to locate the perfect landscape,
Only to find the invisible landscape of imagination
Is what one must paint. I wanted to live my way
As Albert Ryder lived his, inhabit a world of fancy
And stay out of the rest, no more horse-piss in a puddle,
Paint the enduring landscape of inevitable thought.

Jazz-Drift

(1)

Jazz-Drift, beat of night,
blues riding on the black voice,
floating chips of tone grating blood,
syncopated, eager beat of jumping beans,
trumpets, saxophones flaring,
exploding high, pounding through separations:

What did I do
to be so black and blue?

My black woman's face shines like the sun.
Lipstick and powder sure can't help her none.

When asked what makes a good blues singer,
Henry Townsend laughed and said, "Trouble,
that's right. That's the one-word solution. Trouble."

(2)

You've got to rhyme it up a little,
get words short and close in sound
like "ground" and "down," "town" and "now,"
let 'em flow through your ear
till you get a swinging, tight sound;
when your voice aches like the words
then you got yourself the blues!

(3)

If you've got a tight, aching
three or four lines,
you've got the right resistance,
cool, unwavering repetition:

Times is so tough, can't even get a dime,
Yes, times is so tough, can't even get a dime.
Times don't get better, I'm going to lose my mind.

Listening in a Greenwich Village Bar, Joe Gould Scribbles Notes for His "Oral History"

In a real church, remember, dear,
The rage for God requires gargoyles

> *

Lookin' down a sewer the other day,
I know we don't have roots, we have connections.

> *

I fancy a song singing like a full moon,
Not one that hammers rivets like a skyscraper.

> *

There I was, drinking, thinking of heroes,
Their round holes of nonsense . . .

> *

Whadda ya mean, stock market legends?
What goes up has to come down.

> *

Yeah, he's some boss, women padding along
Behind him with their pushcarts, while he
Wears halos like a mockingbird.

> *

13

The trouble with this city is
It ain't got no silence,
Only a raping stance.

The Country Fair of Childhood

Recall the country fair, memory,
Rough canvas tents stinking of manure,
Bright painted clowns laughing in
Evening lights, lights soft as silk.
In holiday clothes the town arrives,
Acrobats leap, the ringmaster stands
In limelight stance, rope hands of rule,
Voice thick and lush as Panama.

Return, cries the country crowd, return,
Flowing through popcorn and palmistry,
Through cunning sideshow barkers
Who know the whiskey spirit's spiny ways.
Return, cry my lost childhood friends,
Through comic horror of freaks,
The fluffy fat lady rolling her flesh,
Sword swallower, tinkling thin man,
Those lost oracles of the pythoness.

Return, oh return to the dumb show's
Ascension of awe and love holding
Within its glow our circus rhythm.
These, our tents, we have raised not for
The splintered eyes of confessed faces,
But to celebrate the Big Sky's lusty cover.

Home Life of the Circus Dancers

Home in the Henhouse or No Man's Land,
Seventy feet of a rambling railroad car,
The circus girls wear mules and snazzy pajamas.

Forty nicknames, family of the car mother,
Eat in shifts of six; and the cold front for
Miss Horse if she blooms into a borrow-body.

Meticulous the life of laundry—Little
White Cloud floats on a sea of wash, while
Princess irons for her friend, Blowing Wild.

On track dates after the show, they whip out
Folding chairs and tables by the car,
Listen with clowns to the record player.

When the train whistles, back to their berths
In their snazzy pajamas and nicknames, Smacks,
Streaky, No Pants, and Cheeseburger Cora.

As the train jerks away, the car mother rules,
Dog and pig-pets sleep, while in her Big Top berth,
Miss Horse pastes up white, waltzing wall paper.

Windowshade Vision

Often I dream I have windowshade vision
Like Maurice Sendak, artist of children's books:
"I sat in my grandmother's lap while she
Amused me, raising and lowering the windowshade."
Slowly, my long-dead mother raises the windowshade,
Takes me on her lap, and we stare out the window
At fog coiling through an enormous bay tree.
She tells me stories of Coyote I do not understand,
Coyote transforming himself, eternal trickster.

As a boy I confuse Coyote with Christ, twin magicians
Who transform the landscape with resurrection images.
I raise the windowshade to reveal the rising sun.
My mother moves through time and religions,
A nervous ghost seeking impossible sanctuary.
Behold how the windowshade curtains of our eyes
Flash up and down, disclosing pieces of memory,
Fractured America in which we struggle to make
Our god-visions into new, magical revelations.

15

Fra Elbertus or the Inspector General

Silky, flowing hair,
Colorful cravat flaring open like the first flowers of spring,
At age thirty-six he abandoned the traveling profession
            of soap salesman
To become a rooted "Inspector General of the Universe."

Farewell to fancy
Buttonhooks for button shoes, farewell to the salesman with his
Sniffer of perfume, celluloid collars, and kerosene lamps.
            The world of print
Lured like the Flying Dutchman on a mysterious sea.

He settled at East Aurora,
New York, prospering in the 1890s by publishing
Proper, wise sayings, an aura of diligent words
            a practical country desired.
He established proud periodicals, *The Philistine* and *The Fra*,

Magazines of uplift,
And printed 170 chapbooks called "Little Journeys,"
Embracing a new, moral frontier of international celebrities
            from Confucius and Christ
to H. J. Heinz and *A little Journey to the Home of a Great Dentist.*

"Take the train for East Aurory,
Where we work for art and glory," wrote a dedicated employee;
Where the great were spirits close as flowers and grass;
            where visitors sawed fire wood
And meditated on the saying: BE KIND—BUT GET THE MAZUMA.

In the industrial dawn
He revered the pastoral doctrines of William Morris, domesticating
The machine, making it seem likeable, a welcome friend,
            taming the crafts
To suit the social pressure for a cozy parlor atmosphere.

A master of innovation,
He supported everything new, trying it at least once
Before racing on to the next exciting possibility:

                    feminism, yoga,
Mary Baker Eddy, New Thought, the healthy Medicine Ball.

                    Though prim about sex,
He created the Topless by allowing his son to appear
Stripped to the waist in a Grape Nuts advertisement;
                    a father of Public Relations
He wrote a Credo for The Loyal Order of Moose.

                    If The Master of Publicity,
Like The Master of Religion, can transform an eager public,
He earned the titles of Friar Albert or Fra Elbertus,
                    sensing romantic glamour
Wears always the spectacular trappings of religious tone.

                    His real name, Elbert Hubbard,
Faded away as he opened the country, reduced it to practical sense.
As the Inspector General of New Glory, he drowned
                    with a drowning age
In 1915 when the *Lusitania* went down, and the real wars up.

Hats and Ears for Charles Ives

I want to make a music with its own ears.
Let the ears remain inconspicuous, at attention,
Sounds penetrating through them into the body's flesh,
Causing the brain to glow burnished with detailed music.
The ears, the ears, from hearing comes soul-knowledge.

The ears of New England sing a joyous peace
Remembering the pleasure of Sunday's raucous noise,
My father in his bright bandmaster's uniform
Playing "Jerusalem the Golden" in the town square
While on neighboring roofs and verandas, musicians

Answered with contrapuntal variations and refrains,
The echoes combining bold secular and sacred worlds,
Uniting a country of democratic promise and desire,
A wilderness land awaiting the immigration rush
That pushed feverish America into ethnic competition.

17

Growing up in Danbury, a hatters' town,
Families worked at home at their own pace,
Shaping practical cover as well as hats of pride;
Then simple hatters turned into Hat Manufacturers
And factories grew with masks of anonymous labor.

The town burst into banks, Savings Companies,
Messages of insurance invaded my head.
I made my wealth by selling life insurance,
Seeking to make it a beneficial science by
Showing men the statistical nature of security.

What I began is now called "Programming"
Or "Estate Planning," figures as machine thought.
My mind full of Emersonian optimism, I wrote:
"As the raindrops falling together make the Rivers,
So men seek common life together for a season . . ."

Discovering that politicians mired in pride are
The chief cause of war, my mind moved to social democracy.
As politicians defend the nature of large properties,
Is not the fighting done by men of little property?
Thus property becomes the red axe of division.

In my lost Danbury town I danced with the group,
Music and hats as the colorful, measured ceremony,
But in New York condemned to the isolation of size,
After work, or weekends, I wrote endless notes on paper
That I could hear only in sharp imagination.

Such sounds are heard by animals in cages,
Listening vainly for a glory of space through bars.
Great minds hang in isolation like vultures
Circling above lost unity with fixed dreams,
Lustful country buzzards above decorous masquerades.

In the concert hall, I sit quietly dreaming music and hats.
When they boo my music, I sit like a rigid patrician,
But if someone boos the music of my friend, Ruggles,
I shout: "You goddarn, sissy-eared mollycoddle,
Stand up and use your ears like a man!"

18

Like Emerson I wish to be an invader of the unknown.
Is not music like an insect buzzing, whirring?
Can it not strike like a clear bell or distant thunder?
In my old age I wear a broadbrimmed campaign hat
To preserve the ears and hats that make a country dream.

Willa Cather in Red Cloud, Nebraska

In summer we begin to live, our small, crowded houses
Open to hot wind blowing through them with sweet smell
Of large gardens flowering in fragrant, spicy odors.

>   In summer the flat land wakes to the horizon.
>   Dust floats back from the slow wagon-wheel,
>   Yellow corn tassels up in lush green dreams,
>   Wildflowers mirror high, sparkling stars.

My eyes are haunted by waving prairie grasses
Whose sensuous names lick at the long sky,
Switch Grass, Buffalo Grass, tall *Indian Grass,*
Grasses honoring pioneers, lost communities.

>   In summer we praise our town's unity.
>   Everyone paints white picket fences;
>   Cottonwoods flicker little yellow leaves
>   As we strut down streets unafraid of mud.

Winters confine us to home solitude, survival prayer.
Families become pressure time for privacy.
I work in Dr. Cook's old drugstore to earn
Exotic wallpaper for my attic room
Where my childhood fantasies can flower.

>   Slowly I learn how to make plain objects
>   Into simple words, direct language cutting
>   Sharply into the center of unruly life,
>   Singular voice masking complex sexuality.

I am one of the first writers ever
To recognize male spirit in a woman's body,

19

The woman's sense of justice overpowered
In man's new world of farm machines.

    By high school I know who I am,
    How I want to live my life. I wear
    Boyish clothes, hat, starched shirt,
    Tie, refuse to be called Willa,
    Prefer Will or Billie, grin with delight
    When friends call me Dr. Will.

Infrequently, a magical man or woman appears
In Red Cloud, who reads Shakespeare or the Bible
Aloud for soaring images and uncanny rhythms,
Transforming the everyday search for literal facts.
Most of our good townspeople are worn hard,
Leathery from weather, long monotonous workdays,
Backbending agony of farming that grassland
To flower one day with tractors and harvesters.

    When there's a rare cultural event I gape:
    Blind D'Arnault, the Negro pianist, playing
    "Musical gems taught by the finger of God!
    Three airs at once! He is a Wonder!"

I dream who is the Wonder, Blind D'Arnault or God?
My desire to write knows I must leave Red Cloud.
Our agricultural success leaves no corner for beauty
As commercial greed washes out sensuous grace,
Cuts, parcels the land into the isolation of money,
Security's masked illusion of independent power.

    Leaving Red Cloud, I know I will never leave.
    No matter how many cosmopolitan cities I visit,
    Nebraska looms like a lantern beckoning my eyes.
    Successful as an editor in New York's steel towers,
    Respecting my cook, Josephine, or in my small
    Maine summer cottage, vacationing with my friend,
    Edith Lewis, guarding the essential tranquility
    The lost country returns with its immigrant dreams.

My phobia about fires, my oddities of masculine attire,
My eccentric refusal of a bathroom in our summer cottage,
My desire for privacy against neighborly intrusions—

All increase accusations of haughtiness against me,
Conceit of literary fame. The illusion of American fame!
I endure guarding a boiling cauldron of memories.

My only aim is bare words with a redemptive feel,
The restoration of wonder to our immigrant memories.
In that wild, open land I name vanishing places,
The Silvery Beaches, the Uttermost Desert, escaping
From boredom in my home to the Huge Fallen Tree.

Red Cloud, my crucible. my obsession,
The sunrising paradox our childhood homes create
Shining lost through time's furrowed patterns of change.

Ma Rainey's Boilin' Rhythm

Damn right, that old title, *Ma,* sucks,
They wanta stamp me a home-puddin' Mama,
But that pushy little white scarecrow reporter
Interviewin' me called it "Ma for Mountain,"
And I kinda liked that. *Ma Mountain* is
What I had to be, standin' cold before
Those agents and producers who run me wild.
They like to use me hot for singin',
Then chuck me out like a used-up whore,
But you can't chuck a mountain so easy.

When they talk, I shuffle like a big snail
Back and forth, oozin' along in my music.
I pretend I don't flow, only my music flows.
What the hell do they care so long
As I open my big mouth wide to sing
And out comes gravy mixed with gravel.
I gotta sound nobody heard before,
It took me years to pour gravy over gravel.
Then tired folks in clubs began to listen
And stop their fidgety, restless chatter.
Ma Rainey began to get the hush of respect.

"Shut up, and listen to Ma with the big black
Bottom, she's turned into a southern institution.

She's got those huge tits large enough to nurse
Every southerner with down and out blues.
She sings blue milk, that old momma
When she starts to waddle off stage
Speakin' so mean, pretend you don't hear her
Cussin', cussin' as if she were a boss-man."

Didn't you never hear a mountain cuss?
If you've rested your ass in a black toilet
Or tried to drink from a fountain marked
Whites Only, you'd plan your life like a
Tough mountain too. Way I look at it, I give
Up my life to a mountainous voice, makin'
Folks listen to the sound of trouble, but
Black trouble ain't like white trouble,
Black trouble got boilin' blood rhythms
That make you bleed your ass breakin' out.

1930s

VOICES IN THE DEPRESSION
SPARKING THE NEW DEAL

Wallace Stevens at Ease
with Marble Cake

Last weekend I spent the afternoons
Sitting in my garden at home,
At ease in a solitary situation.
I drank a glass of White Burgundy
And watched my neighbor's pigeons.
A black and white is an old friend
I call Marble Cake. Sitting near him
With a little Kraft's Limburger Spread,
Pouring myself a second glass of decent wine,
That big, fat Marble Cake moves around,
Strutting, keeping his sharp eye on me,
Doing queer things to keep me awake.
Marble Cake, my fat Pigeon Master,
Teaching me the drift of imagination at ease,
How the grace of sound reflects
A still point in time dancing in the light,
Where imagination reveals its proud presence
Transforming the commonplace into points of brilliance.

Hershey's Chocolate Kiss

What's more American proud than candymaking?
Aiming at it big-scale I learned to pour molds,
How to make hard penny candies, dipped sweets,
And *French Secrets*, with messages hidden in the wrapper:
"Roses are red, violets blue, sugar is sweet, and so are you."

I failed at candy in New York, Chicago, Denver, New Orleans,
Writing new failure maps in rushing economic gloom.
Switching from caramels to chocolate, my life began to hum.
I dreamt white cows, pure milk from green pastureland herds,
Of plumping down my sweet chocolate factory
In open country land safe from urban filth.

25

Over forty, a wound-licking bachelor, I married a
Bouncy, pert Catholic girl who made me laugh,
Catherine Sweeney whom I called "my Kitty."
We laughed a lot until we couldn't have children,
But that didn't stop her. We started an orphan school
For boys, lost foundlings, financed by a chocolate community
Humming country rhythms, summer crickets chirping in grasslands.

Everybody said I was crazy to leave rich cities,
But, driven by a dream of chocolate independence,
You can't sweeten it up in stinking smokestacks.
My wife and I aimed to create a new chocolate life,
But she caught sick, died young. I lived on lonely,
Trying to help my workers build their own town
That somehow earned the name of Hershey.

I told my people our religion is the Golden Rule,
Benevolence must stand up to hard work, loyalty.
Still they called the first strike against me in 1937
And that ended my benevolence. Good will don't
Go anymore. Labor unions want their own power.
They want their committees to run everything.

Here I am dying at eighty-eight, alone with a
Chocolate fortune, thinking it's easy to make a mold
For a rectangle bar; it's easy to stamp your name on it
With pride, but you've gotta be a lucky bellringer
To create a chocolate kiss that sweeps the world!
All I did really was marry chocolate to the country
And watch that marriage surge up fresh into a kiss.
When you shape 'em pretty and wrap 'em glittering in
Silver tinfoil on every store counter in America,
Europe coasts in, kissing back your chocolate kiss.

The Artist of Escape: Houdini

> Magic of the savage
> As Frazer showed is always practical,
> Translates mute theory into action,
>   burgeons crops,

Brings rain and bouncing deer to the net,
                    beauty to the dance,
                    a blessing on barter.

                    Born in Wisconsin,
He was circumcised with the name, Ehrich Weiss,
Son of a rabbi fled from European bigots,
                    a sober, humorless boy
Who learned at eleven the touch of lockpicking
                    with a tumbler-clicking ear
                    and a poking finger.

                    To eat well,
He endured the cracked rules of compromise,
Slaving in dirty cabarets and dime museums,
                    roaring with lust
As a painted Wild Man in the Tent of Freaks.
                    Next to the Bearded Lady
                    he longed for magic.

                    He succeeded as
Conjuror, a short, stocky man summoning illusion
With fast, agile fingers, a conscious fool of grace
                    who took
The imperial title, Houdini, crying at trick's end:
                    "Will wonders
                    never cease?"

                    Trained wonders
Were not magic; he yearned to be the artist of escape.
Handcuffs were easy, boxes and coffins more difficult,
                    but prisons loomed as
Awesome concrete walls frozen over the eye of logic.
                    Freedom was a spirit,
                    not a lock.

                    In the supreme test,
Contemptuously he broke unarmed from a steel "carette,"
A Russian police cage designed for transporting prisoners
                    to Siberia.
Throughout the world, jailers watched complacently.
                    Prison was an idea
                    beyond escape.

At last he
Wanted to set in the sky a sense of logical magic;
He stormed to expose the spiritualists' fakes.
              A French scientist
Reported that spirits were warm with hairy heads.
              Science was a spirit
              beyond illusion.

              All his life
He sought to prove, when the deer of magic leaps,
A body trained by reason performs the baffling dance,
              but died when
Enthusiastic fans hammered his unbraced stomach,
              acts beyond
              the reach of reason.

              After his death
He was buried in time with the heroic monsters of legend,
The poisonous spirits seeping from Pandora's Box,
              who jeered
The master of rational mysteries forced at last
              to rest under
              supernatural skies.

Hank Snow, the Evangelist
Prays for the President

Let us pray for the President in this time of Depression.
Let us pray he will do the right thing for the unemployed.
Let us pray he will work to right the economic ship of state.
Bismarck once said: "A statesman must listen until
He hears the steps of God sound through events,
Then leap up and grasp the hem of God's garment."

I pray that our President will hear God stepping
Through city traffic bedlam, frantic stock market,
All those typewriters clicking below screaming planes.
Let's all pray for our President to listen for
God's footsteps ringing through this alarm.

28

And when our President responds, perks up his ears,
Let's pray that our leader and our great country
Will soar up and hang there in God's heavenly sight,
Ride safe and high in the sky on His golden hem.

A Funeral for Hinky Dink

At Hursen's Funeral Home
on Chicago's South Side,
under the polished glass cover of a bronze casket,
with five thousand dollars
of sculptured ornaments,
Hinky Dink sleeps in the turmoil of the forgotten past.

Master of the First Ward,
the Loop, and near South Side,
his tiny pumpkin shape, five feet four inches short,
ruled a roaring time
on dollar cigars
as fifty luxurious years folded up and rolled away.

At twelve an orphaned newsboy,
he sized up the city
from cold corners cut by icy flares of Lake Michigan winds.
At twenty-four he owned a
saloon with upstairs dice game,
the gambling lure of Chicago Democratic politics.

All his life his Front Man
was a Turkish Bath rubber,
a handsome stud called Bathhouse John, a tower of muscles
shouting loud, bell-like
words of pompous strength,
rung by clearthinking tones of the musical Hinky Dink.

As elected aldermen,
they ruled with benevolence
over the bawdy paradise of the feverish First Ward,
Little Chevenne and *The Levee*,
flop houses and peep shows,
bordellos jangling with jazz piano players and hoofers.

29

The benevolence was beer
in Hinky Dink's saloon,
The Workingmen's Exchange, foaming in fine mugs,
gleaming with two handles
twenty-eight ounces full—
and free lunches handed out lavishly to the poor.

While Hinky Dink poured
free-flowing suds,
Bathhouse John led the Grand March at their First Ward Ball,
flowing in green cutaway,
with high silk hat,
mauve vest protruding colorfully over lavender pants.

Hinky Dink was a sober man,
(his wife a temperance worker),
and he knew the rule that a favor was good for a favor;
for a job or recommending push
the payoff was votes
and often subtle bribes under the table of benevolence.

Mayors came and went, dancing
to the tune of Hinky Dink;
the law grew cross-eyed under his quiet, benevolent stare,
this gimlet-eyed small man,
shrewd and feared
throughout his empire, the Honorable Michael Kenna.

Death honored the Front Man.
Smothered by funeral flowers,
Bathhouse John was eulogized in a crowded church,
while Hinky Dink lived on,
his power sinking
beneath the machine-gun heavy weight of prohibition gangs.

Retired in hotel rooms,
attended by a male nurse,
alone with a couple of million dollars in the bank,
and the dozen dollar cigars
he smoked every day,
puffing slowly, frantically, against diabetes and age.

At his official funeral,
the church was half-empty;
as the organ loudly engulfed the Priest's mumbled Latin,
only three carloads of flowers
whitened the dark church,
compared with seven carloads brightening walls for the front man.

Greasy Thumb and Loud Mouth
sent their condolences,
and a ward heeler sighed: "Poor Hink retired too long.
If you don't go to funerals
and pass out flowers,
you won't see·expensive bouquets celebrating your funeral."

Jazz Drift II

Duke Ellington: "I don't listen in terms like modern jazz. I listen for those individualists. Like Charlie Parker was."

(1) *Bird*
Listening for take-off, he grew wings,
Measured out distant notes of space
Which his saxophone could sound.
Cool synthesis, *mocking and bird,*
In a time of absent birds, he brought
Bird-cries to steel-clanging cities,
Sounding the missing image of flight.

"I'm blowing high, turning into a queer bird.
I blow all the instruments into bird-song,
Sing you mockingbird songs that hurt and soar."

Where is the song of a man-made bird?
In those smokefilled rooms, some crazy nights,
Clean and polish the air, flying bird-man of song.

(2) *The Risk of Improvising*
Duke Ellington: "Do you know the diference between worry and concern?
Worry is destructive, but concern is a thinking mind solving a problem."
Out there *improvising*

31

we have to be anticipating,
we can't be worrying,
have to swing into each other,
hit the beat just right,
keep jamming and soar,
take off from the center,
let that tone soar high
as you can fly.
If you don't risk nothing,
you're gonna be nothing.
Risk begins when
you think about it with concern.

American Gigantism: Gutzon Borglum at Mt. Rushmore

"Why should not art be as big as mountains?
Think, if you can, of faces the dimensions of
A five-story building carved into a mountain peak,
Clouds folding about them like a giant scarf,
The moon glowing, half-hidden behind a lock of hair.
If Bartholdi can create a giant woman,
Her torch summoning America to liberty,
I'll wave to her grandeur jauntily and cry:
"I have a feeling, old girl, my giants on
Mt. Rushmore will outlive you by a million years."

In Jefferson's eye, often two men work together.
A mole in Lincoln's face is sixteen inches across.
Celebrating freedom, a monument must be colossal.
Every facial line requires gigantic imagination.
When President Roosevelt dedicates Mt. Rushmore,
I want a plane to circle overhead and drop down
Little parachutes, each with a flag and mountain chip.
Frank Lloyd Wright writes to me, "You are a
Sorry old warrior—all scarred up and bleeding grandly."

Learning how to blast a mountain gently with dynamite
Is like learning how to stroke a porcupine's back;
And getting congress to appropriate money is like

Lobbying squawking seagulls flying over a ship.
To tell the truth, I get a little weary of doing
Colossal works—then I enjoy making busts of friends.
But the mountain looks down at me in my dreams
And I know a big head is not like a little head.

Size is what space must always respect.
I cannot match the mountain's lofty grandeur,
And that's why I let my son grow up carving mountains.
Someday I hope someone will say I had a genius
For the small as well as the colossal,
But when you've lived to carve a mountain
Which only wind and rain can wear away,
After your death that massive monument rises
Through dawn and sunset like an eternal sphinx.

The Corn Palace in Mitchell, South Dakota

Staring dumb-struck at a true American corn palace,
I gape at red, white and blue Byzantine domes towering
Over yellow corn panels rumbling with buffaloes.
Every year the brick main walls are redecorated
With three thousand bushel-mountains of corn,
Grain, and grasses leaping in natural colors,
For which taxpayers fork up 30,000 dollars.
Every corn cob is soaked carefully, sawed in half,
And fitted with precise fingers into the right design,
A true corn tribute to Indians hunting buffalo,
Wagontrains traversing the Great American Desert,
Crazy, dogged homesteaders settling, farming
The desert into a dream of the world's breadbasket,
Earning for themselves a Corn Palace of entertainment.

The greatest entertainers in the world played here,
Every name from John Philip Sousa to Duke Ellington,
Even Rayburn's Variety Girls who brought a flavor
Of that old hot hootchy-kootchy. When he saw the town,
High and Mighty Sousa wouldn't leave his train, protesting:
"What is Corn Palace? Are you people aware that
Sousa's famous band commands a healthy fee, cash down?"

Corn Palace stared at him with silent scorn and money
Changed hands in hidden style as it does in America.
Walking gingerly through mud, Sousa dirtied his
Fancy button shoes to play his rousing marches,
Starting the imperial reign of Corn Palace. All right,
Corn Palace, as its rulers say, is "a little bit of everything,"
But we built the country in a wild combination style,
Jumbling together foreign fantasies with American
Dream images of democracy shining in cornfields.

Trailer Dweller in Miracle Valley

Seems like in hard times poor people have to move,
Follow the Star of Hope into a quiet place.
Sure, these western names are a bit spectacular
Like Chariot of Fire Drive, but that's
Just because it's a place where God lives.
In every desert there's a Miracle Valley
Where the cactus wren pecks past thorns
And Holy Water flows out in sweet concern.

Sitting on my trailer steps, reading my Bible,
I know we read strong words into true world,
Real Hell-Fire shines out of God's syllables.
His breath is so powerful it singes His beard.
America's the land where poor folks move on
In search of God's fiery eye. Can't you see, it's all
Writ down by His moving finger, and read
By us trailer folk moving out of the Dust Bowl.

All you need to create your own Miracle Valley is
Learn how to read the blazing way God moves.
If we was meant to live locked poor in city slums,
He wouldn't write no sunsets to move us west.

Off the Sea into the Merchant's Life or the Search for Quality

Off the sea into the merchant's life is
No way to go; it's got no quality.
I don't care if you sell a fortune of goods.
It's like the old shepherd's staff, crooked,
So I became a big merchant of secondhand books,
Running a racket like the rest of them,
A lunatic business, only my racket don't pay.

My momma had a breast as big as a watertower
For me to suck on forever; she thought I was
Going to be God the Doctor, Lawyer, Intellectual
Like her pet Rabbi, but I came to fancy systems
Open at both ends, nothing closed in secrecy.
So I never went much for religion, I don't care
What faith, they're all a Jack-In-The-Box world.
They want to tie up your nuts, Jack, in the box
And shut the top so you've got a closed bottom.

The only way out is to pop up like toast in a toaster
And squawk to Old Daddy Skin of Wrath in the right
Tone at the right time. I never knew the right time
For nothing. Back home all the Pittsburgh mommas
Wanted me for their daughters till I was caught
Naked in a black whorehouse in a police raid.
After that I was a colored Jew and shipped to sea
For thirty years, thirty god damn long years
Staring off the stern of dirty, lousy freighters
At the phosphorescent wake, wondering was
That the way life drifted, little bubbles of presence
Vanishing into the pressure of endless waves.

Son, I've failed so many times my teeth chatter,
My false teeth that is, I chattered the real ones
Away long ago. I hope I've got a little quality left.
It's a poor, abstract word, but what else is left?
I've got an ancient Mother-In-Law I should hate,
But she's dying with quality, she don't whimper,
She don't complain even though she's Christian
And had to get used to a Jewish son-in-law.

Stuck here in this store with hundreds of dusty shelves,
I think quality's like a secondhand book.
You gotta be tough to survive the lonely time,
The rot, greasy fingers, the isolation when
Nobody reads the bareassed lies on lost pages.
Quality's when you take it down into sunlight
And you stare at it, crazy-like, to find at last
If there's a real piece of you left in the wreckage,
A real piece of skin covered with blood
That shines and endures in the dark of your life.

Indian Summer

Sometimes in chill fall,
Winter approaching,
Warm air floats across America,
Causing memory to stir
With frontier dreams.

In dawnlight,
The plains grow hot,
Buffalo shadows stalk the grass.
An autumn flare
Disguises winter death.

Indian ghosts stand
Staring in displaced weather.

The Exterminator

I invade cheap apartment houses, 1920 dingy style,
Owned by absentee landlords who enjoy rental profits.
Early mornings I saunter down dark corridors of
Dirty brown paint, scuffing faded, red carpets
Glittering with worn-out dreams of former wealth.
I start pushing doorbells with prohibition slits,
Where suspicion stares out at fear when I ring.
In my loud voice I call, "It's the Exterminator!"

And wait for the long pause, letting the words sink
Deep until they recognize it's only The Cockroach Man.

I catch them in all crazy, waiting positions,
Lovers waking in bed, housewives with frizzled
Morning hair, pale lips before the paint of recognition;
Old men with their teeth out planning toothy smiles;
Yelling kids with toy guns and planes already at war.
I spray their garbage cans, run my hose up through
Broken plaster to liberate their walls with my poison.

Some people don't like my early visits, but they need me
To stink up their places, keep 'em free of bugs.
Sometimes I get a cup of coffee from a widow
Who keeps her pot steaming hot for gossip.
She talks about her life's rhythm which has no beat.
I'd like to tell her some about the way of cockroaches
Crawling in the walls around her, the complex way
They love to multiply, how they die in my strong perfume.
But all I do is smell her cheap scent, listen to her chatter,
Sitting there drinking her lousy coffee in my clean,
White uniform lettered with my name, *The Exterminator*.

The Connoisseur's History
of the Bathroom

My bathroom has a fireplace of white brick,
Sliding glass walls and a lovely carpeted floor.
I live there in seclusion like a sybaritic hermit.
The glass walls open outside on a terrace.
As I sit in my black terrazzo tub, I watch
Luxuriant orchids grow behind the dressing table,
And remember other familiar, classical bathrooms.

The Greeks and Romans thought of the festival bath,
A center of sublime conversation, rejuvenated spirit,
A leisurely soaping and steaming in public baths
Provided by thoughtful tyrants. Christianity taught
Man was sinful if he removed his heavy clothes,

Hence scorn of the bath as Satan's lurking temptor,
And hiding of that room in dark shadows of necessity.

Believers in ornamentation and aromatic bath elegance,
The lush, invading Moors horrified devout Spaniards.
By the 18th century, the bath was "convertible,"
Disguised as an inviting *chaise longue* for the aristocracy.
But a Queen could indulge her private privileges:
Marie Antoinette's bath, wrote Mary Gray Humphries,
Glowed with a tub room paneled in marble,
"Fed by swans whose necks and heads are of silver."
Behind the tub hung a mirror "painted over
With lovers pelting each other with flowers . . .
Mirrors were set in the ceilings, like crystal lakes
Upside down amid garlands of flowers."

In the 19th century plumbing brought new elegance.
Scarcely was there a workable toilet; instead, a sculptured,
Porcelain dolphin held a conveniently shaped shell
In its teeth. Petals and roses gilded the washbasin.
Bathtubs were hidden in copies of period furniture.

By 1903, the century turned proudly to progress.
The *Woman's Book* proclaimed: "The exposed tub and
Exposed plumbing all make for health and cleanliness."
Happiness too, concealment resolved, bathrooms
Finally freed from pleasure to health rooms.
In 1908, the Statler Hotel in Buffalo advertised:
A BED AND A BATH FOR A DOLLAR AND A HALF.

As we build our way out of the depression,
The modern tendency is back toward the elegant bath,
Glass-enclosed tub in gray mosaic tile, radiant heat
In the floor, bright towel ladder, handsome wall boards.
Usually, it is men who insist on ornate bathrooms.
A terrifying thought: the bathroom has replaced women.

My bathroom designer says, "People are mad for cherubs,"
And so I have them dancing on the wall next to
The counter basin with foot pedals instead of faucets,
Which leave my hands free to pluck at bright yellow towels.
My clothes hang from a hook designed as a jutting peacock's tail.

My melon taffeta shower curtain guards the floor
And the mirror walls are lit with incandescent bulbs.
I think of an old party jingle:
    "Come into my bathroom, Maud,
    The plumbing Cranes have built.
    There let us carouse with guilt.
    Come into the bathroom, Maud."
My wallpapers tend toward the mildly naughty.
This is the place where I forget I must wear clothes,
And nakedness shines across the room with its lost grace.

Old Salesman Planning the Fit
of His Death

Sitting here dying slowly, I want smallness,
Think of one fence post, not the whole fence,
The hang and weather of that special post.
When I open my closet I want to see
One suit of clothes sparkling alone
In the right set of buttons, hang of pants.

When I was young every gadget I sold
Grew bigger, more ambitious in dream
Until I woke up sweating managerial
Visions, sweating bigness and booze.
I could set any catalogue on fire with words.
I believed the integrity of advertising words
Could help to create a great, growing country.
Once, at a convention, a thousand salesmen voted
Me the biggest sense of language in the business.

Evenings now I just sit on my porch, listen to crickets,
Listen for simple sounds, watch the Evening Star,
Try to find with my dog a quiet relationship.
Days gardening, I search for the perfect shape,
The one brilliant flower, as time cuts money
And power ambitions down to grace of smallness.
When I die, I want every small thing left to fit.

Parade at the Live Stock Show

In lazy light, dust drifts over the small town,
Where the summer pose of life is parade,
        hullabaloo prance.

The proud Grand Marshal leads, fat owl's face
Puffing cigar next to the high school Queen
        in her cardboard crown.

Bounding bantam rooster, the home-
Painted Indian swings his silver tomahawk.
        "Big Chief from Hong Kong,"

Jeers a barefoot girl with laughing, nasal joy.
Christ rides in the Catholic Ladies Float,
        crucified on flowers;

Beneath the cross, a thin, pale boy reads
From a Giant Bible, his stiff, white shirt
        illuminated by roses.

A grotesque, comic fire engine, river-curved,
Flows to spray the School of Scottish Dance
        dancing Scottishly.

In high-button collar, with derbies, canes,
"Two Business Men from Nicasio,"
        push a toilet marked

CURB SERVICE, and, gleeful, lift out beer.
In a small town the formations are loose
        until night edges

Main Street with soft, deepening shadows,
And late, lonely, the sweepers sweep up the
        horse dung with huge brooms.

Mr. Castle's Vacation Drive

Humming a virtuoso vacation tune,
Fancying himself as the owner of fluid time,
Mr. Castle drove south on the coast highway
Ignoring the sign, ROAD CLOSED BY SLIDE.
Along the two-lane road blasted from the cliff,
He stared down happily at long ocean views,
Free at last from routine of office work
Where he drew precision as a designer,
His labor the deft re-modeling of stores,
Interiors of supermarkets, shelves arranged
Cleverly for tempting cans to caress the eye.

At night, relaxing in his bachelor home,
Mr. Castle dreamt of naked men ideally muscled
By Renaissance painters, chained to trees
Beside the sea with its maternal hissing,
Promethean forms stretched on granite cliffs.
"It's not that I hate women," he assured himself,
"But in a purely decorative society,
Fascinated by the glittering surfaces of change,
It's easier to live where everything can be
Arranged in terms of masculine order
And neatness, no messiness of sexual births."

As he drove on, fog settled over the mountain range
Until the sudden lights of bulldozers
Grinding at the riotous rock startled him
Out of his fantasies and he stopped abruptly,
Gaping, in the middle of the vanished road.
High on their bulldozers masked behind goggles,
Two burly men dug into the rock and pushed it
Over the cliff, pounding down on the beach below.
Mr. Castle paused to admire the experienced deftness
Of their machine handling. He ran to the guardrail
By the roadside and stared, entranced at the
Avalanche of tumbling rock. Down, down,
He peered and heard a sudden, muted wailing
Like distant dogs whining in isolated hospitals.

Staring deep, he saw through swirling fog
Some wounded dots where bouncing rock had

Smashed some sea lions waddling to mate
On the rocky beach. The rest of the pack
Had withdrawn upshore; their barking echoed,
Rising in indignant protest against the wailing
In a cruel counterpoint of injury and shock.
"A tragic disaster," mourned Mr. Castle.
"What a pity, such a tragic accident!"
Turning, he fixed his eyes slowly on the powerful
Drivers enthroned on thear roaring machines.

At last the bulldozers finished their passage
Through the slide, and the drivers stopped, wiping
Sweat from their eyes with huge, red bandanas.
"Hey, Bud, you're free!" An enormous arm
Waved at him from the sky. Leaping gladly from
His confinement, Mr. Castle drove through
The narrow canyon in the rock and stopped
To wave his thanks to the grinning drivers.
He saw them pass a whiskey bottle from hairy,
Muscular arm to arm, and was surprised to hear
His light-belled voice say in sudden protest:
"Too bad about that flock of sea lions below."

"Can't be helped, dad," snickered a high giant
Over his hand wiping whiskey from his mouth.
"It's a tough shit world for men, daddy,
We clear the coast for traveling fairies."
The last in drunken mockery with an obscene finger.
Speeding away from sacrificial whines and barks,
Mr. Castle felt an angry shock expand as the
Blood of recognition flowed through his body.
He pressed the accelerator down, sharp,
And felt a surge of hatred overcome his reason.
Driving faster, faster, over the dangerous road,
He saw the windshield flare with visions of women
In childbirth creating the chained gods of the world.
As the car shrieked rubber on curves, he dared himself
To crash and heard the glaring, naked bodies
Of gods howling in agony like wounded sea lions.

Neighbors in a Coastal Town

Next door
in a shingle-sliding house,
paint curling off like worms
              in their crawling pace,
lives the neighbor whose guts I hate
              with his miser-face.

His house
is a jungle of mice and junk,
and he means to cut my property value
              with his ugly mess
of broken furniture, decaying wood,
              nothing to bless.

In the morning
he stakes out his property line
with a tall, imaginary fence;
              I feel barbed wire,
though he only hammers sticks in the ground
              with eyes of fire.

His little head
sits on his neck like a grape,
and the rags of his clothes fill with dirt.
              To treat him mean
I give laughing parties for my friends;
              he watches behind a screen.

I think he was born
to live a hermit's isolation
and serve himself with trembling hands,
              trapped in a shell
of darkness where cold air blows
              no saving church bell.

But every time
I look at him with hate he changes;
his shoulders sag, his head sinks,
              he decays with his house,
as I paint desperately to keep my house alive
              and set traps for any mouse.

43

Boy Watching a Light-Bulb Death
in a Country Town

Tight to an old man's shack
I smoke, watching his light
Burn speech into silence.
His bulb blazes just
Above his skinny reach,
Bright, round, a naked glow
Hung from a butcher's cord,
Some kind of execution show.

That stingy oldster, his messy house,
Make me shifty, angry,
I don't know how to help, just stare;
I watch his light-bulb death
Hating that lonely glare,
Knowing he lies invisible below
The glaze he never shuts off in sleep,
An old puzzle, stiffening slow.

One winter night, his long cord
Wavered, swung, cracked.
He lashed the light up and down
As though it were a whip
Attacking enemies in the town.
Somehow the bulb stayed weird
With light, flaring wildly through
Shadows that soared and disappeared.

When the light stopped swinging
And stood still, I wanted to hope,
"Maybe he's dead or blind at last.
It's just a light now
Burning up something past."
But I keep on watching the light,
Growing older in my room,
Learning a different kind of sight.

The Old Woman and the Cat

White hair spiky in the wind,
Deep eyes set in dried-out skin,
She lifts the full bell of her skirt,
Out pops a cat like a bloated balloon.

"I'm pushing ninety," she says with a push,
"I got that old cat down by the road.
He was slung against a tree like a tin can
By a truck making time for the city.
His pelvis or something was broke,
That's why his stomach hangs down."

As she speaks, she feeds him a sandwich
While scraps of fish smell up the porch.
"I never saw a cat so round," I say.
"Is it only a broken pelvis?
You sure you're not feeding him too much?"

"Yeah, I can't stand that busted cat.
Last winter rain poured through my roof
And I set out plates to catch the water.
Pretty soon there's food in all the plates.
I don't know how that damn cat gets it.
There's nothing to do in this town,
But watch that cat lap water up
And gorge himself until he dies."

Muttering, quivering, she walks in the house
And comes back with two cans of cat food.
"I'm not staying another winter," she says,
"It rains too much for an old woman here.
In the city I could ride around on a bus
And talk to people on the telephone
Instead of watching this busted, old cat."
With a blue-veined hand, she scoops out food,
Stoking the cat's impatient greed; his tongue
Licks out, and his yellow eyes shine
As his stomach of death sags on the floor.

Frontier Photographer:
Sumner W. Matteson

In 1900,
I go with the new technology,
bicycle, and proudly gleaming
Kodak portable camera
    with roll-film.

I pedal away,
test my lonely strength in the West
by photographing strangers and scenes
exactly as they look,
    precision pictures.

Photography is
not yet an art, only a new-born
vision like a child's stare,
capturing innocence, or evil's
    sudden revelation.

I capture
the essence of communal time:
ladies gossiping in markets,
a water carrier caressing his jug,
ritual fear of rattlesnakes
    in haunted caves.

How I exult
at the task of honest recording!
Like an ancient scribe with perfect
penmanship, I show twelve-horse freight teams
    on wilderness trails!

I portray
sacred Indian dances in Montana—
The Grass Dance, The Fool's Dance,
The Giveaways, last rituals of
    dancing societies!

Peddling my bicycle
furiously into desert clay, distant sunsets,

my forbidden bisexual desires rise and
flow daily into the vast impersonality
        of western space.

Finally, I photograph
my mocking bachelor self in a cistern
near Mesa Verde, Colorado, naked, safe,
luxuriating in water up to my beard,
        naked feet, muscular legs

spread apart under water;
holding the snakelike, pneumatic tube
between my thighs, I squeeze
releasing the shutter to preserve
        my voyeuristic stare.

Here I lie content,
naked reporter of the new machine,
ironic voyager escaping from money minds,
hardworking immigrants creating
        the new capitalist world.

Or was I born
anonymous quicksilver in vanishing time,
snapping the flash of frontier visions,
images that once disappeared in the night,
        and now shine on?

Frank Lloyd Wright Desperately Designing a Chair

Sitting is an
Unfortunate necessity.
Everyone knows
Reclining is the
Only attractive
Posture of relaxation.
So I will not let you relax!

Let us all sit
Straight at attention
Enjoying the requirements
Of eating and conversing.
With good talk
Flowing into our ears,
We must not sag
Or slump into disarray.

Between contempt and desperation
Rises the vision
For designing a chair.
As you sit in my chair,
Entering the world of desperation,
On guard against contempt,
You encounter the
Clear, sharp lines
Of my design,
Sit ramrod straight
With the angels of necesssity.

The Big Room

(1)
Believing in a radiant, visionary time
When imagination rides on spectacular wings
Beyond the confined pride of small-scale art,
My stubborn mother conceived and built an
Extraordinary living room she called the Big Room.

"When the community dances, everything comes
Alive," she smiled, "but it takes a Big Room.
In a small room you can hide, my son,
But in a Big Room you must observe
How the community connects. In the end
You will find that the minimal glows in
Time's mirror only as a lovely, minor image."

Spying on the parties in the Big Room as a boy
Through a peephole in a gold Chinese Buddha

Fixed tranquilly on the balcony wall,
I peered down, fascinated, at the dancing guests.

All those people dancing around in impossible joy!

Transformed in the foot-tapping
Thrust of that rhythmical music,
I heard my mother whisper exultantly:
"Anyone who is afraid of wonder
Dares not enter the Big Room! This Room
Attacks the common, restricted possibilities!"

    (2)
Older, I remember the Big Room aspiring
To a jubilant sense of communion, the pressure
Of light through majestic, high laddered windows
Revealing the moon in a star-fused sky,
Eager dancers flowing below in joyous bursts
Like an enchanted white-rapids river.

Still, the Big Room questions me:
"Can you sing? Are you a natural phenomenon?
Can you perform magically in my presence,
Present yourself as a paragon of movement?
Can you see yourself as a strong shadow
Following masterly motion without being mastered?
In the Big Room can you dance with others into
The impossible rhythm of happiness?"

My Father, the Scholar

    (1)
One morning, annoyed by my father's retreat,
I pushed open the closed door of his study
And accused him angrily, "Father, why is your
Library piled so high with so many dull books?"

Hurt by that accusation, he answered slowly
In a sad tone that I did not understand:
"I am that man sentenced to study dullness."

49

Is not a boy sentenced to search for excitement?
A poet destined to the search for exaltation
Even if living in a time of dogged materialism?
Is a scholar sentenced to study dullness
As the paradoxical opposite of creativity?

"Scholarship is for those with shovels," wrote Mark Van Doren to John Berryman. *"You're a man of the pen, the wind, the, flying horse, the shining angel, the glittering fiend—anything but the manure where scholars have buried the masterpieces of the world!"*

Here speaks the ironic Double,
The poet to his scholarly self, delighting
In the reflected mud of scholarship,
Yet great scholarship flourishes
Close to the critical stare of creativity—
Coleridge, Arnold, Schiller, Unamuno—
Poets and critics both taking from manure
The illuminated roots of redemption
Growing fiery through terror into light.

(2)
San Francisco: 1937, during the Spanish Civil War that foreshadowed World War II.
I wait for my father to speak in a waterfront union hall filled with huge workers smoking, laughing, drinking, shouting. To my awed teenage eyes, every foot wears a heavy shoe, every muscled arm can bend an iron bar or smash a nose. Speaking to these men is like addressing lions—where are the words that snap like a whip?

My father, the distant scholar, has turned into an activist. He heads the West Coast Committee for the Defense of the Spanish Republic attacked by General Franco's military insurrection. With Fernando de los Rios, Spanish Ambassador to the United States, my father is to speak in defense of the Republic at this rally sponsored by Harry Bridges' longshoremen's union. To my startled eyes these longshoremen are the champion weightlifters of the world.
Suddenly, my father and de los Rios appear on the stage. No! They're trapped in formal tuxedos! I gape in terror. In formal dress they look like stiff dolls standing lamely before roughly dressed demons. When they speak surely straw will spurt from their mouths! Instead, the restless workers listen to passionate appeals for democracy, unions, civil rights, peace in Spain. De los Rios condemns Lorca's recent murder by Franco's Civil Guard, the impending threat of Franco's military dictatorship. Brawny workers stand cheering, passing the hat for donations. Abruptly,

50

to me my father's absurd rented tuxedo becomes Don Quixote's armor attacking the windmills.

Later I learn that the absurd tuxedos are on their way to a formal civic dinner to raise money for ambulances for the Spanish Republic. I begin to understand my father's unique dedication to Cervantes and the cause of Spanish freedom; why my father wrote at the end of his Cervantes biography: *"Spiritual poise and the triumphant heroism that greets the unseen with a cheer . . ."* My father marking the scholar's stance in his absurd tuxedo; my father to be blacklisted for these efforts by the Un-American Affairs Committee.

"Clothes are only a costume, son, to create the role you must play in the theatre of life."

Running blindly to maturity in sweatshirt and jeans, I could learn only by experience the white speech of ghosts. Now, in dream, I walk with you, father, through the Prado staring at Goya's Black Paintings, the dark fantasies that rule our destinies. I hear with you the ghostly voice of St. John of the Cross protesting against death, *"Muero que no muero."*

"Spanish, my son, is the language of romantic opposites, the balance of cruel death against redemptive death in the double battle in which eternal life is the goal.

My father's romantic stance transforming dull facts, five feet four inches tall like his hero, Don Quixote, blending honor with chivalry, where the difficult discovery of brilliant, sane words shapes the insane battlegrounds of history.

(3)

My father's voice singing through library dust,
Summoning us to the visionary scholar's task:

> *"Breaking the seals of forgotten boxes,*
> *I search darkening, lost pages*
> *Of unknown poets. So many puzzles*
> *As if history consists only of rages*
>
> *For order, violence assaulting peace,*
> *Creating a complex, formal mystery;*
> *The art of learning how to feel*
> *Through the knowledge of how to see.*
>
> *I sit at my table in time's historic dust,*
> *Puzzling out the dull, demanding facts;*
> *Watch, slowly rising, dust's dancing lesson*
> *Trace honor's enduring, defining acts."*

Death of My Brother

Today, I still see him, real ghost.
He was twelve-years-old that day
In 1924 when he died suddenly
From influenza's searching virus.

Although I was only four, I remember
A kind shadow indulging my antics
In the garden, as he quietly observed
The look and flight of every canyon bird.

The day he died he was sitting up in bed,
Joking, laughing, his tousled hair waving
Over his forehead, our doctor optimistic
About his recovery, his fever lessening.

If his death had been more violent,
Not so peacefully quick, perhaps my mother
Would have suffered less. She could not bear
To bury him after he was duly cremated.

Instead she kept his ashes in a box
That the mortician presented to her,
Hid the box in a corner of the dirt-floor
Basement near the furnace as if for warmth.

Years later, my boyish, poking curiosity
Discovered the box, presented it to her,
Demanding to know this box's contents,
Triumphant in my search for treasure.

My father intervened, and she buried,
Reluctantly, the box, buried my
Brother's sweet spirit in a cemetery
Grave next to her selected site.

Still, the image of a puzzling box
Springs out in my dreams, and I see
My brother's youth confined there;
Death, the harrier, closing a fatal box.

In dream, my mother still confronts
That box, perceiving it contains forever
My brother's living, unfulfilled spirit,
Youth's promise locked safe in a box.

A Dream of High School

Still a boy-man, you think you're a man. High school because you're
reaching high, stretching between adolescence and college. The inbe-
tween world is wandering purgatory, you're neither up nor down.
Wandering inbetween.
I learn how to wander by car. At sixteen, I learn how to drive from my
remaining brother, Karl. He drives up the steepest hill near our house,
stops halfway up, gets out, says, "You drive." Under his furious com-
mands, I almost strip gears as the car jerks uphill. Still, I'm learning es-
cape routes, commanding the car exuberantly, youthful illusion. Best of
all, I command the car to high school; father likes to walk to work.

Long corridors of wandering
And all those required courses—
Everywhere I walk
I search for a girl,
But my face is too pimpled
And the ones I like feel
They're too old for me.
The bright kids are the ones
With a knack for finding
A secret corner to smoke in.
An unwritten law states
Don't stand out in class
Or you'll be too conspicuous.
Borrowing the family car,
I drive by school several times,
Hoping I'll be noticed.
If I can't find a parking place,
Sometimes I just cut school
And drive to the movies with a friend.

A thousand ambitions tug our high school eyes, conditioned by films. In
pre-television time, I lose myself in luxurious sweep of Baroque film

53

theatres. Films are palaces, not video mini-dress. . . . Every film promotes romance, touting the right look, upward way of life to wealth, or "the terrible power of fortune." In high school I'm a blotting paper for films of powerful fortune, tuned to fantasies offering pleasure of escape from confining classes.

Yet high school is where I learn to live beyond the racial barrier. One-third of this Oakland school is black. Many years later the Black Panther movement will emerge in this building, transformed into a community college. A high school dreams of unity, not racial separation brought about by suburban growth after World War II. In the 1930s we're lucky to have art programs that are the first programs eliminated in later years for economic reasons. If high school is not a training for the senses, what is it? Reading, writing, arithmetic require sensual training too. In high school you learn to live together, or discover isolation is an evil eye. Wandering and wondering time. My high school trains student teachers for the University of California. We rapacious students have an instant test. Like tigers we wait for apprentice teacher to enter the classroom, write his or her name on the blackboard. With back turned, a volley of spitballs results. If teacher shows fear, hostility, undue confusion, forget this profession. Cool is when the teacher turns, as does one former baseball player, and hurls spitballs deftly back. If teacher is able to joke, transform crude behavior into disciplined respect, that's *Cool*. From black friends, I learn the origin and broad meaning of that curious word, *cool*. Learning how language flows despite well-intentioned, bland teachers struggling to cope with large classes, aggressive, needy kids. Teachers marking time of long, repetitive hours, boring time, education chopped into quick fixes, where the quickness doesn't fix. My senior English teacher times his own poems in strict, conservative metres, marking out rhythms on the blackboard, turning the flowing blood of poetry into boredom. Unfortunately, I turn away from him, losing the possible sense of tradition that he might give me. I study music, voice, sing in a church choir to help pay for voice lessons. In an increasingly specialized society, how can I learn that the musical voice is the poetic voice? Wondering time.

Learning names, races, habits, moods, advantages of public schools over private schools which my parents wanted me to attend. I wanted the public world, not the private world, so I forced my parents to consent to public school. Sometimes I curse my choice, confronted by the whirling mass of immigrant names seeking American recognition, suspicious, assumed names, names of beauty, names of ugliness, fractured, melting pot names struggling for unity. I learn to be careful when I open my lunch bag. Someone may insert shit in your sandwich as a mocking joke, or warning against an outsider trying to muscle in. Cruel jokes as hope or death-wish of high school gangs. I learn costumes, clothes of conformity, indifferent, casual look. The right sag of clothes I learn from sports. Basketball is my game. Despite my bad, myopic eyes covered with thick, hornrimmed glasses that break easily, I am a good outside shooter, so I make the junior varsity team in my junior year. But I don't stay long. Glasses broken constantly are too dangerous. No plastic goggles in those days. The surge of black athletes, playground-tuned to tough play, is beginning. If I can't play, I can still cheer, love sports. The age of legendary coaches is beginning, our lunchtime talk praises winning teams, ambitious coaches who will do anything to win.

High School Football Coach

How to fire up my players—
When I see a guy sag in my locker room
I yell, "Son, you've gotta get fired up!"
Then I just reach down for a little frog,
Grab it, bite its head off . . .
The player's eyes get big as saucers
And he jumps up with a head of steam.
Trouble is then all the boys bring me frogs
And I have to say, "Naw, boys, no!"
My players and I, we scream and carry on.
We psych things up till they whistle like a kettle,
We go stark raving mad, jump and holler.

The other day it hit the fan.
My high school principal defended me to parents:
"I haven't seen him do any of these things.
You know how a controversy is often created
Out of nothing. The coach gives
Twenty-four hours a day for his players."

When you're hitting hard twenty-four hours a day
You grow some teeth, you develop a real bite.
I don't eat frogheads. I'm married and all that normal stuff.
I wouldn't put frogs in a coaching handbook,
But every day at school you do things

Spur of the moment that you wouldn't do
If they were made known to the public.

Last year to motivate my team I shaved my head;
We won nine games, lost only one.
Tomorrow I'll wrestle a bear if I have to.
Only sometimes a frog's head stares at me.

In my senior year, asthmatic attacks overwhelm me. Confined often to bed, struggling to breathe, I wander deep into my imagination. Asthma sears the isolated loneliness of breath into your mind. I listen to myself too much. Is that a slight wheeze? Laughter. Afraid of catching cold. It hurts to breathe. Don't be so damn self-conscious. Time of hormones as well as illness. I dream of girls. How can I find a girl friend if I can't breathe? Masturbation and asthma, tests of adolescence. High school means *high*. Do I feel guilty about masturbation? Yes, but I feel guilty about asthma too. Feeling guilty is stupid. Do something, stupid. Breath, I yearn for breath. Singing I need breath. Reading hundreds of adventure, sex and sports books I need breath. The line of words breathes, has a rare breath. I read haphazardly, anything to relax and catch a breath.

Fantasies of Europe

(1)

At age of seventeen, summoned into the living room,
    Mother's ambitious Big Room of dreams, I know the walls
        Glow no longer with communal pleasure, the house is cracking.

Mother's face quavers in a mask of tormenting nerves,
    Father moves cautiously like a snail over slippery surfaces,
        The three of us alone in vast space, a curious triangle.

Mother speaks, each word a splinter from deep wounds,
    "Your father tells me that he wants a divorce. After all these years!"
        Father says awkwardly, "I want to be fair to everyone."

"Fair!" Mother shrieks. "He's fallen in love with that woman.
    "It's absurd at his age. Can't you tell him he's wrong!"
        I mumble in confusion, "I can't take sides."

I have a sense of "that woman," as I've seen father,
    Age evaporating, speaking romantic Spanish
    To a comely young graduate student in his department.

Although I'm walled off, struggling to hold one hand
    On each side of the wall, I'm sentenced to be mother's
    Companion in separation, a cheerful son of comfort.

When a family breaks apart, intense tears remain private,
    Friends take sides, create new barriers for children to confront.
    Passages of change result in fusions of new knowledge.

At seventeen, one must believe in the future's possibilities.
    I'm told I will accompany mother to Europe; a friend my age is to
    Join our journey into a dark fantasy beyond all fantasies.

(2)

Europe, 1938. Broken, trying to find some balance in her corkscrew life, mother travels to Switzerland to renew her psyche with Jung's counsel. We travel to England first, the people and Neville Chamberlain believing that peace and reason will prevail. Suddenly, in Switzerland, trains reveal blackout curtains, reserve troops called up for training, newspapers report border tunnels mined against invasion, Jewish refugees move, anguished, along unfamiliar streets.

As mother seeks inner peace again with Jung, I struggle to find myself as a singer. I start lessons with Albert Emmerich, a rare Viennese actor-singer, bald, with a huge smile masking a hundred characters from sinister to serene, and a firm belly like concrete on which he asks me to fracture my hand constantly to make me aware of his breath control. Often, when I am unaware, he hits me in the stomach to demonstrate my lack of support. At night I watch him perform Mephistopholes and Sarastro at the Zurich opera house and marvel at his transformation from devil to wise man. Frequently, during lessons at his home, the phone rings. I hear the Nazi ambassador to Switzerland urging Emmerich back to Vienna, now under Nazi control. Afraid of impending war, struggling to remain in Switzerland with his wife and children as long as he can, Emmerich bangs down the phone, barking out mockingly the new communal greeting, "Heil Hitler!" spitting out his anti-Nazi hatred to me. Then he hits me extra-hard in the diaphragm: "Strength! You must have strength there to look up at this crazy Nazi world. If you don't have strength there, how can you breathe the air of freedom?"

To increase my German-speaking ability, I study with a distinguished refugee, Frau Wassermann, widow of the distinguished novelist, Jakob

57

Wassermann. In Germany and Austria, Wassermann was considered the equal to Thomas Mann until the Nazi invasion of Austria confiscated his royalties and property.

Fortunately, with Wassermann's death just before the invasion, he did not have to witness the anti-Semitic soiling of his reputation that sought to eliminate him from literary history. Bereft of financial support, his widow fled to Switzerland, forced to work as freelance critic and German teacher to foreigners. A sensuous, middle-aged woman living suddenly in a burning world that has branded her *Jew*, she takes a liking to me and begins to teach me German poetry. "Poetry endures beyond politics," she counsels me. "How can you find the breath of singing if you don't know the sister-breath of poetry?" She forces me to memorize Goethe, Schiller, Nietzsche, Heine. "Learn Heine so the Nazis cannot make him disappear from literature like my husband." Sometimes we sit on her meagre sofa in her small room holding hands. She taps the poem's rhythm into my hand. I try to suppress my growing erection, but she is in a world beyond sex; poetry assumes a new sexual, romantic meaning to me.

(3)

Three encounters with Nazi fantasists of power: The Salzburg Festival, summer, 1938. Of the supreme conductors, Toscanini and Bruno Walter are gone, only Furtwängler remains, riding lonely, haughtily in the rear seat of his open sedan, driven by a chauffeur. Nazi flags blaze everywhere, a fire of burning, triumphant swastikas. The few remaining Jewish stores are marked with boycott signs, *JUDENGESCHAFT*. Inside one I see a pale white face strangely isolated in time as if a society has discovered an obscene fossil.

In the park with my American friend, John Partridge, we discover a typewritten order on a wall banning Jews from the park. Impulsively, we rip it off with disgust, walk away hurriedly, afraid that someone has seen us. John and I are too young to realize the intricate effects of power and corruption that we are witnessing. Ezio Pinza, Italian citizen and one of the last international stars, is singing Don Giovanni, a superb Don, forceful, romantic, corrupt.

Why is the relationship between corruption and romance so compelling to Mozart? Because of his court experiences? The Nazi military presence is incongruous with Mozart's spirit. Stern, goosestepping troops with their mechanical strutting smother Mozart's impetuous, graceful melodies.

Second, a trip to Munich with mother and friend, John, to attend the premiere of Richard Strauss's opera, *Friedenstag* (Peace Day). In Munich John and I visit the Memorial to the Nazi Martyrs with its eternal burn-

58

ing flame, guards standing at rigid attention. Every German citizen walking by stretches out his or her arm in the Hitler-salute. Impulsively, John stretches out his arm too, in mocking, clown-like obedience. He joins me, laughing, while Germans stare at us annoyed by crude American youngsters. The opera celebrates Strauss's homecoming to Munich after years of disagreement with civic authorities. Strauss, a buoyant, waving figure, receives seventeen curtain calls. The central box, illuminated brightly with a spotlight on a huge Nazi swastika, is deliberately empty, a censorship of absence. To Nazis the opera's theme of peace is worth only contempt of a military flag.

My third and greatest traumatic encounter: In fall I journey from Zurich to Freiburg in southern Germany to visit my American friend, Jack Kent, studying there on an exchange fellowship. Freiburg, where the famous philosopher Heidegger, teaches, *Das Nichts nichtet*. Nothing nothingizes. Jack meets me at the station and escorts me to the room he has rented in a boarding house. Toward midnight, at the end of the street a fire is blazing, surrounded by uniformed men. Forbidden to move closer to the fire, we watch as several uniformed men push an elderly couple into a waiting car. The next morning I discover that I have witnessed Kristallnacht. All over Germany stormtroopers burned down synagogues and smashed Jewish stores. Here in Freiburg, I was an unconscious witness to the burning of the synagogue, and the arrest of the rabbi and his wife. By morning a tall fence was built around the burnt-out synagogue as if to pretend accidental fire to innocent civilian eyes, including Heidegger's sophisticated, abstract, cloud-high vision. The next morning when I read in the newspaper and hear from Jack and his friends the planned attacks throughout Germany, I write my first poem. Angry, shapeless words on paper. Emotional fury without the power of form. Something abstract in music that I have loved begins to fade into the concrete action of language.

(4)

Time is not eternal; it sags, changes, vanishes, returns flickering.
    Thanksgiving time, 1938, American celebration with Dr. Jung as
        guest of honor.
      In the Hotel Sonne in Küsnacht where I live with mother and
      friend, John,

Jung rises to speak, his face lined with the study of mythological traumas.
    Once he wrote of a patient; "She had no mythological ideas; therefore
      The most essential part of her nature could find no way to express
        itself."

Possessed by a recent dream of blood flowing down a mountain,
   He prophesies darkly, "Europe is being overwhelmed by a
      Demonic mythology, shadow-forces of war overwhelming reason."

Throughout the banquet hall laden with food, sweets, drinks, older
      guests
   Marvel at this grim prophet, master of serenity, whose forceful
      personality
      Looms suddenly like an aged, afflicted tree fighting oblivion.

We young people listen, disturbed, youth cannot stand darkness of doom,
   Must live in the fertile moment, so sitting at a table of young people,
      we elect
      Jack Kent, who is returning my Freiburg Kristallnacht visit, as our
      speaker.

Jack delivers an optimistic tirade against twentieth-century corruptions.
   Choked with emotion and wine, a future city planner after the war,
      He speaks of youthful ideals, Lewis Mumford's plans to change
      urban tyranny.

Outside darkening lake skies reflect Jung's vision of unconscious fury
      raging amuck.
   The time has come when Jung's dream of blood, "gigantic blocks of
      stone tumbling
      Down upon me," will reveal the abyss of conscience creating
      concentration camps.

Mass-war beyond knowledge, beyond imagination, will penetrate our
      emotions,
   Conceal dangerous images in our fantasies, images we must
      recognize, Jung says,
      Or risk descending into unconscious nightmares flowing with
      rivers of blood.

1940s

WARS WITHIN WAR

Perhaps a Prayer

I would say a few words
Though they stumble.
Perhaps the man on the frozen corner
Will hear me and the scars
At the peak of my night vanish
And my hate change to praise.

I live in a time of unknown masses.
Over the notched fields of war
I hear only pins of voices,
Huge, impersonal hate,
Unknown soldiers obliterated
In massed divisions,
Ruling idols commanding
The automatic service of acolytes.

Call the kings of today mass masters,
Administrative bumble-bee men,
Pollinators of red tape
Who beat the language to its knees.
There on the impeccable standard of living
Sits a title, the anonymous name.
Our problem is one of identity.

Have I no name?
I would have this war become
Personal, who will recognize me?
The man on the frozen corner is
Silent as a shelf, as a closet.
Nothing belongs to my eye.

The Refugee and his Library

At a New York party, the small, grey-haired man
Clings to his wife. They whisper together,
Uncertain foreign accents in a foreign land.

"Ancient lovers," a guest guzzles fondly.
"The war separated them for many years.
He used to be a wealthy publisher."

I try conversation with a refugee eye,
Float questions to open broken streets.
The eye lives in its socket like a trench.

"You must have had a remarkable library?"
"Oh, he had thousands of books," his wife says proudly,
"That was years ago when he was a famous publisher."

The eye begins to shine with memory:
"When the war began, I escaped and sent
Half of my library north, the other half, south."

The eye turns north, south, inward:
"The Nazis bombed the free, northern half,
And the Allies bombed the free, southern half."

The eye smiles at the irony of freedom.
"You see, I believed books were more than people,
But I learned books are less than life."

He squeezes his wife, she squeezes him back,
Death to the library. Life has triumphed.
After their war, refugees cling only to themselves.

I ask a final, floating question:
"They say you have a clever bird at home?"
"A Budgie. We are his refugees. He is ours."

The eye retreats again into its socket
Like a piece of flotsam, waiting in water,
Floating on a dark wordless underworld.

A Fantasia for Harvard

(1)
Worried California boy trying to climb the thick-leafed,
              impenetrable ivy;

War in my head, Nazi occupation of Europe,
      when would I be drafted?
In Boston my cousin, Bill, oceanographer, meets me at the train,
      escorts me to an oyster bar
Where I celebrate my arrival at education's crimson pinnacle
      by throwing up violently.

As a sophomore transfer student from the University of California,
      I search for a house to live in.
My first encounter, the mathematician master of Lowell House glances
      at my application with disdain.
"You're from California. Why do you wish to live in Lowell House?"
      I croak like a frog.
In his elevated, accented tone, California is a mysterious swamp
      from which strange creatures crawl.
"I'm sorry to say that we have no room left in Lowell House. I'm afraid
      you will have to try elsewhere."
Sorry, afraid assume diamond-hard meanings, his house
      requires scholars and gentlemen,
Not green youths handicapped by raw birth in frontier swamplands

   (2)
Odd man in, I find at last a place in Eliot House,
   Begin to make friends, join the Glee Club where voices sing across
      barriers,
      Pursue my studies as an uncertain music major
      Although writing poems has become a deep desire.

I take a course in Shakespeare under F.O. Matthiessen,
   Who seems at first a poor lecturer stammering "ohs" and "uhs,"
      Soon proves extraordinary teacher challenging closed minds,
         Showing brilliantly how nature and myth shape Shakespearean
         drama.

Many teachers I encounter deliver mere facts, self-centered opinions,
   But Matthiessen, quiet, intense, small, bald-headed explorer,
      Delights in probing how public actions relate to private obsessions
      Lifting Shakespeare's characters off the page in historical fire.

He makes us memorize passages from relatively unknown plays
   Such as *Troilus and Cressida:* "Time hath my lord a wallet at his back
      Wherein he puts alms for oblivion"; metaphor becomes a gold rush
         of comparison.

65

One day Matthiessen produces a guest lecturer: Harley Granville
   Barker.

Legendary Barker, actor-director of Shaw's plays, playwright
   Scornful of commercial theatre, visionary critic, voice glowing with
      translation lessons,
      Reveals how Shakespeare's skeleton script translates into bright
         flesh
         When actors and stagecraft illuminate the magic of poetic
            suggestion.

In Eliot House, where Matthiessen tutors, I encounter him frequently,
   enroll in his
   American Literature course, tranced by his opening words: "Reading
      American literature
      (He is about to publish his great book, *American Renaissance*), you
         must not believe
         That Cambridge is the center of American writing; westward
            opens a vast country

Breeding a multitude of styles promising at last the creation of a
   literature
   That does not merely pay debt to British and European ancestors."
      A multitude of styles . . . *The creation of an American literature* . . . These
         words haunt
         As I witness faculty, hiding provincial roots, ape British manners
            and speech.

   (3)
Beguiled, drawn by old operatic yearnings, I enter theatre timidly.
   Theodore Spencer casts me in the chorus of Sophocles' *Oedipus*, a class
      project.
      Yeats's adaptation, two masters training my ear and mind to
         mythical images.
         I.A. Richards smiles benevolently at our bumbling, earnest
            production.

In May, 1941, because of Glee Club and music major activities, I'm cast
   again
   As Greek Chorus member in the Student Union production of
      Aristophanes' *Peace*.
      A desire for peace floats in the air, though inevitable war
         approaches;

66

In a month the Nazi war machine will roll massively into the
Soviet Union.

Disguised in the chorus, I sing music of Leonard Bernstein, a cocky
recent
Graduate studying conducting at the Curtis Institute with Fritz
Reiner.
This is Bernstein's first experience conducting a small orchestra and
chorus,
Featuring four sarcastic, blasting trombones, piano, wild, jazzy
percussion.

Occasional soaring tunes transfommed into *On The Town* prefigure
Broadway talent;
Ego-energy, acrobatic conducting sweep us high into bright, youthful
exaltation.
Uncanny energy, we sense, is the wild source of art; at the cast
party, Bernstein
Jams at the piano, his sister sings with him in fused Grecian flesh.
Music is miraculous.

(4)

If internally Harvard is exclusive, wealth and racial superiority marking
entrance to clubs,
Harvard attracts the world, slowly forcing Harvard to change.
Incredible visiting voices
Pierce my mind, Harry Bridges, labor leader the government is
trying to deport,
Robinson Jeffers, speaking granite poems from a solitary, hawk-
like face;

Most dramatic, the frail, ancient figure of philosopher, A.N. Whitehead,
lecturing in the chapel
On "The Immortality of Man," his opening words causing whispers in
the front row
Of dignitaries: "The trouble with the world today is the self-conceit
of so-called learned men."
Enigmatic Harvard, where the ego's creative and destructive
power dances in the Yard.

(5)

One evening, the humped, fur-coated, fur-hatted figure of Igor
Stravinsky appears at rehearsal.

67

Mesmerized by the legend, we are to sing his *Oedipus Rex* with the
  Boston Symphony;
    His conducting puts us off at first; twitching out compulsive
      rhythms like an electric beetle.
      Set in hieratic Latin, his opera-oratorio is distancing, history
        sculptured in time

Like a marble monument before Brecht thought of the idea of
  alienation.
    All over campus excited Glee Club voices resound practicing difficult,
      Quickly shifting, syncopated rhythms; the choral sections become a
        secret code
        Only youth is privileged to explore, hearing eagerly new
          standards of music.

When orchestral rehearsals begin, some players resent the work, too
  difficult.
    After one rehearsal, winking scorn to friends, a percussionist envelops
      Perspiring Stravinsky with a huge bath towel, collaring a bad,
        mischievous child,
        But in performances, professional mastery prevails, the work
          triumphs.

Standing with first basses directly behind the mezzo-soprano singing
  Jocasta,
    We stare into her naked back, watching her flesh tremble with
      passion,
      As Stravinsky leads her through her sensuous aria revealing her
        growing fear of
        Incestuous marriage to her son, myth flaring in Latin's sexual
          distance.

Writes Stravinsky: "I have always considered that a special language, not
  that of current
    Colloquial limits, was required for subjects touching on the sublime
      mysteries.
      That is why I finally selected Latin. The choice had the great
        advantage of a medium
        Not dead but turned to stone, monumentalized, immune from all
          vulgar risks."

Torn in studies between music and poetry in an age of specialization,
    Too young to realize the bondage of sister muses, studying just
        enough to stumble on,
        I fall in love with a darkhaired Radcliffe student, another music
        major singing in the chorus.
            Blood flowing like notes in a musical romance! We sing together
            with Koussevitsky

And his Boston Symphony, soaring education beyond all plodding,
    required courses.
    Holding hands on the subway to Boston, concerts glow with sound
        magic.
        Youth is contrapuntal love, trumpets heralding wartime search for
        union.
        She is Jewish, I fighting renegade Christian roots, we dream all
        barriers will fall.

Under Koussevitsky we sing Bach's B Minor Mass, "Dona Nobis
    Pacem," while Nazi-Russian
    War rages, and all leftwing dreams of peace collapse around us in
        malignant separation.
        Koussevitsky possesses us, master aristocrat, slim, elegant, aloof
        theatrical figure
            Commanding space and time, last orchestral tyrant raging at a
            cellist in rehearsal,

"You murder ze moo-sick!" Humbling himself before Bach, tyrant angel
    serving only
    "Ze gawds of moo-sick!" Koussevitsky addresses us hordes of chorus
        members as
        "My deer chill-dren," heavy Russian accent creating apocalyptic
        sentence structures
            Hypnotizing us into laughing imitations, reverence for a blessed
            teacher.

(6)

Dazed, strengthened by love, I write feverishly, ignoring my required
    courses.
    One afternoon drinking with my diabetic friend, George Taylor, beers
        held high,
        We challenge each other to a contest of poetry—how many poems
        can we scribble

Into the night before passing out caught in the fever of Dionysiac exaltation.

At the summit of fourteen poems, we sag into blissful, triumphant oblivion.
A few nights later, convinced of our brilliance, we read imitative masterpieces
At a gathering of experts in the Poetry Room of Widener Library, trembling before
Faculty members Matthiessen, Spencer, John Berryman and Delmore Schwartz,

Schwartz recently annointed as "The New American Yeats" for his first book, *In Dreams*
Begin Responsibilities; I read my whirling Hart Crane-inspired poem, "The Crucifixion,"
Suddenly an argument erupts over my presumptuous poem, angelic Schwartz defending,
Bow-tied, scholarly Berryman attacking, friends delighting in argument

Disguised as critiques of my poem, others smiling at effrontery of my youthful lines.
Never mind; my passion stands revealed; for a moment I am a public poet, young, green,
Trembling as I assert my imitative metaphor of agonizing crucifixion,
My search for love in a world where war plans to summon my eager body.

History Flowing Around Harvard

At Plymouth Rock

Liberty! Teach me again. No one taught me
That Plymouth Rock is an old worn stone
In a cage beneath an imitation Greek temple.
I'm tossed back in time by a trick of light.
In winter wind, amidst two hundred spectators
Honoring memory of the *Mayflower* invaders,
I learn to praise, feel silent, accusing eyes through time,
Hear swelling, violent voices, Indian ghosts
Calling the Puritans, *White Devils;*
Accusing Washington, our First President,
As a murderer, *The Burner of Villages.*
It can't be true. I was taught in school
That the Puritans were religious zealots,
That Washington is *The Father of our Country.*
Why then, struggling around this rock,
Do Indian spirits clash with white settlers,
Lost cries of anguish merging with the wind:
"Liberty! Freedom! Teach us again.
If the world is true, memory must always be new."

How to Create Music
by William Billings

A tanner who scribbled music on hides with chalk
Put out his racy flag: BILLINGS, MUSIC
One mystic eye saw the virgin unspotted,
The other eye shone barnacled with death.
One arm hung down, dry withered weed,
The other beat a rhythm into radiance.
Legs uneven, one limping from poverty,
The other trotted in a juicy jig.

71

In church they smoothed him down
With careful smirks, he bellowed back
A fuguing tune. They called his music
Smut within a smoke-house; his Voice
Rasped over all their prickly hymns.
When English tea tasted Boston water,
He hollered out his war song *Chester*
And rebels shrieked with raven's joy.
When critics called him coarse,
He jabbed them with his *Jargon*,
A concussive swordfish laughter.
More choirs jigged within his tunes
And his massive head rehearsed
Quick, merry notes at noon
To jibe the strict Puritan night-shade.
When he died, Mistress Music knelt
In silence to the Singing Master,
Then began to sing his starfish songs
Twenty lustres more than old, worn hymns.

The Peaceable Kingdom
of Edward Hicks

When the heart leaps in a world of wonder
Where lion and deer wander together,
Hope shines like a star of charity
And peace sings from the clear weather.

No time can be killed or wasted,
Hands of love move the hours and days.
The lost animals rove home with joy
To a rich election that houses the strays.

Laughter from the eternal world sounds
As God blesses each animal's eyes;
Bright, ascending acts of compassion
Dazzle the dark surrounding lies.

Simple kingdoms soar in true reality
Through the mind stunned by desire,

Drive towards the sun the ideas of light
Where meet the words and acts of fire.

In the Peaceable Kingdom a Man Sings of Love

Sing the simple word as the word of love.
The word of love is a singular stare
Disdaining the garden of satire.

Love's word is a light-charmed word,
Belled and soft in the peeled glare
Glowing above the hawkweeds of death.

When the angel began his descent to die,
He sang of love as the wisdom of quietness
Winding on the spool of God's quiet eye.

Jefferson Dreaming about the Declaration of Independence

(1)

Learning is like lightning. It never reveals itself unless you learn to live
in thunderstorms. Struggling with facts means grappling with intense
weather. Only when facts explode with imagination are they illuminated.
For a moment knowledge glows with beauty and truth before the curtain
of time is drawn concealing another layer of civilization. Last night I
dreamt the United States shone with this singular learning, these light-
ning facts revealing beautiful edifices, landscapes, a real culture standing
alone in proud independence from Europe.

(2)

I designed and built my own world, Monticello, on top of a lovely hill in
Virginia overlooking a fertile valley. Classical architecture, books of all
cultures, music: Purcell, Handel, Vivaldi, Haydn, French wine—mostly
European indulgences I admit. Can one build a sanctuary in American
wilderness? My dream was to support myself, my library, my family, my

slaves, in an ideal, natural setting free from the peril of urban cities. In every true society there is a hierarchy of learning. Not the rank of money and patriarchal power, but the rank of respect. The great American dream of equality trapped me, the beautiful paradox of equality when there can only be the equality of opportunity. Yet the paradox is so forceful, mysterious, daring, that I praised it, while at the same time forced to endure slavery of masters, slavery of servants.

(3)

Monticello became the one peaceful place where I could fulfill the goal to which I had sentenced myself and my fellow Americans—the Pursuit of Happiness. In this judgment, pursuit becomes the mask of performance. If we run, move, travel, seek, we will achieve. But I wished to stay in one place, design, build, decorate rooms to achieve a unity of scale that is an illusion of happiness. The United States creates its enigmatic destiny by turning property into creative power. That is why I bought the West from Napoleon. Property would become creative power. Was it not I who forced the materialists to change "property" into "Pursuit of Happiness"? As we declare Independence, behind the free word lies the chained word of property as profit and power.

(4)

My dream of Napoleon is a curious nightmare. A tall man, I look down on the short, pompous Emperor. I command him to sell me the West, the Louisiana Territory. Instead he invades Haiti and I feel my own slaves revolt. How cruel to own human flesh, yet how do we escape classical forms of bondage in a new Republic? His troops festering in tropical heat, murdering and murdered by Haitian Blacks, Napoleon marches into Russia to counter his American losses. As he moves eastward with his armies, the West becomes free. How long can we Americans expand to the West? How long can we live in simple obligation to a vast, developing land where government cannot rule by imperial force from the center?

(5)

Unspoken, love exists beyond law. Martha, my wife, my delight, sang with musical flesh. She loved the harpsichord and sang sweetly. When she died young, I was devastated. What could I do with my passion? If a man is forced to wear the mask of law, often the time comes when passion forces him to live behind the mask. The social code governs only surface manners. Did I love Black Sally? She was my devoted slave, mistress of my household. When we lived in France she could have been free. Can slavery contain love? I never loved her, she never loved me, some unknown fathered our children. Who can deny black dreams, black desires? *We hold these truths to be self-evident, that all men are created equal* . . . In "self-evident" is the deception, the deception of self. The true national flag is white and hidden black, though it flutters only red, white and blue.

(6)

Whenever I see three physicians together, I look up to see whether there is not a Turkey Buzzard in the neighborhood. What is it in man's nature that will not temper judgment with humility? The Greek philosophers teach us that truth is great and will prevail if left to herself. *Herself*, this feminine truth? Nurses nurse, doctors pronounce, and the power of healing slides into the dark where every man must treat himself and mend his own soul.

(7)

Politics is insufficient reality. The beauty of Monticello is insufficient vision. Can the clash between reality and vision ever be resolved? Is my dream of endless land a peril because of the wilderness where the Indian lives, where the slave flees, where the wild animal lurks, whose wills are as strong as ours? What if we tame all wild, free spirits and my dream of endless land becomes illusion? Will Hamilton triumph with his federal and international banking dreams and banks become the center of government? If money conquers and every city is centered in banking, insurance and legal buildings, then my dream of western freedom vanishes in the winter of time. I am caught in a trap between the dream of land and the dream of freedom.

(8)

My architectural vision of the University of Virginia is a classical drawing of rational education. If an ideal symmetry of buildings can be achieved with a marvelous library at its peak, men must learn the real source of creative energy, the soul's expansion by training the senses. Is not false specialization our American danger, where we educate only for pursuit of goods, not aesthetics or the beauty of ideas? My cursed word, *pursuit*, makes us run into the net of exploitation and false profits.

(9)

"We hold these truths to be self-evident . . ." The revolution of change was my natural and spiritual goal. Yet I was an excellent committee man. When compromise was needed, I was the personable compromiser.
"Almighty God has created the mind free . . ." But mind is servant to body and body is bound to family and society. When body revolts, it must suffer

though mind soars free. Thus ideas glitter in sunlight while flesh shrinks in terror. Hamilton dying after thirty hours of agony when he was shot by Burr. What was it Burr sneered to Hamilton in 1800? "Our Constitution is a miserable paper machine." Does not the paper machine endure and glitter in the sun?

(10)

A ripeness of time for death is essential, though we do not stop dreaming of eternity. Clinging to the past does not merit the wisdom of history. History teaches us present actions, how to learn from the past. Men call the marks of physical combat badges of honor. How can war be a badge of honor? Only peaceful, eternal revolution that continuously purifies men's souls can be such a badge. The Capitol and the Presidency fade away. Virginia and the Frontier are my only rest, but slavery will not let me rest in time. We have a wolf by the ears. All men are born equal until the points of equality dim and are taken away. In the dream of equal opportunity, in my struggle for human rights and justice, my death will be my dream of resurrection.

Ralph Waldo Emerson Receives a Visit from the Sane Man and Rejects Him

By way of showing authority he knocks
On my door as if there were no locks.
Perhaps he is a joker of my brain
This sane man unwet in the rain.
Optimistic as an apple, decreed
To conformity in word and deed,
His mind is straight and never leaning
Pressured in progress's single meaning.
He knocks to prove himself the image
Who drives this new Industrial Age.
How shallow is his doctrine of beauty!
We have lost the classical, perceptive eye,
Drained the dependence of form on soul—
The eternal sane man has become our goal.
Yet I believe in one soul related to the world.
I see this world man by woman, not hurled
Down from radiant skies to shine in goods

Caging our spirits with hawking hoods.
Only the fixing of soul-fragments together
Shall discover the white-bait weather,
When mind and soul unite in the eye
As sea and earth are one with sky;
Then the soul will speak free from terror
Of isolation, and the poor sane man's error
Will soar into the jagged soul under
The nailed cross and sing in wonder.

Whitman Stock-taking, Cataloguing

"Stock-taking, inventory, is the first effort of the mind to make itself at home . . . We see it in the Homeric catalogue and poetic inventory of Whitman. But how does one do it where the home will not stay put? Where the stock of items on the shelves changes every day?"
                    Wright Morris, *The Territory Ahead*

Me imperturbe, standing, imperturbable, surveying the big country in rough-hewn, limping language, seeking the barbaric yawp;
Allons, rushing ahead in pseudo-language, fighting out of immigration's Tower of Babel to a new American tone, stock-taking, inventory, a bursting catalogue of fresh vision;
Ya-Honk, wild gander leading his flock through the Big Sky back to the frontier dream where Indians wait with grave faces contemplating the meaning of Reservations, lost land as restrictive, confining camp-metaphors;
Pent-up, aching rivers driving pent-up, aching language down the Mississippi to New Orleans, following the terrible currents of slavery, "a woman's body at auction . . . the teeming mother of mothers," slavery as incestuous relationship, grotesque purchase of sexual mistress-mothers;
A woman waits for me, "They know how to swim, row, ride, wrestle, shoot, run, strike, retreat, advance, resist, defend themselves," these Amazons know everything, new society of aggressive force, women warriors on the frontier, schoolteacher, nun, whore, wife, impossible future fantasies hiding slaves and masters, haunted homosexuals becoming isolated singers;
The demand for facts, endless naming of objects and characters, "but woe to the age or land in which these things, movements, stopping at themselves, do not tend to ideas," ideas vanishing in Civil War, nursing

wounded comrades, O Camerado, a great feminine nurse bending over
desperate physical and spiritual wounds, washing off the blood of insan-
ity, feeling the uncanny "body electric," flesh as leaves of grass;
The long line gathering, flowing out into space in a curious procession, low-
hanging moons, solitary guests from Alabama, demons and birds, me-
chanics, journalists, opera singers, the pure contralto singing in the organ
loft, the noiseless, patient spider, the carpenter dressing his plank, the
driver with his interrogating thumb, the Good Grey poet camouflaged in
the en-masse searching for the cradle of liberty endlessly rocking; *Out of
the roughs, a kosmos,* all of the illegitimate word-children eating, drinking,
breeding, probing the darkness of our Captain's continuous assassina-
tion, transformed into military scientists, impersonal, technological as-
tronauts, pursuing happiness into space, time, earth shrinking to a tiny
orange below, up, up with "oceanic, variegated, intense practical energy,"
to land in triumph on the moon where, suddenly, down the ladder "dis-
orderly fleshly and sensual," he emerges singing to the moon's wasteland
his song of rugged independence, the Song of Myself.

Mr. and Mrs. Herman Melville, at Home, Isolated in their Rooms

"Herman has taken to writing poetry,
You need not tell anyone,
For you know how such things get around,"
His wife writes to a friend . . .
She is sitting in her bedroom
Across from his study, worried about him.
He has taken to closing his door,
Shutting himself up, writing obscure poems,
A great manhole of isolation
With a peculiar, concealed look
That marks the losers of fantasy.
Some scholars laugh at her cautious words,
Some guess frustrations of sex, religion,
A somber, puritanical heritage, decorous duty
Masking, controlling the crawling visions . . .
Perhaps she also feels poetry is dangerous,
A possibility . . . Does she fear insanity
Closing the door, tense in his study,
Writing his labored, difficult poems?

They are still there, sitting in history,
Wife and husband together, apart,
Disciplined boarders pursuing separate lives
In vision, secluded rooms,
Worrying that poetry is
The shining grave of eternal language—
That we write only to preserve
A myth of words opposed
To the acts of love.

Horatio Greenough Writes of Reason

Give reason but a cock-boat,
She will elaborate a battleship.
She can modify but cannot find,
Adopt, yet she cannot create.
    Putting down his pen
    He began to work on reason's sculpture,
    Stiff Washington with Roman sword,
    The honest pioneer, savage loin-clothed Indian,
    And Cooper, dry, meagre as a tit-mouse.

This was his paradox, to know
How form functions, know the tools,
The power of hands searching new themes,
But still create monuments of stiffness.
    Around him the states were young,
    The people old without a childhood,
    No legendary past, no myths for growth.

He wrote that reason was a dry nurse
To the young states, feeding them
With hardened bread, cold meat of facts.
    Out of banks, factories, came
    Cues for culture, masks of sentiment,
    As power flowed across the land.

Learn from Greece to be American, he wrote,
And watched with joy the clipper ship go
Flat against the wind. This was beautiful.

Man had learned the building lines
From wind, wave, study of the sea.
    His chiseled stone would mock,
    But on the page his words would point
    The future's formula—form follows function.
    He smiled and watched the gliding clipper-ship,
    All her white wind-muscles pulling the sky.

James Gates Percival Pleads
for a Unity of Vision

Our curious society
Speaks of gentlemen and ladies
Writing verses of entertainment,
Dreaming apart from machines
Of singular science,
As if this dry disunity
Creates angels of song.
I speak of the imagination's need,
To take from the air
The full flower and frame of form.
What kills is knowledge without humility,
The roar of certainty like an arrogant crow.
True vision sings to unify
The severed eyes of science and poetry.
Behind all forms a simple unity shines
Like a flowering tree,
That lovely foam of light

In Nervous Motion: Charles Willson Peale

        He began as a Maryland saddler;
A humming bird of nervous motion who taught himself
How to make everything from carriages to chairs,
A fusser at trades and the first home handyman,
        even dabbling in portraiture.

Failing in every craft
And caught in the laws of debt, he fled to freedom,
Hotfooting it from the debtor's jail with his brushes.
Patrons sent him to London to study the genteel painters,
        the posed velvets of tradition.

Back for the Revolution,
He painted propaganda pictures for the street,
Patriotic canvases of freedom-shouting marchers,
And seeing they were crude, deceitful art,
        threw them away like junk.

Peace could not pacify.
He carved and painted a rage of puppet shows,
Promoting them with pride as "moving pictures."
His puppets bounced through naval battles, storms, and
        Milton's "Pandemonium."

Restlessly, he built
A world in miniature, a museum of natural history
With stuffed animals before prim, painted backdrops,
Searching driven nature to a stop for frontier men
        to catch their shadows.

Rushing America required
New gadgets, new sets of equipment for unknown ends;
He turned to the force of invention, eyeglasses, stoves,
And one day when words failed in his decayed mouth,
        a jaw of false teeth.

In his late 70s,
Wisps of white hair wild, false plates jiggling,
He accelerated savagely down slanting hills on
One of the first bicycles built in America,
        self-designed for speed.

He died at 86,
Searching with sexual pulse for a fourth wife,
Having produced for an artless frontier society
Many solid, material sons whom he named Rembrandt,
        Raphael, Rubens, and Titian.

Emily Dickinson in the Asylum of Poetry

Some nursemaids thought she was a witch;
They liked to frighten children
By pronouncing her name sharply:
    MISS EM-I-LY DICK-IN-SON
Staccato, like the flash of a carving knife
Thrust into the savor of a Sunday roast.
Even her friends saw her rarely;
As they sat in the stiff parlor,
She would speak from the hallway shadows,
And some had the sense of a spider.
But she sent them notes frequently,
Brief, not barren, cryptic, uncaged:
    "Do you look out tonight?"
    "Mrs. S. gets bigger and rolls down the lane
    to church like a reverend marble."
Poetry or prose, one lucidity to her,
Language, not flesh as illumination.
After she was forty, she gave up colors,
Took to wearing diaphanous white with a cameo pin.
She flowed "as quick as a trout,"
Said her sister, Lavinia, *a human trout* . . .
Her father provided the river of pride
Through the house, punctilious, severe,
A lawyer of abstract love in broadcloth coat,
Beaver hat with a goldheaded cane,
And time, time, eternal time on his mind . . .
From her father she took the isolation
And the invisible glow in knowledge,
Shining energy that links the static facts.
She knew the difference between her father,
Selecting the proper depth of books for Sunday afternoon,
And a pseudo-scholar, and wrote of the latter
    "He has the facts, but not the phosphorescence of learning."
    (When she was too witty, her father arose,
    a thin, succulent clam, and left the table.)
She wrote poems on sheets of notepaper
And stitched them together carefully,
Then rolled them up and tied them safely
With a ribbon, her unity, her publication.
Out of her father's house, a fortress of Calvinism,
She made an asylum of poetry, sensing

That both fortress and asylum are barred,
But in the battle of asylum and fortress,
The asylum must be favored to survive.

The Glorious Devil at the Dovecot:
Edgar Allan Poe and Sarah Helen Whitman

"I see by the *Home Journal* that your beautiful invocation has reached the
'Raven' in his eyrie and I suppose, ere this, he has swooped upon your
little dovecot in Providence. May Providence protect you if he has! for
his croak is the most elegant imaginable. He is in truth 'A glorious Devil,
with large heart and brain.'"
                    Mrs. Osgood to Mrs. Whitman

   (1) *Sarah Whitman Conducting a Seance*
In the dark, motionless,
A veil over my eyes
To enter the second darkness,
I wait for him to strike.
A Glorious Devil, he will come.
I listen for the lilt of his voice
After I wrote to tease him:
"A low bewildering melody
Is murmuring in my ear."
Bewildering hides the poison,
The jealous play of loss that struck
When mother whispered his infidelity;
He was courting a bitch-stranger
While he whispered to me of roses.
The table begins to move!
Through the shaking wood
The poisonous Doubt flows out.
Drink, drugs, his knife-like tales
Fade into his poetry of praise.
We walk in the summer-flowering graveyard,
The Devil assumes his courtly Glory,
Love speaks through Time to crystallize the first dream
Of Helen (my name too!) of the Thousand Dreams.

(2) *Poe: The Song in the Darkness*
In a timeless song
Love sings to the woman lost:
Doubt—Doubt is the spectre, Fear,
Master of the killing eye.
Let love break free from wagging tongues
That death looks down and cannot die.
The gossip and the spite rise up to haunt us.
Rumors, not earth-bound spirits, move your table.
My croak is termed so eloquent—I am a Raven
Sentenced to the mockery of *Nevermore.*
The Yale President explains why the Hall of Fame
Refused to admit me among its immortals:
    "Poe wrote like a drunkard and a man
    who is not accustomed to pay his debts."
Two lies. I wrote from my divided spirit,
From deep knowledge that debts are paid
Not in money only, but in loss of love.
All that remains of me is false portaits.
In a daguerrotype I'm shown untrimmed
With pasty skin, a mass of flaring hair,
Satanic, proud mustache, a drooping eyelid
As though I squint at dream before reality,
One hand in my coat-front like a mocking actor,
An actor like my parents' last debauch with time.
Do you hear my song? This drunkard's search for love?
Do you think I prefer liquor, drugs, to flesh?
I'll knock your table out of your classical hand,
Helen, I'll sing you my glorious Devil's song:
    Soft from the moving table
    A dream is flowing
    Into nightmare, into love.
    Touch if you can its glowing.

(3) *Mrs. Whitman Clipping, Pasting in Her Notebook*
Wear wild robes, ornaments against desolation,
Shock the smart town with eccentricity,
Behave with arrogance against a commonplace time,
This Providence hiding a difficult Providence.
What's left? This small lock of his hair
That coils around to make its own planet.
Scraps, scraps . . . Obsessive flowers from tombs
To remind me of our summer walks in the cemetery,

84

A pansy that I picked from Keats's grave,
A flower from the ruined Areopagus in Athens,
A daisy from a newly found ancestor's tomb—
Marguerite Le Poer—*Power*, my maiden name akin to his,
Power . . . *Poer* . . . *Poe* . . . I spend my failing time
Searching in scrapbooks lost names from graves,
Anagrams, puzzles, linking me forever with Poe:

SARAH HELEN POER
3 6 5 1 2   8 4 9 10 11 7 12 14 13

12   3 4 5 6 7 8   9 10 11 12 13 14
AHSERAPH LENORE

(4) *Poe Walking Past the Deserted House where Mrs. Whitman Died*
Wild winter now,
Bones of trees break
Snow's frozen flesh.
Lost that sultry summer
When we met, loved
As roses reddened night
Under visionary stars.
A stranger is playing music
In your last, rented house
Where you summon my spirit.
The dark blinds are down.
The house is empty . . .
Harpsichord fantasies
Pluck frantically
For immortal sounds,
Music pursuing the wind.

(5) *Mrs. Whitman with the Spirits*
He was a great magician, a God peer,
Whose spirit speaks to me forever.
Our separation glows with more love
Than the usual marital complacency.
Baudelaire, Mallarme . . . This French resurrection
Of Poe which I helped create, the Raven spirit
Spread as Manet drew his black-winged spectre . . .
What does this clipping say? *"Baudelaire, like Poe,*
Died from artificial excitement."
Artifice is what we make, not how we die.
His suicidal nature plagued him after we parted.

85

With his alcohol, his pain-killing laudanum,
Perhaps he was impotent . . .
How could I save him with my flesh?
New England graves tremble with guilty touch.
To flaunt naked fears we dress ourselves in fancy.
Husbands guard our safety, not our pleasure.
The risk was mine, I faltered,
Our fleshly nerve-ends failed to connect
Despite a quick magic of tentative touch.
Yet enduring spirit prevails.
In his fiery moments of high inspiration
Poe speaks to me, immortal,
A singing, burning essence,
An alabaster statue melting into white fire,
A fire that lives and burns the Raven down.

(6) *Poe with the Actors*
The human brain leans to the Infinite
And fondles the phantom of the idea.
Seek me with the ghost company of actors,
My parents's masks, more comfortable than mine.
They dance their dressing room obsessions,
Sentimental brief performances
That mask a deeper ritual of fear,
A ritual that left to me the tales of horror.
I was born to wander from imaginary to real stages,
Create phantoms in a haze of alcohol and drugs.
Somehow every actor always looks like me,
Impoverished, disolute southern aristocrat
Dragging, as I wrote in a story, my headless head,
My southern curse of nigger and poodle behind me;
Scorning the genteel yet sucked into its world
To survive a little, play the gentleman's role,
Capturing feminine attention with my casual air.
My fate is to found a Theatre of Cruelty
That festers in the mind as on the stage.
Artaud, that mad Frenchman,
Twitching with plague and magic,
Writes that he became my character:
"My life is that of Mr. Usher and his
Sinister hovel. The soul of my nerves is disease-ridden."
No wonder we are condemned, Sarah.
You love the actor for my act of love.

You fear the actor for my failed life.
One day in the trance of morning, vision
Blazing with bright eyes of wonder,
You will see our love survive the literary games.
As listeners we will step freshly out of books
Into the world, the living, listening time
When history stops its dream of action,
And our redeemed flesh praises the dawn of love.

Out of History into the Army, 1940s

Limited Service, 1942

Standing in stoptime, hot July morning in California, draft-summoned.
One of many misfits classified 1B, healthy bodies pure in 1A. Drafted as
Limited Service slaves in World War II. Eight four-eyed misfits blinking
feebly through thick lenses, three heavy-breathing asthmatics inhalers
at-the-ready, four medically certified allergy victims subject to food, pol-
len, and dust disorders, two depressed, isolated neurotics faces sunken as
fallen dough, two incredibly flatfooted slumping shufflers, one limping
straggler with artificial foot. After long stoptime absorbing the army
motto, "Hurry up and wait," we fill up a bus like slow water poured into
sand, ship off to the Reception Center in Monterey.

Stripping civilian clothes, I enter a long tunnel in time.
With my first uniform, skin jumps, prickling, into a mass-tuned world.
First night, a long double-bunk barracks full of coughing, snoring men;
One depressed 1B neurotic sleepwalks at 2 AM into the urine-smelling
    latrine,
Lowers his shorts, squats on one of the long row of oval-shaped toilet
    seats,
And cuts his wrists with a razor. Trickles of blood flow slowly down
Scrubbed floorboards, until dawn brings a scream from the first draftee
Finding the corpse stiff with sacrifice. Morning of the second day,
Mr. Ulcer, my grey-haired companion aged 44, collapses, slumps
    moaning
On the floor, holding his stomach. "God damn army food," he grunts,
"It devours my gut." A rigid Major appears, regular army doctor,
Chest covered with ribbons. "What the trouble, private? Anything
    wrong?"
"Sir, I've got an ulcer . . . Can't tolerate army food . . . Read this
    letter, please . . ."
"Don't you know, private, letters aren't worth a fuck here. You're in the
    army."
"Yes, sir, I'd like to serve, sir, but . . ." "But what, you god damn faker!
Get back to duty or we'll have to give you the Mussolini Treatment!"

"Mussolini Treatment, Sir? I never heard of that. What is it, Sir?"
"Castor oil four times a day until your faking body swims in shit!"

LIMITED SERVICE, category of contempt. Huge stamped letters on our papers. Limited, handicapped, secondary, superfluous, sacks of shit they call us, shit service we call it. After three lost, insomniac days at the Reception Center, I'm assigned to Station Hospital, Fort Stevens, Oregon, coast artillery station at the mouth of the Columbia River. Dazed on our rolling bus, I gape at a huge sign at the fort's gate proclaiming with surreal pride: THE FIRST MILITARY BASE IN THE UNITED STATES FIRED ON BY THE JAPANESE. No signs of destruction, but a total blackout at night. After Pearl Harbor, it seems, a toy mini-submarine, one of several the Japanese built to threaten the North American continent, surfaced offshore and fired two torpedoes into the coastal wilderness. Not even close to the fort. A couple of trees injured. An attack warning to forest foliage and seagulls. Groping through the dark, blacked-out fort, I find the only buildings with blackout curtains are the hospital and movie theatre. Impossible even to read at night in the barracks. Lying on my bunk I listen to the radio and dream of my fiancée lost in the east. Or, off-duty, I go to the movies. In the next two months I see thirty bad movies, implanting television eyes before television exists.

Assigned to the nightshift in the hospital's reception office, my two
        typewriting
Fingers blunt with bureaucracy, I'm reading a book in deadtime one
        midnight,
Fog covering the building in a white shroud, when a bus arrives,
Disgorges twenty Limited Service misfits exhausted by a trip from
        Pennsylvania.
A weaving, punchdrunk ex-prizefighter leads them in, shouting at me:
"Christ, is this ghost-house the end of the world? God damn, I bet they
Don't even have any fights here! What's the name of this fucking place?"
"Fort Limited Service," I reply. "This is the fort's sacred hospital."
"Limited Service, hell!" he yells. "I'm in shape, I'm ready to fight!"
He begins to shadowbox, fighting his way out of a trap, stops suddenly,
Poses, pointing to his head: "Which one of my eyes you think is bad?"
"I don't know," I shrug indifferently. "The right . . ."
"How'd you guess?" He reaches up, pulls out his right eye,
Puts it, glass, like a piece of ice in my hand.

Sharing is not Limited Service. Limited Service classifies you *alone, special, inferior, alienated dreamer.* How to escape. I study every army bulletin like a convict haunting a law library. The Adjutant General's Officer Candidate

School in Fargo, North Dakota, invites applicants. Three months in winter's heartland, January to March. Extreme cold for a California boy. As a college-educated, two-finger typist-clerk with filing experience (I can file anything alphabetically), I qualify, but my eyes confront the eye chart as if the large E is the original invisible man. Think like a thief. Forge the physical! As a forger, I can't even imitate my own bad handwriting. Safer to get a medical officer to lie. Every doctor is trying for a transfer from this barren coastal fort. I approach a major, an oldtimer always cursing his boredom and the fact that he should be luxuriating in the salary of a colonel.

"Son," he grins. "You got my sympathy. You're an ambitious boy. I like ambition, but I'm trying to escape this creepy place too. I can't lie and turn your bullshit physical condition into shining glory."

Age is too cagey, try bitter, rebellious youth. I find a First Lieutenant with one eye and a black eyepatch. Sympathetic eye comrades! "I'll sign for you, Private," he says, "But if anyone finds out, it's your ass, not mine. You're the forger, I'm just the innocent, harried signer of endless forms. I don't have time to read what the small print says. Agreed?" "Thank you, Sir. You're a Limited Service fiend." "A fiendish friend. Find me an escape too," he says, his good eye gleaming.

The forgery of fate. Accepted at officers' school.
Several days before I leave the alarm bell rings.
A bomber on a practice run crashed in the ocean.
Three of us medics on duty jolt over the dirt road
To the beach, searching for fliers from the plane.
Low fog, limited visibility, intense wilderness
Of sand dunes, pine sentinels, hawks hovering, sea gulls
Soaring, vultures waiting to attack any movement.
Suddenly, plunging out of the booming surf,
Washed back and forth in endless tidal surge,
A body's battered on the beach. Parachuting
Down into spindrift waves, grappling free from harness,
The navigator swam blindly for shore, almost arriving.
The other three crew-members vanish, ocean-missing.
Hoisting the navigator into the ambulance, as we bounce
Back to the hospital, we medics take nervous turns
With futile artificial respiration. No possible luck.
A doctor pronounces him dead, orders me to pack
The body in ice awaiting arrival of the distant Portland
Mortician. As I chip and shovel endless chunks of ice,
The young, shining white flesh sinks beneath snow.
Time stops in slow silence of freezing death.

90

Eyes shut, I sit waiting for the summoned mortician.
His step rings confidently through the basement morgue;
An experienced eye surveys the iced corpse on the table,
Uncovers a naked, tagged leg with critical admiration,
Pats it, pronounces judgment, "Too bad, nice boy."

Marriage in Wartime

In wartime marriage is a sudden escape from frenzy
As if a small, special room slides quietly free
From broken houses shattered by indifferent bombs.

A warning time hovers over this sanctuary.
In January winter our private room will disappear,
The bitter landscape again will ask questions of survival.

Meanwhile, strive to create a blessed, private ceremony,
Transform the agonizing, real world into this room
Where the imagination is still capable of wonder.

For a few brief hours our private room is the world
Filled with the sound of remembered awesome music
And poetry speaking valued sounds beyond time.

What does it matter if time slips and bleeds away
And the future contains difficult absurdities?
A miraculous room measures the limits of wartime love.

Song of Misgiving:
Officers' Candidate School

Living four to a room
In the Adjutant General's school,
I dream of love in the snow.
Tests, test after test,
March, march, march
In the flatland of winter,

Older guys sagging behind
Into the dark-lettered ambulance;
Inspections and no rest.

And then more tests.
Study dolt-faced to become
A clever master of forms
In the Adjutant General's school.
A million combat soldiers will rejoice,
Count on your bureaucratic skill
To solve the complex difference
Between tests of true and false
And the puzzle of multiple choice.

As final physical proof of war
They give you ten more tests,
March you out in five below zero
Down an endless icy road.
Your company officer yells,
"Fall on your face!"
As a fighter plane attacks
Twenty feet over your head
Buzzing you flat on the ice.

My wife pins me with two gold bars
And they call me Lieutenant
Master of endless forms,
Covered with administrative scars.
Cheers ring out as I put on
My officers' cap like a lamp,
And I'm shipped off
To guard duty in a
German Prisoner of War Camp.

In the Arena of Ants: German Prisoners of War

Papers glow huge headlines: ROMMEL DEFEATED! ALLIES TRIUMPH IN AFRICA!
As if from an underground arena of ants, 370,000 German prisoners of
    war emerge slowly,

secretly, scattered throughout the United States in isolated, wasteland
    camps.
Combat troops from the Afrika Korps paratroopers tank crews artillery
    infantry
still believing fervently in Nazi victory Heil Hitler!
    1943. Europe remains under German domination Throughout the
        United States in
prisoner of war camps, Nazis install their prearranged plan:
    To enforce political morale, German officers masquerade as enlisted
        men.
    Secret kangaroo courts punish anti-Nazi offenders.
    Swastikas are burned in the backs of rebels.
        Bravura Nazi newspapers are published from material clipped
            out of American papers.
        At blazing campfire ceremonies, *Mein Kampf* is read and
            venerated like the Bible.
        Under bright moonlight, songs and speeches promise a
            new Aryan Europe.
        In bizarre force across the United States, Nazi
            communities flame into existence.

"A denial of our most trenchant assertions, the desert is a question to All
    and horizon of Nothing . . .
Never will sand disown sand."
    Edmond Jabes, *The Book of Shares*

Nor will the desert's arena of ants ever disown sand.
I remember the implacable desert outside of Trinidad, Colorado,
    hypnotizing red ants coursing relentlessly out of deep, eternal tunnels.
I remember barbed wire fences, created to contain western cattle, rising
    to new heights defining the vast prison world of modern wars.
I remember guard towers towering darkly in cold, electric nights,
    manned mostly by Limited Service guards with little or no experience
    in firing weapons.
I remember a one-eyed guard panicking, firing into the German officers'
    compound, killing two German officers with one shot, the bullet
    penetrating one officer, richocheting off a wall, striking another
    officer.
I remember dust-storms blowing up phantom forms, twisting in thick,
    gritty air. Through the dust, soccer-playing prisoners looked like
    sand-dancing ghosts.
Always I remember the remote majesty of snow-capped mountains

south-west of the camp blocking escape to Mexico of which prisoners dreamed.

I remember mocking duality of guards and prisoners, guards feeling confined by prisoners, all of us caught in the vice of sullen waiting for invisible freedom.

I remember wondering if universal prison camps mark poetry's endgame as camp numbers replace verbal identity.

I remember German troops, perfectly drilled, marching, singing triumphantly with Nazi pride and arrogance. Nodding his approval of these machine-like troops, the American camp commander mutters: "Our troops should be so well-trained!" "You know what they're singing, Sir?"
"I don't give a shit, Lieutenant. They're god damn well-drilled."
"They're singing the Horst Wessel song, Sir."
"What's that?"

I remember guard duty, finding a jagged hole in the perimeter fence. Two prisoners escape, a boldly lettered sign marks their exit: AUSGANG/EINGANG—exit and entrance to the absurd world.
Two days later I remember a tobacco-chewing, leather-skinned rancher driving angrily through a dust-storm into the camp. In the truck's bay, sit two prisoners, large whitepainted letters PW still marking their shirts and pants. A stuttering ranchhand holds a rifle on the prisoners. They complain indignantly: "We almost got shot! In America, it is not safe. Everyone carries a gun! We Germans believe in law and order!"

I remember the blond-haired, handsome German ranking officer, a Lieutenant-Colonel in charge of camp prisoners under the Geneva Convention. He wears a medal for hand-to-hand bayonet combat in the Russian invasion, a General Staff officer trained in the Prussian aristocratic military tradition. Despite his rank, he's forced to obey the Nazi political officer, a stocky Captain with darting, suspicious eyes who dictates the strident tone of loyalty expected from German troops. Philosophically, the Colonel clings to the metaphysical General Staff belief of aristocratic gentlemen creating victory from defeat, a belief fostered by the famous military theorists, Clausewitz and Gneisenau: *"Defeat must result in inevitable victory!"* Though the Colonel mocks his cruel, plebian Nazi captain, politically he has to conform. Staring at a silver-framed photograph of his wife and children, the Colonel struggles to reconcile his Nazi compromise with the mystical goal of losing to win.

I remember escorting two German prisoners dying from tuberculosis to a prison hospital in Arizona. Pistol I have never fired strapped around my waist, I lead the two prisoners into the station restaurant in El

Paso, where we change trains. A crescendo of enthusiastic rapping erupts against the large, plateglass windows. Black faces in American uniforms stare in at the German prisoners. The pale prisoners stare back dully at the clamor outside. Suddenly, I realize that since the army is still segregated, black American soldiers are not permitted in the restaurant. Here I am eating inside with two German prisoners, while black Americans, forbidden to enter, rap on the windows. As we eat, white officers hustle the gaping black soldiers away.

I remember prisoners inventing the game of red ants, bored tribute to the Horizon of Nothing hovering as prison vision. Kill two flies, throw them into the arena of scurrying red ants. Bet eagerly on the time it takes for desperate ant teamwork to dismantle the flies' wings, drag them as sacrificial prey down into their tunnels.

Always, I remember prisoners cheering as the flies disappear, checking their watches to verify the winning time. Always I remember the arena of ants swallowing fly-victims.

One-eye and the German Prisoners of War in Colorado

(1)

Why do I feel I'm fishing in the desert? Glaring sun makes the desert ripple like water. Somehow the barbed wire fences dangle men instead of fish. Lining the Limited Service fishermen up for guard duty makes me squint they're so lopsided. Limping is my new angled perspective. Most guards have never even fired weapons. Hunched over his machine gun in a guard tower, One-Eye, the private with a black eye-patch, looks at the menacing machine gun and his rifle stacked against the wall, as if they were sharks.

(2)

Am I going to spend the rest of my life guarding prisoners? These German Africa Corps soldiers are so healthy their skin shines in the sun. I can hardly wait for winter to shut down on their muscles. They play soccer and volleyball with grim intent as though all games are mythologies. Inspecting One-Eye's tower as Officer of the Guard, I see him looking at me through his single window as if I were a lifeguard. "Lieutenant," he says, "I'm glad you're visiting."

95

(3)

I show the Nazi newspaper, a surrealistic collage put together from American papers and magazines, to One-Eye in his tower. Bad idea, it makes him more nervous. Taking a telescopic look through his good eye, he says, amazed, "They're trying to steal Superman." I don't tell him they believe in another kind of Superman. He recognizes only one kind who soars away over barbed wire with a big S on his chest.

(4)

One-Eye is getting more aggressive. He fingers his rifle in the guard tower, blows dust off the machine gun. He reads about how they work, although there's no place to practice. Officer of the Guard one stormy night, rain spotting my glasses, trickling down my jacket, I climb up into One-Eye's tower. Through fogged glasses I freeze, seeing One-Eye's machine gun pointing at me. I scream, "Stupid bastard, what the hell are you doing?" "Sorry, Lieutenant," he apologizes, "I thought you were Superman climbing up my tower. I wanted to show you I was ready to help." How can I answer the sudden unity of war and comic books? Shaking, I sit down, wipe my glasses for freedom vision.

(5)

In deep night I wake to a siren wailing emergency. One-Eye has fired his rifle into the compound killing two German officers with one shot. The bullet goes through one officer, ricochets off a wall, hits the second officer in the heart. In the hospital I visit One-Eye under arrest sitting on a cot in a locked room. "What happened?" "Lieutenant," he says, agitated. "It was an accident. I was firing to save Superman and I killed him. I thought he was flying over the fence and they were after him."

(6)

The Nazis are on strike. No prisoner will work until the American camp commander lets them conduct a Nazi martyr funeral. Under huge swastika banners made out of blankets, they march in goosestep formation to the burial site outside of the prison in the desert. Their band plays Beethoven's Funeral March, poor Beethoven. Nazi flags and flowers drape the coffins. German officers take turns reading from *Mein Kampf*. The whole ceremony makes the bright desert sky seem full of rigid plaster casts. One-Eye has been shipped out to Cloud-Cuckoo-Land. When they examine him they'll find his good eye is a real tunnel.

(7)

A Nazi world in an American desert is like watching a machine operate in a block of ice. The machine and the landscape operate with the same

96

cold, impersonal designs. A hawk in the sky becomes a hawk in the heart. When winter whistles down from the mountains, we wear fur hoods on the night watch. Limping in the fur along icy roads, we look like crippled storks. Guards and prisoners, both full of barbed wire fantasies.

(8)

One-Eye writes me a postcard: "I miss you, Lieutenant, your tower calls. They're going to try me for killing Superman. My lawyer says they can't convict a one-eyed soldier. I want to get up in court and ask the judge, "How can you kill Superman?" But my lawyer won't let me. I guess I have to follow the law even though there isn't no law these days."

(9)

The desert fishing goes on. The barbed wire is a net. The net spreads into camps around the world. Men are learning a new fishing mentality. They hook souls on barbed wire as One-Eye thought he hooked Super-man. Goodbye One-Eye. You disappear in time like a fisherman pulled down in deep water by huge shadow-forms knifing through the currents. I go on living with barbed wire and desert as day and night become the same intense reflections of slow time. At night searchlights make the barbed wire dance in cold, glittering points to match the stars above.

My Wife's Dream in the Midst of War

In the first night of spring,
Soft air swelling with growth,
Confused by humming sounds,
My wife dreamt that God took
From man the gift of language
And gave it to the towering trees.
While men with arms groped
Wildly through destroyed cities,
And desperate, illiterate symbols
Were painted on dark walls,
The trees stood rooted in time
And spoke with wind-shaped clarity.
Flowing from tangled roots, their language
Shaped a pride of leaves in the sky,
Praising those who live in place
Free from the wild wanderers of war.

Shanghai Stories

Everything   big
goes on   all
around me   small

shanghai 1

Toil and trouble
on the double
   hyphen, oh missing hyphen—
alas, oh military punctuation!

Never sing why   or wherefore   in the army
orders appear   suddenly   on smudged paper
I'm transfered out of the prisoner of war world
Can it be? A flyboy high in the sky in the
Army Air Force   Brookley Field   Mobile, Alabama?
Yes-No   A military police combat company
En route to Africa   guarding air bases
To qualify for overseas duty   At-tenshun! For-ward Marsh!
I lead my company to the shooting range
"Sergeant," I whisper with hangdog eyes, "Shit, please
help me   I've never fired a gun before."   *Never?*
"Jesus Christ, what turkey did they give me!"
Suspicious as a bank robber coaching a recruit
on his first mission   he loads the heavy pistol
hands it to me   I lift its hard weight
like a shotputter   hoisting his Sisyphus stone
aim   wavering   at the distant target   fire wildly
missing the target completely   soldiers fall down
laughing   the furious sergeant thinks   "What kind
of four-eyed clown-shooter is this new bastard?"

Examining my papers, they transfer me again   assign me
Base Classification Officer   what do I know about planes?
misfit alarm   what if I send a pilot to kingdom come?
where am I, where?   In the confusion, General Marshall,
Chief of Staff, calls from Washington   "What the hell is
going on? A lost officer is roaming somewhere   He's absent
without leave from a German PW camp   Have you got him there?"

98

All powers converge on my ghostlike state   because   because
I was transfered because a hyphen was left out of an order
the order read   "Transfer so many officers *over-age in grade*."
some dull renegade clerk left out the hyphen   the reluctant hyphen
vanishes   at the age of 23 I'm not *over-age in grade*
but I am overage   excessive   too many second lieutenants
The Chief of Staff commands, "Restore the missing hyphen!"
and I'm shipped   like a glittering new postage stamp
back   back   to another German prisoner of war camp

Toil and trouble
on the double
    hyphen, oh missing hyphen—
alas, oh military punctuation!

shanghai 2

Toil and trouble
on the double,
balancing books
in the officers' club
rub-a-dub-dub!

In the new German prisoner of war camp   Greeley, Colorado
one of my duties   running the American officers' club
Accountant Master, what?   balancer of money books
profits   debits   another language to learn
The Colonel, the American commanding officer, orders
"Keep the club in the black, Lieutenant, or it's your ass
That's all you have to do" "Yes, Sir, what are the assets?"
"You've got plenty of asshole assets, kid   Slots and booze
Slots and booze!   Here are the golden keys to the slots"

High in the gambling world   dangling slot machine keys
checking the bar for supplies   outside on the other side of
the barbed wire   German prisoners under Nazi discipline
build a theatre inside a barracks for Nazi festivities
and a production of *Faust*   A heavily made up, stocky,
middle-aged blonde haunts the officers' club   drinking highballs
banging the slots   playing bridge with her friends
every day she leaves a personal check to pay her bill
Often the check bounces   my books are screwed

99

Three times I let her re-write the bouncing check   after all
Mrs. Blonde is the Commanding Officer's wife   after the
fourth bounce   stupid me   I take the check to the Colonel
He looks at it with a frown   a frown opening into a coffin
"My wife has a problem, Lieutenant   You should try to understand . . ."
A week later I'm gone   on another shanghai trip
this time to a Quartermaster hell   Fort Warren, Wyoming

shanghai 3

Toil and trouble
on the double
in this idealistic war
against racist Nazi tyranny
where is the American star?

Fort Warren   huge Quartermaster training center   supply troops
army still segregated   black soldiers drawn up in waves
for reveille and retreat   the day before I arrive a race riot
occurs at retreat   drunk, a black soldier returns from Cheyenne
strips off his clothes   parades naked   mock salute to his white officer
The white officer loses control   slaps him   as one, black troops
break ranks   rush the white officer   he runs for his office
locks himself in   a riot develops   black troops break into the arsenal
seize weapons   tanks and troops are called to put down the riot
two black soldiers killed in the battle before cool heads prevail
strict censorship   nothing in the papers or radio news   I'm fastened
like a white clothespin into this tension   assigned to a company of
black soldiers awaiting discharge   a transient company of soldiers
from the south   blacks with advanced syphilis or criminal records
drafted illegally to prevent priviliged white boys from serving
blacks shipped immediately to Fort Warren for discharge proceedings
Monday evenings I cry, "Fall out!" assemble advanced syphilis cases
march them to the hospital for their shots   weekly, we white officers
conduct a barracks search for knives, razors, guns, drugs   three months
of racial turmoil   constant turnover   arriving, preparing discharge
   papers
departing   presumably, in other sections of the vast fort
the war is proceeding   here it's a strange kind of
civil war   until I'm transfered hurly burly again
back   back   into the German prisoner of war program

100

Toil and trouble
on the double
in this idealistic war
against racist Nazi tyranny
where is the American star?

The Saga of Walter Schoenstedt and the Re-education of German Prisoners of War[1]

(1)

Immigrant. The word, stone of promise. Is a stone promising? An immigrant carries a stone pressing his heart, stone of the past, his lost country. Even if the new land accepts the immigrant. embracing his new home with zeal, the stone remains, invisible, a singular weight. United Stones of America, melting pot full of stones that do not melt.

(2)

1909. Born in Germany, father a Berlin bricklayer, poor, working-class family. Schoenstedt is five years old when World War I erupts to pulverize the century. The boy grows up amongst women, father drafted into the army on the western front. "Women ran the streetcars, made hand grenades, tended furnaces, shoveled coal, unloaded boats."* Mother commutes three hours every day to and from a factory making grenades. Worn-out when she arrives home, the boy has already boiled their dinner of potatoes. Occasionally a turnip. No meat, no vegetables, no milk. "We had forgotten the lovely desires that a child can have . . . And with our increasing maturity grew our bitterness and there appeared a new brutal manner of thinking and seeing."*

(3)

Brutal manner of thinking and seeing. Hunger. Skin grows pale as flowing blood fades into invisibility. "When we stripped for the school medical examination we looked like walking skeletons in colorless skin."* A pompous, nationalistic teacher nicknamed Tomcat rules over Schoenstedt in school. Tomcat teaches only "the community of hatred against the enemy." Blind duty is Tomcat's password. He punishes strictly, "swishing the cane down on our palms so that they swelled and became red."* Dur-

---

[1]All sentences in quotation marks and with asterisks are excerpted from Walter Schoenstadt's novel *In Praise of Life*, Farrar and Rhinehart, 1938.

ing recess, Tomcat marches his schoolboys around the courtyard like Prussian soldiers, thick glasses reflecting dreams of military glory.

(4)

Germany defeated. The Kaiser gone. A feeble republic, economy too weak for democracy. In 1918 Tomcat teaches nine-year-old Schoenstedt and his friends that Germany's defeat is due to "a stab in the back," traitorous elements at home betraying the army. Several boys protest, asking "Which traitors?" Tomcat beats them on their palms with his blackboard pointer. One day an educational miracle. A new young drawing teacher presents a laughing parable: An Emperor rules over people forced to accept his every word. To astonish the world, the Emperor commands his tailor to create the most magnificent uniform ever, or else! Despairing, the clever tailor draws in the air with acrobatic gestures a gigantic uniform covered with glittering braid and hundreds of battle decorations. The air is radiant. Afraid to offend the Emperor, servile ministers praise the new uniform's magnificence. "A new standard of excellence for our country!" they cry in unison. Pleased, the Emperor struts with naked glory into the astonished air. Only one impudent, little boy cries out, "That man is showing his penis!" Laughing, the art teacher draws a caricature of the naked Emperor. He looks like the Kaiser! Befriending Schoenstedt, the art teacher praises the boy's drawings, speaks of a possible future as scenic designer, entering a theatre of dreams! "You taught us to see . . . When you talked of the great masters, and the times in which they lived, it meant for many of us the beginning of a new way of thinking."*

(5)

Disillusioned, bitter from war, the boy's father returns to dream of laying bricks into a new sky. No bricks, no building, no sky of hope. The boy dreams of forests, mountains, escape from the swamp of poor unemployed in Berlin. Hating Tomcat's world of prescribed nationalistic books, he haunts the public library. Sensing the boy's grey, sunken heart, a spinster librarian gives him a book by Jack London. "I went to the little park and sat down on a bench. Then I read the American writer, Jack London. There were dogs and wolves, and indescribable white men and Indians in snow and ice, in a land called Alaska."* Alaska's free, open wilderness submerges shabby Berlin slums. Schoenstedt imagines Tomcat's Nietzschean superman blending with "the sinewy, powerful man Jack London described, striding victoriously across the earth, conquering at every step. Was it the call of the wolf, or the man in him? No matter. It was a strong call, as powerful as the waters of the river called the Yukon." A boy's call for manhood and space, friendship with animals, escape from a turbulent city torn between rightist military power and leftist political rebellion.

(6)

Graduating despite Tomcat's critical comments and poor grades, he seeks Wanderschaft escape time from gloomy parents into difficult nature. Pitiless landscapes, indifferent to human pretense. Glory of trees, wildflowers, clouds flying across lofty sky. Long hours of farmhand work. Milking cows, huge eyes staring passively. Dogs barking, fierce territorial protectors. Days of tramping roads with homeless wanderers. He roams eastward with a band of friendly gypsy horse traders. Villagers slam doors on them, cursing: "Thieves, gypsies, panhandlers!" Evenings the gypsies sing songs to a guitar. The boy discovers performing ability. People laugh and clap when he bellows out a hoarse song. At wayside inns, in return for food, he takes to singing. Lure of nature fades in rigorous winter. Needing money he returns to Berlin, works as load carrier for a construction company, then for two years on the new subway. Joins a strong leftist union, struggling for workers' rights. Witnesses growing Nazi demonstrations, with his union friends fights the demonstrators in the streets. Aged nineteen publishes first story. In 1931, at twenty-two, first novel, *Kaempfende Jugend (Fighting Youth)*, sells twenty thousand copies. A gifted, young, working-class novelist! Two days before Hitler becomes Chancellor in 1933, Schoenstedt's second novel, *Motiv Unbekannt (Motive Unknown)*, is published, seized by the Nazis. He goes into hiding, friends help him flee across the border. His third novel, *Auf der Flucht Erschossen (Shot While Escaping)*, is published in France and England by a small refugee publisher, falls into quick oblivion. Europe does not want to believe in a new Nazi danger. Schoenstedt emigrates to the United States, and finds New York.

(7)

Confusion and promise of the powerful vertical skyscraper enigma. Literary friends offer publishing prospects for new novel about his youth. Works with German refugees building international support against Hitler. Writes his best novel, *Das Lob des Lebens (In Praise of Life)*, published by Farrar and Rinehart in 1938. Dedicated to "The Youth of Germany and the United States of America." Jack London solidarity, youthful future of hope. Published in a limited edition, the novel receives a few good reviews, vanishes as creative words transform into universal military language. Hitler invades Poland in 1939, youth is conscripted throughout the world. As World War II spreads, Schoenstedt enlists in American army. Applies for infantry officers' school. Hunting ability learned in Wanderschaft year, youthful lessons in survival help him endure rugged officers' training, earn sharpshooter's medal. One day in a secret conference at the Provost Marshal General's Office in Washington, D.C. meets Major Edward Davison, soon to be promoted to Lieutenant Colonel.

(8)

Spark of immigrant, New World spirits. Davison, newly appointed head of the Top Secret Prisoner of War Special Projects Division for the Re-Education of German Prisoners of War. Top Secret because it violates the Geneva Convention that war prisoners maintain their national customs and military discipline. A project suggested by Eleanor Roosevelt to her husband when Nazi tyranny created violence in camps throughout the country. Kangaroo courts sentenced anti-Nazis to death or had swastikas carved in their backs. How could the United States tolerate contemptuous flashes of Nazi rule in its own domain?

Davison, imposing, ruddy faced Scot from Glasgow but reared in Leeds and South Shields, gifted Cambridge-educated poet destined for British literary fame, transformed into professor at the University of Colorado. Natural orator and teacher, when he spoke everyone listened, "words, and the song of words convinced his life," as his son, poet Peter Davison wrote. Linked to Schoenstedt by immigrant myths. How to be American writers? English and German tones hamper elusive American language rhythms. Both from working class poverty sensitive to how wealth controls power unjustly. Locked together suddenly in powerful Army positions dependent on each other, Davison without German; Schoenstedt requiring Davison's administrative skills to create an aggressive, democratic, anti-Nazi program. Davison, expert administrator, who could sharpen ironic language to satisfy high level demands for a less propagandistic word than "re-education" and wrote in an office memo:

"The term 're-education' will not be used in referring to the mission of this Branch. The term 'I.D. Program' (Intellectual Diversion) will be used whenever reference is made to the program."

Davison and Schoenstedt, stubborn, temperamental idealists, fighters for the Statue of Liberty immigrant dream, "Bring me your homeless, tempest-tossed, yearning to breathe free." Frustrated, proud men with suppressed writing ambitions; ambitious men with sudden power to affect the war of ideas; men with historical convictions that the war of ideas can be as important as the war of slaughter.

(9)

Here I, narrator, enter the Special Projects Division as Schoenstedt's assistant in the Programs Branch. Our secret, camouflaged business office

104

at 50 Broadway near Wall Street in New York spews out programs to prison camps. With Schoenstedt I visit the "Factory" at Fort Keamey in Rhode Island, an abandoned coast guard station. We plan *Der Ruf (The Call)*, a bi-monthly newspaper for prisoners written and edited by anti-Nazis Schoenstedt has screened and quartered in this secluded camp. Sharing ideas is joyous freedom, no sense of prisoners and guards here. Schoenstedt works closely with gifted men he's recruited, including future novelists Alfred Andersch, Hans Werner Richter, literary historian Gustav Rene Hocke, publisher Curt Vinz. Veteran anti-Nazis, they believe in democracy with a socialistic bent. They reject the "collective guilt" that Washington officials impose. The Kearney group aid in developing film, book, and history programs that circulate to all prison camps. Under the title New World Books, German writers banned by the Nazis, are re-printed, sold in cheap editions—Thomas Mann, Heinrich Mann, Franz Werfel, Carl Zuckmayer, Leonhard Frank, and others. Bertolt Brecht's anti-Nazi play, *Fear and Trembling of the Third Reich*, is vetoed by a high-ranking American officer in Washington, a German refugee distrustful of Brecht's "leftwing propaganda play." Arguing for freedom of ideas, Schoenstedt and Davison get the decision reversed. Schoenstedt takes me to see Brecht in New York for permission to reprint his play. Climbing several flights of stairs, we hear a loud babble of arguing voices. Cigar in hand, Brecht opens the door, gestures at the radio: "That's the most exciting theatre in the world!" A United Nations session is arguing about aid to the devastated Ukraine. Epic Theatre.

For final permission to publish a secret newspaper, *Der Ruf*, I am sent as trustworthy courier to the Pentagon. My day as Hermes, winged messenger in beehive frenzy of relentless corridors, maze of ambiguous signs, turning, twisting, where am I, where is General So and So, never heard of him, around and down, then up? All day I run, walk, wipe perspiration, salute, answer skeptical questions, present authorization papers, gather endless signatures. Humming, an autograph hunter I, pursuing signatures till I die. One signature away from nightfall, I descend into the secret printing office deep in windowless bowels of this surrealistic war fortress. Huge presses hum arrogant, clandestine rhythms. No human presence. Am I in some mad, secret world of machines operating mechanically? As I grope desperately around machines, a huge, bear-like man with thick glasses, shaggy beard, baseball cap, tangled grey hair, long filthy printing apron confronts me. "Secret paper in German?" he mutters. "Shit, son, that's kindergarten stuff. You know how many languages my babies can print? Thirty-two." I salute his languages, stagger out of the Pentagon into darkness. What kind of war involves the printing of thirty-two secret languages?

105

(10)

Davison and Schoenstedt drive the program with furious, twin-like energy. Our fervent staff, only some twenty officers, labor frantically. Washington frowners work to keep our program small. Counter-Intelligence is spying on our "leftwing, intellectual" program. Davison and Schoenstedt have begun a program training anti-Nazi prisoners to work with military government in Germany. War is ending, Hitler dead a suicide in his bizarre Bunker. No, his ideas are alive in the United States. A new larger camp is set up at Fort Getty, Rhode Island, then one in Virginia. Well-known educators are recruited to help train these prisoners, Howard Mumford Jones, writer and professor from Harvard, Henry Ehrmann, refugee historian, T.V. Smith, former congressman and professor from the University of Chicago, and many others. Schoenstedt is often away, recruiting, interviewing prisoners. Who knows better hidden Nazi words, corrupt tones of compromise?

One evening Schoenstedt invites me and my wife to meet his new, young wife. A rare social occasion. My first time in Schoenstedt's apartment. But Schoenstedt is not occasional. His pleasant, bland, silent American wife waits, awe-struck, on his charismatic mystery. Little to talk about since we cannot talk about a secret program except when Schoenstedt takes me aside and tells me privately what he wants. My wife resents the way Schoenstedt sentences his naive wife to silent servitude. She seems like an eager, empty well waiting mysteriously to be filled with water by a veteran dowser. Schoenstedt is too obsessed by mission and secrecy to fill his wife with anything but his body.

(11)

Every secret program breeds absurdities, opening envelope within envelope, inner contents stamped TOP SECRET: "Someone is tampering with Coca-Cola machines in various Provost Marshal General offices. Report any observed misconduct to senior officials." One day I carry a secret mssive to an unknown destination near Rockefeller Center. What am I delivering? Approaching through guarded military security doors, suddenly I hear an orchestra, then a husky familiar voice singing in German. Am I in heaven? Marlene Dietrich is recording a program for transmission to German troops everywhere. Captive, put me on the receiving list. I never learn the mysterious message I transmit. Can it be Schoenstedt's list of suggested cabaret songs from his old gypsy days? I never learn. He pretends he doesn't know.

(12)

Fear of communism spreads like false butter. The so-called McCarthy era really begins in World War II. Writers are suspect because they read

106

too much suspicious material. Classified hostile by non-readers, Davison and Schoenstedt are warned Counter-Intelligence is spying on us. Assigned to burn confidential wastepaper at end of day, I and colleagues begin to watch a young, redhaired Second Lieutenant in charge of security. He puts his feet up on his desk, sits twirling his revolver when he isn't typing. One afternoon we discover in his wastepaper basket—miracle of beneficent miracles—a copy of his report to Washington Counter-Intelligence. In his diligent manner, he types five required copies with a plethora of carbons so one copy comes out on the backside without his noticing. He crumples what he thinks is a blank page, and throws it away. In his report he accuses us of fostering intellectual, impractical ideas; reading leftwing magazines and newspapers. He confuses our names with different names in the notorious redbaiting book, *The Red Network*, claiming that we belong to unknown organizations. With proof of these lies, Davison fends off Washington attackers led by a Colonel commanding Counter-Intelligence. The climate of time is against us. Our program is too successful in filling prisoners with hope about a new democratic Germany. In early 1946, as we prepare to take the prisoners we have trained to Germany to help military government, our program is disbanded. Davison, and Schoenstedt who was busy in France setting up another camp to train German prisoners, receive high decorations. Davison receives the Legion of Honor as head of the Special Projects Program. The rest of us are given Commendation Ribbons, signs of bureaucratic Machiavellianism: *If you want to eliminate someone, promote or commend him into exile.* In Bavaria, American military government refuses to hire many of our anti-Nazi prisoners. Andersch and Richter re-create *Der Ruf*, criticizing both Americans and Russians. Their neutral stance transforms into the influential literary movement, *Gruppe 47*, in 1947 when *Der Ruf* is shut down by American authorities. The cold war is freezing.

(13)

For a time, Schoenstedt remains in the Army serving as head of a War Crimes investigation team preparing for the Nuremberg trials. Back in California, rejoicing in my civilian status, I hear from Schoenstedt in August, 1946:

War Crimes investigation is not a romantic business. If the grave is discovered somewhere in the deep woods of beautiful Bavaria with deer and bear watching from the underbrush, and the light comes through the tall pines at just the proper angle with specks of dust and butterflies dancing in a hazy sun, the belief that plain murder could not have been committed might grow strong. But then you're thinking back: your own experiences, old and new, and the human head chopped cleanly in half—now on exhibit in Dachau—or the lamp shades made from human skin, and the collection of twentieth century torture instruments, and the expression on faces you have seen and will never forget all your life long—just a few seconds remembering and you make sure the bottom of this soft forest will be dug and the sand searched for even, perhaps, the knuckle bone of a little finger . . . Near here in 1945, a boy from the vicinity of Chicago parachuted to safety, You know what the rules of land warfare are, but safety? He came down all right, but his mother is still waiting for him. Now you get down to business. The farmer, shrewd eyes, stocky, ruddy, clicks his heels: "Ja, Herr Hauptmann." Then you crack down on him, fast, surprise him. He is not alert after a while. Make him confident, scare him, and smoke, and give him a puff too. Finally "I fired two shots at the parachute." Yes, he did. And he is such a clean, peaceful looking bastard, and he adds happily. "As a Christian I took good care of him. I gave the American pilot a nice clean bunch of straw." Everything is nice and clean around here. Even the cow shit. There are Americans who believe this Bavarian cow shit is the cleanest they have ever seen . . . When you leave and tell him the boys will take him to Dachau tomorrow, he cries, the Christian.

(14)

Silence and separation except for brief, drifting letters. Schoenstedt's handwriting bold, hurried, skipping across the page with his familiar, great energy:

My old War Crimes team has been dissolved and the boys have gone in all directions. God only knows how long it will take them to get rid of several thousand war criminals still not processed. I have taken a job with Military Government as Refugee-Welfare officer. My job is civilian . . . Next year and especially this winter people will suffer more than before. There is no fodder in the silos, the fields and meadows are burned. It is as if this war will never end, as if there was a Lord who intends to extend the usual seven lean years into a decade of hunger everywhere. The Fourth Reich of abundance and without occupation is being promised in whispers. Already the U.S. army is recruiting former SS for the final war against Russia . . . Operation powers, I am sure, have been returned to German administration at least one year ahead of time. It would have been better if we had returned powers to those cities or districts which had earned

108

that privilege by proving the proper attitudes, and by establishment of proper examples of democratic behavior and action . . .

(15)

Years of silence again. Working hard I publish poetry, a play, a biography. My wife and I now have two children to support. I begin to teach. Suddenly, in January, 1952, Schoenstedt writes from New York: "I have just returned from Europe. There are many things I should write to you about, but they remain better unwritten. Unfortunately, the Gestapo is still pretty much alive. Can you help me translate my new novel, *Union of Wolves*, for which I've sold rights to a Swiss publisher?" I start translating. Amidst scenes of war crimes investigations, the first part describes brilliant hunting episodes (Schoenstedt's major recreation) in the Bavarian mountains. *Hirsch*, is it just a deer? "Not an elk or deer," Schoenstedt says, "something inbetween." In February, 1952, a more urgent note: "I am trying desperately to get to Denver. You don't know it, but I have some kind of family there. Do you remember . . . (a chief administrative officer of the Special Projects Division)? He actually told an interrogating Inspector General that we were all impractical intellectuals. The bastard." In February, 1952, more desperate messages: "It is very unfortunate that I have been caught in complete bankruptcy. Asked big shot Davison (fool that I am) for some money. He couldn't even part with one. Poor guy . . . My European publisher pesters me about the rest of the story because they would like to publish this summer. The point is can I hang on long enough without starving to death. I saw the beast, the "Hirsch" at the zoo yesterday. It is called a red deer." Splintering of friendship between Davison and Schoenstedt, Davison in a new high level academic deanship, his poetic ambitions uneasily suppressed, Schoenstedt, bankrupt in New York, struggling to finish an unusual novel based on his wartime experiences. What has Schoenstedt done to cause his present plight? Perhaps the finished manuscript will inform me of missing adventures. I send 120 pages of a rough translation of *Union of Wolves* to his small hotel address in New York. In ten days the manuscript is returned marked: "Not at this address. No forwarding address available." I never hear from Schoenstedt again.

(16)

Rumors ripple on the turbulent surface of time. His novel is never published. He vanishes completely. In Germany? Not likely. After his interrogation of so many Nazis, it is too dangerous for him to return to Germany. Davison, busy university administrator again, has lost all contact. Sad ending of a dynamic wartime endeavor. Schoenstedt is said to have fallen in love with a Polish refugee, perhaps smuggled her illegally into the United States. Was this involved with the bankruptcy he mentioned? Counter-Intelligence always suspected him unjustly of communist leanings. Perhaps they're still after him, along with the Un-American Affairs Committee now that the McCarthy Era has erupted. Maybe he's just in hiding from his debts. Perhaps he is divorced at last from the paranoic confusion of challenging, idealistic words in a world blasted by visual images of nuclear bombs and concentration camps. End of Jack London wilderness, closure of linguistic ambitions. Word has it he may be running a nursery in a remote Connecticut small town. Leave him in impossible peace, at last in the tranquil, open relationship to nature that he always desired. The confusion of immigrant languages, cultures, camps, technological warfare, transformed by the clarity of rooted plants.

1950s
Living Blindly in
the Dream of Victory

Family Fantasies after the War

A Guilty Father to His Daughter

Why are you always glad to me?
Shouts my daughter gladfully
A twist of time a tuneful word
Happy I roll into the glad gully

High father in my Morning Glory
Silk virtue violently in me
I rule my family like an old fox hound
And father my way in fancy

When I curse her she catcalls
And cancels her sparky consent
Carnal her sun foams out and her flesh
Firms between us fixed as cement

Prince of fathers in my glad gully
Hobbledehoy in my fatherly rain
Why are you always glad to me?
Demon down the fatherly drain

The Momentary Glimpses of Women through Windows

At dusk time, the time of softness, I catch
A momentary glimpse of women through windows,
Beautiful, strange, absolute.
I drive home to you through evening fog
Flowing like the smooth sap of a varnish tree
Over Christmas lights brilliant as scarlet fire birds
Flying through old memories of desire.

113

Along the street the domes of evergreens
Sing that women are like shade trees,
And the city traffic stares through smoke
With the sullen frenzy of ancestral strangers
Searching for love through nets of circumstance.
I think of you waiting, my love, like these
Momentary glimpses of women through windows,
Beautiful, strange, absolute,
Rays of wonder like the starfish on some foreign beach
Whose distance measures only my desire coming to your waiting.

The Shape of the Poem

Hot sun cannot shape the poem,
The poem withers in that heat.
Flesh wrinkles the poem,
Minglings and marriages,
Children and fantasies,
As you stand before the mirror,
Naked, in soft morning light,
And the awakening lines of your body
Become the lines of my poem.

Flesh of the Fawn

Vigilant on her door, the vibrant sign
In large letters twangs like lute strings:
        Hello
Knock please—if there is not any answer
        please go away—
After her bath the demons of dawdling begin.
Before the magnet mirror she turns timidly,
Flesh of the fawn, pivoting to please her dream.
One arm reaches for some goading afterglow;
Hip out in the thrust of devotional flesh,
She peers anxiously at sprouting breasts.
Next her comb's teeth arch through hair
That breaks into burnished temple waves,

114

Elflocks over the ears, bangs over the forehead.
The nightgown, flaring with jeweled colors,
Jiggles into place over jump spark skin.
Then the ordering of animals, pillow-piled,
The teddy bear, glazed tighthead; dusky dog
And jumbo elephant; on top she clamps the real cat
Who clings, claws her arm, and the child cries
Until, deep in the mirror, she sees her crying self
And slams the mirror shut. Ordered again, neck high,
Swashbuckling, she slides into bed with a baroque bloom.

Death of a Cat

A sultry summer evening, my children playing jacks
     in the hot, grimy garage
     under their grey cat's yellow eyes,
     when the rubbery jack ball
     pops like a bubble into the street
And the cocky cat after its red-streaking path.

Brakes scrunch, the cat shoots up in the air
     hit harshly over an ear,
     and the children scream
     at the death of their pet.
     While I haul a hose to clean
the clotted pavement stains, I remember mother's Irish legend:

In the Irish Golden Age, three fasting clerks on pilgrimage
     sail hungrily off to sea,
     praying with soft, folded hands
     their serene faith in God's care.
     For trust the youngest clerk says,
"I think I will take the silence of my small grey cat."

Reaching a rocky island, they beach the boat
     and kneel to speak the Psalms;
     the cat creeps to a wild wave,
     snatches a salmon from the foam.
     Still the clerks doubt the Lord's hand
until the fish begins to burn on a sudden fire of coals.

Kneeling humbly on the pavement, I see
  some lost jelly of the cat's brain,
  a little mound of curious cells
  clinging against the asphalt
  and lashing water.
Only the hose's full fury washes the cells away.

The myth of the legendary cat fades
  in grey evening silence
  lost in the glittering air;
  though as water smashes the cells,
  they flicker in fading twilight
as sparks snap brightly out of a flaming fire.

Girl Covered with Pigeons

Laughing pigeon-girl
Which are the pigeons
And which you?
Through a frenzy of
Fluttering birds
On your shoulders and hair,
Wings grow from your head.
You fly out of inner joy
Where the will to ascend
Sings into soaring light.

A song of flight begins
That separates sea
From clinging earth,
And in your young, fresh eye
Creates the free, invisible sky.

The Watch of the Live Oaks

Across the street from my childhood summer house,
A twisted strand of live oaks rises in the sky,

Boughs locked high in a green vault. Beneath their watch
A neighbor boy was killed, shot through a window,
As he stood drunk and cursing on the lawn.
I think of Robert Louis Stevenson,
Walking in dark groves, who called the oaks
"Woods for murderers to crawl among."
Compelled, we blaze our images on trees.
They only watch us from their silent peaks,
And yet without their arch of greenness
Who would walk out singing in the morning?
As among a grove of live oaks in the mountains,
Father Serra ordered the bells unpacked
For his new mission, hung the bells
From the sinuous, gnarled grace of an oak.
Seized by his writhing search for peace,
He rang the bells exultantly, crying:
"Hear and come! Come to the Holy Church of God!"
And the heathen oak became a Christian church.

City Funeral

Four black suits led by a snout-beetle
        with down-curved beak
Heaved in the coffin—that great, carved walnut weight—
On it a small wreath of roses.
The long-headed, low black car
Swam in sultry light like a snake-bird
        down the street.

After the hearse, a procession of used cars
Filled with relatives, dilly-dally,
With signs on their windows:
        FUNERAL.
I thought, in Japan, the festival of lanterns—
Those huge, scampish shades with wanton colors—
        is for
        the souls of the dead

The Japanese Tea Garden
in San Francisco

If you wish to create
An expert difficulty
That defeats destruction,
Build a Japanese bridge.
Arch the wood in a high curve—
Block it with steep, splintery steps,
Flow under it a clear stream
With red fish for contemplation,
Assemble families for the climb.
Vary ages, sizes, forms, minds,
Quiet, ugly, lazy, combative temperaments;
Children to scream, stare, giggle at danger;
Frantic, laughing parents to warn of falls,
Broken legs; grandparents to mutter "impossible,"
And watch with resigned pleasure
The high, difficult crossing.
Shouts of triumph should be an absolute joy
Aimed to clarify the air, not muddle the fog.
At night, let the aging, wooden bridge
Rest in the silence of its lofty curve,
Worn, mirrored in the moonlit water,
The wheel of life that turns,
Extending the joyous invitation of difficulty.

The Washing Machine Cycle

"A poem is a machine."
WILLIAM CARLOS WILLIAMS

SPIN
    the whirling motion
    pressure of the
        cyclical return:
    earth around the sun,
        around, around,
    the beginning dance

118

TUMBLE
   the roughness, hitting
   of word against word
   syllable against syllable,
   the tension between phrases,
   to sing and not to separate

WASH
   to clean the sound of errors,
   pierce through the merely smooth,
   create the true texture
   that the glistening shines
   dimensional with depth

DRY
   out of the damp mystery
   to dry the final language
   on the bodiless page,
   the word without water, air, earth
   that speaks and cannot die
      as the action
         becomes the poem

The Dream of Fathers

After his father's death, William Carlos Williams
Dreamt of his father descending the staircase,
Looking over his shoulder severely,
Remarking casually, "You know all that poetry
You're writing. Well, it's no good."
Father, father, what have I done?
Teach me to find the independence vision.
Proudly he appears, father after father,
Speaking with love and secret knowledge:
"Success is the goal of all proud fathers.
Always, my son, your success is my goal.
With your own children you'll learn to understand
That after success comes symbolic revenge—
To see each son defeated like his father's death,
And the father's image shine like Mars, god of war."

119

Youth and the Abyss

Youth falls into the abyss,
But the abyss is friendly.
Family stands around the edge,
Looking at you in the muck below,
Advising, counseling, praying.

Fortunetellers and moneychangers
Consult with fast-food merchants;
In the midst of crowds, the abyss
Offers its own consoling identity.

Come, embrace me. I, the abyss,
Will devour your challenging youth culture.
In my depths, old age disappears,
My chasms absorb all flashy rebellion.

I, the abyss, will transform your youthful energy
Into the cutting angles of eternal revolution,
The slow geology of immortal change.

First London Press Conference in the American Campaign to Bring the Yo-Yo to England

Fifty hard sellers will divide Britain
To sell my new, electric yo-yos
In plastic, with whistles and lights.
Technologically, we're beating the Thirties
When I discovered the yo-yo in the Phillippines,
Where natives threw them at each other.
To sell it, I got the Duke of Windsor,
Even Hitler to play with it;
Napoleon, too, in a cartoon, of course.
Toys are like dreams; they fade out,
You have to analyze them back.
You have to find the time of ripeness,
Just like your old master, Shakespeare, says.

Forty years ago, I bought a bankrupt,
Climbing-monkey business for $400.
Ever since, money's been climbing me,
Though children are getting lazy.
They like to sit and dream . . .
That's why my toys have electric motors.
Kids want to sit and press buttons like Mom.
Toys are like any other business;
You have to keep up. I go to college
Fifteen weeks a year for the latest trends,
And wear this Latin motto on my ties:
Dum vivimus vivamus:
Translation: *"You've gotta live it up, boy."*

Confessions of an American Viewer
Of the Large Screen

"At the American Exhibition in Moscow in 1959. American life was depicted, simultaneously, on seven screens."

To depict American life, simultaneously,
    on seven screens,
The theory is tumultuous, a panic for the eyes,
A smash, a shivering, a shock, a hit;
On seven screens, gigantic, probing space,
Showing the endless energy, the engineering
    mind and heart.

I see a peasant in his threadbare clothes,
    unwilling Communist;
He hopes for hope and on the seven screens
He sees the sparkle of the racing life.
"Dear God," he thinks, "They have it made.
Life is a race down endless freeways,
    so why not run?"

I am that peasant in my business suit,
    upon my seven screens,
My television in my home, my radio,
My car with fins that swims from my garage,

121

My frigidaire that purrs much like my cat,
The charcoal tang of outdoor barbecues,
     my life on telephones.

So, gape, oh peasant, at my secret life,
     my soul of seven screens.
I joke at gadgetry, I love my mortgaged home,
I laugh at lovelorn columns where analysis is free,
I go to church, I pay my loans, I work, pursue
     my search for happiness.

The Corporation Lady in Bughouse Square, Chicago

Before a sign commanding, BUY!
The drunk staggers to a stop, mumbles:
"Corporations! Always bucking noses!"

Floating papers kill time,
Flicker in gusts of autumn wind,
Whirl over red leaves tumbling in the park.

Through ornate, gold-frame glasses
A sumptuous lady sits pigeon-staring,
Skin shining with a summer tan.

Her long earrings sway,
Tinkle softly in the wind,
Gentle music like Chinese garden glass.

Stumbling up to her, bowing,
The drunk eyes her regal perch, exclaims
"Hey! You're tinkling, Corporation Lady!"

New York Subway Rush Hour

Chaos, the churning time.
I watch a fur-wrapped matron,

122

Grey glow of hair preening for place,
Imperial gaze of the proud gourmet,
Squeeze into a corner of stuffed bodies,
Raising her arms high, a defiant tower
In this servile subway of darkness.
Upon a praying pedestal of soft-groomed hands
She guards a chocolate cake against the crush.
Two stops to safety and sweet chocolate . . .
First stop: An anonymous, salivating tongue
Beneath a beret, plucks the cake
From her sheltering hands, darts out
The slamming door. The train grinds on
Its sentence of predestination.
One stop to safety: no more sweet chocolate.
Her lighthouse tower battered by invasion,
She stares in wonder at high, empty hands . . .
Crumpling, she rages at sullen straphangers,
Indifferent riders through mass mirrors,
Reflections of private dooms, public destinations.

Mr. Martin in His Advertising Agency

In a high tower I sit, the new writing master,
Commanding words in the air, as well as on the ground.
My words glow in paint, flare in neon at all altitudes.
Master of verbs, they flash below my office, melt in fog
Like grease sizzling, sliding on a frying pan.
From my high perch, I look down upon
Aisles of perfectly trained commercial artists
Designing flaming missiles of make-believe.
Instinctively, they know how to decorate
The perfect slogans that shine in my eyes
As I heat up word-pictures for gaping commuters,
Burn advertising joy into their eager, lonely eyes.

123

An Astonished Listener Hears the Radio Announcer Bat Out the Long Balls of Verbs, Nouns, and Adjectives

Swing on the cripple and hit the dying quail.
The roundhouse curve, the swell wrinkle, and the
Big dead fish all fail if the slugger
Rammycackles a liner over the advertising sign.
At the break of seven spasms take some of that
Good beer, for the Little Professor's at bat.
The sprayhitters are breaking out with
Five o'clock lightning and Old Casey the Cagey
Calls in a new repair man. It's Cautious Joe!
He's deep down in the barrel and has to
Swim out of it, but boy he's swimming!
Watch those fielders put on the chain,
Skid, gobble and throw. They know it's
Hang tough, root hog or die, and they want the
Poke ball hit in the well. You never know in baseball.
In the last gasp or never inning, veterans can wield
The willow and play some beautiful tunes
On ancient fiddles. Then the cripple and the
Dying quail and the big dead fish are all
        Stashed in the deep freeze.

The White Writing of Mark Tobey

Liars!
        (who write white with your skins)
        This is not white writing.
The old Chinese used to say:
        "It is better to feel a painting
                than look at it."
So much today is only to look at,
        poor vision strewn on walls,
        a politics of art, skin-painting.
Yet the mind flows on
        infinitely,

line merges with idea
at the sensuous source,
touch searches time
for the tactile discovery;
White writing as a window to
    blackness,
Lucid, black discoveries
    for white writers.

The Painter Studying Trees
without Leaves

Why study trees without leaves?
Like Cezanne in his drawings.
Because the naked branch reveals the curve?
    No.
Because the stripped vertical line soars free?
    No.
Because the true source needs stripping.

A Drip Poem for Jackson Pollock

Put this paper   on the floor
    drip words on it   sounds
SWOOP   drip poem   SPLASH
        SPLAT-TER
        SWIRRRL
        CIR-CLE
    SPLASSSH-SHING   CO-LORE
dripline dripline dripline   TANGLE NET
City ity *City* ity *City* ity
run *running* run *running* run *running*
Height fall *Height* fall *Height* fall
Ver-ti-*go* Ver-ti-*go* Ver-ti-*go*
        fall FREE fall FREE fall FREE
        RAGE
Vision   Vii-sion   Viii-shun   Viiiii-SHUN   VIIIII-SHUNN

125

Drink   drinnkk   Driinnkk   Driiinnkk   DRINK
     RAAAGE!
          ATTACK   EN-DEAR-MENT
          (call everyone horses ass)
SPLINTER-SPLATTER   eateateat
SPLINTER-SPLATTER   lovelovelove
SPLINTER-SPLATTER   dripdripdrip
EN-ER-GY
     drin-king waves of seeeee
Lady ask:
          "Mister Pollock,
HOW do you KNOW when you've finish-dead
          a pic-ture?"
Answer drip-pi-ly:
          "Mad-damn,
How do you KNOW
WHEN you've finish-dead
          ma-king love?"

The Abstract Expressionist
Searching for the Angel Track

Four feet from the canvas he points
His brush at the white emptiness:
"You have to know where to begin.
These young guys start painting anywhere,
All they want is to go fast.
What way can they fight twenty,
Thirty years of experience? NO WAY."
For an hour he tries to start and fails.
He advances, circles, measures, stares,
The canvas, pristine white, remains intact.
"The beginning is the curse, the crime.
Once you get started you hit the rhythm.
The whole thing grows like it was forcefed.
But the beginning, you've gotta be bold,
You've gotta hit the deep stuff where it hides.
It's like looking in a mirror or lake.
If you don't see more than your reflection
You're in trouble. There's a whole world

126

Under that reflection, all those images
Connecting you to time, space, history.
See that blank white space singing to me?
It's an angel track. To fill that angel space
You've gotta dance around with demons.
A painter's trapped searching for invisible angels.
The real beginning is finding dim angel tracks."
Suddenly he splashes a black line on the canvas,
Smears it up, down, searching for the angel track.

Graveyard Aesthetics

Begin in *Wrecker Service*
Collect smashed car skeletons
Soon you have a graveyard.

Wounded, broken forms grow
Into astonishing natural artifacts.
You're known as a sculpture collector.

No one knows more than you about
The happenstance of chance aesthetics.
You've become a sudden cultural historian.

With pride you turn your metal sculptures
Into a glowing, prominent museum
Of remarkable grotesque forms.

You name your transformed business:
> *The Auto Sculpture Graveyard*
> *Last Chance Historical Museum.*

Jazz-Drift 1950s

Duke Ellington: "The old way was like a kid playing
with blocks. Now they don't say it, they just play it."

(1)

Usually after hours in the clubs,
sit in and search the nature of jamming—
many jump in and are cut down,
young players hanging on the fringes,
it takes more than a dream now,
the music flowing behind us
in a current as strong as the Mississippi.

(2)

A lot of that pounding in the current
is oldtime piano music, back to the basics,
the old whorehouse, gut level style,
call it ragtime, call it this new bebop,
call it as every new wind calls things,
still there are ancestors pounding away,
Jelly Roll Morton, a "Professor" in Storyville,
Fats Waller's father, a good minister
calling jazz "music from the devil's workshop."
Why shouldn't we play a lovely,
grotesque slant of keys like Fats,
jiggling with music at 285 pounds,
gin bottle at hand, derby hat cocked
on his head, cigarette dangling,
his eternal smile a challenging mask.
As James P. Johnson said: "Some little people
have music in them, but Fats, he was
all music, and you know how big he was."
Did you ever hear one of Fats'
legendary organ recitals of Bach?

Blues from a Thunderhead

Her voice flowed out of
An old rain-barrel body
Full of wet, wild tones.
Who expects wet weather
In a dim, blue-lit bar?
It was all showery there.
She sang her Blues

Out of a thunderhead
Till all of us listeners
Began to feel wet.
Outside of that sleazy club,
Stars leaped to control the sky,
And I shook myself like a dog
Free from her drenching voice.

All Day Driving across Kansas

This Kansas distance
stretches so far
you drag it
around after you,
no stopping lights,
no ending doors.
The highway engineer
says when you build a road
straight
there's never a return.

The Fury of a Midwestern Thunderstorm

Where the wind strikes, nothing remains.
This is not true, wind-music remains,
Lashing, searching, music of fury
Hollowing out the stones of time.
This is not true, man makes music.
Beyond musical order, nothing
Remains when the wind strikes.
This is not true, a song unites,
Wind and flesh singing together.
This music splits the rock,
This music cleans the air.
This wind, these strange people
In vast space planting immigrant dreams.
Always the fury of their music remains.

129

Oklahoma Farming Song

Farmers make love on Sunday afternoons
Solomon suggests in the good Book's script.
Worship, pray, sleep with your wife
And learn how to love the rest of your life.

Farmers make love on Sunday afternoons.
Weekday mornings it's early to rise;
Slave at the chores with your sleepy wife
And struggle to love the rest of your life.

Farmers make love on Sunday afternoons.
Weekday nights it's tired to sleep,
Early snoring sounds with your wife
And dream how to love the rest of your life.

Farmers make love on Sunday afternoons,
The day of rest is the springboard to love—
In the waving corn lie down with your wife
And learn how to love the rest of your life.

Clown at Crafts Fair

Sitting high on the bannister, atop
A Victorian staircase, the clown freezes,
Right hand upraised, immobile,
Enormous painted shoes curved like boats,
White clownface a fabulous sunset
To the gaping crowd of children below.
"Is he real or rubber?" asks a kid.
Frozen in time, the clown does not answer,
Holding his hand up to the children
In a warning. Holding a trance
Until it transforms into a benediction . . .
Suddenly, his gentle hand moves to salute,
Moving slowly through infinite time
Proving the comic master of courtliness
May be a saint conquering invisible stress.

The Alcoholic's Imaginary Dinner

Does it all come down to duty
Condemned like a tiger or a butterfly?
Alcoholics forgetting, dreaming oblivion.
"The dinner is cooked," and there's
Nothing there except the imaginary dinner.
Duty demands we take care of someone
And the tiger and butterfly tasks begin,
Duty as aggressive attack or gentle fluttering.
With booze we fade into inner worlds,
The imaginary dinner appears, I'll cook
Exquisitely for you, dear, don't worry.
Can't you see I'm preparing your favorite dish?
One moment while I snitch another gin.
The imaginary dinner becomes an immortal song.

The Confidence Man as
Soap Opera Salesman

Cuddle with your old Confidence Man, ladies!
Hook yourself on goodtime, crazy characters
The way your grandmother hooked herself
On those lovely nineteenth century novels.
What is television anyway? A burning box to please!
A free travel ticket to the old land of love!
You know fifty-five per cent of women watch soaps;
Even a solid twenty-seven per cent of men turn on.
Hate a villain and increase your love, that's a fact!
Stretch your eyes, I carry a full line for you soapophiles:
Mugs, glasses, keychains, bumper stickers, buttons,
A *General Hospital* laundry bag for your secret undies.

Enjoy yourselves, ladies, slip around on the soap a bit,
You don't want to knock me out of a job, do you?
Ladies, soaps are just old melodrama colored up
With new technology. Crash, your love's dead!
Surgery, he's reborn as Dr. Miracle stitches him new!
Come on, wash your eyes with death and resurrection,

131

Join a community of women pursuing happy dreams!
Meet the First Lady of the land presiding at our
Birthday Party with a shower of free birthday gifts!
Do you know, ladies, the stars of your favorite soaps
Receive thousands of real happy birthday cards?
Soap yourself up into a Birthday Lady of Happiness!

Co-Pilot to God

Bravura flare of bumper sticker:
   "God Is My Pilot—I'm Only The Co-Pilot."
To be only a Co-Pilot to God!
Lightning splits around you,
Thunder crashes as you drive
Afraid, through windy peril,
And turn to your Pilot for advice—
That invisible uniform behind the wheel,
That whitecapped wisdom frozen with wonder
At the new, roaring technology in the air,
That inaudible voice sounding
Enigmatic parables out of eternity
To every confident American Co-Pilot.

The Immigrant Tailor Stitches the Singer's Concert Dress

She would sing like white oleander
To absorbing summer eyes,
But the church is tuned
To evangelical songs:
"Please sing 'Amazing Grace.'"
"Sorry, we don't have the music."

As a singer, her big operatic voice
Yearns for European tradition,
But her "American upbringing,"
Pulls her into popular song.

The scissors of the immigrant tailor
Cutting her colorful concert dress
Reflects her dilemma; one blade
Glitters with European training,
The other cuts plain American style.

So the resolute tailor stitches a
Tight black cloth around the singer's body,
Trying desperately to blend classical
Tradition with the audience's love
Of popular songs, while the singer
Sings frantically to all paying audiences,
Creating a beguiling voice for talk shows—

And the new American tailor regards his
Adopted scissors style with astonished,
Questioning eyes counting his cash.

At the Mexican Border

Definition, damn you, be accurate:
A border is a fence between houses and languages.
If I marry across the border, I marry the fence,
Yet to know it, must learn language beyond the fence.

I am a native who lives behind the fence.

A foreigner is one who comes to visit my house,
But never learns to speak my language.

A false foreigner is one who lives in the distance,
Knows neither my customs nor my house,
Nor the falseness of his isolated distance.

A border is a line that meanders cruelly
In and out of history's savage mirror,
Glitters with patriotic flag-sitters who chant:
"Build our tradition, fence in our culture . . ."

Grim grotesques flock to the border,
Hunch in bus stations, faces like lime-pits
Scour the air, destroy pity.
Legless, hunchbacked, half-bodies in baskets,
Insatiable, they clutch for money
As tourists turn grotesque, beg souvenirs,
Poke at jewelry with sharp word-crutches,
Haggle with hands that hunt in greed.

Listen: the border is obscene language
Luring natives from both sides of the fence,
Language as fat of food, as twisted flesh.
Through border gates walk dark women
Flowing sensuously in red skirts.
They float like birds in bright migration,
Warning of crucial crossings across borders
Bringing bright stars to dominate the night.

A Tongan in a Tree in Utah

Grinning, he materializes out of his Porsche,
The Tongan student gliding in zoris,
Studying in this western university
On a grant from Mormon missionaries.
"I'll trim any tree you want, Sir,
The higher the better." If not a profession,
His act is a dazzling climb to success.
Kicking off his zoris, he climbs the elm
Barefoot with animal skill acquired
Soaring high in South Pacific palms.
Beneath his confident immigrant slashing,
Dead branches, hazardous limbs, crash down.
"Look at me, how fast I learn the power
Of American daring, swagger to conquer height,
And drive off poor in a millionaire's sportscar."

134

Buffalo Man at the Cocktail Party

Looming large, enticing, swaying on gin,
She accused me at the party in the smog,
Attacking my too obvious guilt
As a minor bureaucrat, a small, skeptical urban man.
"You must believe you are a buffalo.
Breathe correctly. Learn to lumber."
"It's tough to lumber when you're small,"
I pled, smiling my weak sophistication.
"Nonsense, don't be so defensive.
You must think you're large, awkward,
Even a little stupid at times,
Unmistakably present, a looming hulk
Of male existence. That will end your difficulties!"

Well, I laughed, and began our relationship.
Somehow she changed my life. I charge her now
With a definite, ironic, dream of size,
Aware of my slaughtered skin and meat,
Surviving proudly in small enclosures,
Breaking out at night from my office cubicle.
Aware of fences in my masquerade,
Ready for treachery, an obsolete, thick-skinned
Animal with bold frontier eyes,
I endure with patience . . . I love . . .
Although I feel like a monument that moves,
She's given me a mask in which to live.

The Newsboy Enters the Bar

"Hey, newsboy!" call the evening patrons,
Sipping their drinks at the polished bar.
Green-tinted glasses over blinking eyes,
He squints down the bar in dim light
And barks at all the grinning patrons.
The first bark scatters tittering jokes,
Laughter of recognition at this dog-boy
In his cracked shoes and baseball jacket.
The second bark begins a silence:

135

This is a grey-haired man, not a dog.
Black headlines on the papers that he waves
Read: "ROCKET SOARS INTO THE MOON."
He barks, and the customers buy,
Twitching uneasily, their laughter lost.
At last he barks and no one buys.
A salesman on a stool bends over his gin,
The tattooed bartender wipes at glasses,
A thick-chinned blonde toys with a swizzle stick.
Barking defiantly, the old newsboy departs
Through swinging doors that shut on faded faces,
Silent, thinking of rockets soaring to the moon,
And the barking mind with which man soars.

The Traveler of Lavishness

We are all members of the best motels,
I can't remember any even winters.
Hunters of lavishness build lavish hells.

"Godly Devotion Is Not Lost Motion," tells
The sign where Mad Face hooks his thumb undone.
We are all members of the best motels.

Covered with refuse, hair and orange peels,
The back seat for children is the Bear Pit;
Hunters of lavishness build lavish hells.

The white line is the guide that sells
Our fireball ride, a searching string in space.
We are all members of the best motels.

Blueberry hotcakes and the clanging bells
Possess our joy as each hick town attacks
The road from which it feeds and pays its hacks.
We are all members of the best motels.
Hunters of lavishness build lavish hells.

Confidential Data on
the Loyalty Investigation of
Herbert Ashenfoot

Until the birth of my thirtieth birthday
I walked in the wide harbor of illusion,
Wind and war of parents over my silent head
While the curse of identity tinkled
At my window like the Good Humor salesman.
Around me the black armies like bats
Lay darkly in their caves of caution
And for security I joined the Civil Service.
Rating P-3, almost a pristine transport plane,
I roared from basket in to basket out
And all my days were clocked and carefree.
At the dawn of thirty my reform began.
My loyalty was cleaned and prodded
And my dreams divorced from all emergencies.
Propped at a desk of quinine I typed
In the tears of my time like the frozen sea.

In the Blind Years

BLIND
        escape from his boring suburb home
        to X-rated organs of decaying Beehive City,
        the boy sits on a sidewalk, casing the action,
        reading a paperback, *Classical Ghost Stories.*

        Fading out from his routine family life
        in turtle-slow suburb, he is testing the
        reality of fantasy ghosts, will ancient
        ghostly power survive in city turmoil?

BLIND
        "Reading, I hope they'll think I'm weird,"
        The boy dreams hopefully amidst the Korean War,

sacrificial victims in body bags haunting television,
United Nations mission, but our "police action."

Supreme Commander MacArthur, ego shining,
leading his troops on a spectacular "end run,"
war as football sport, dashing in triumph
until the Chinese explode across the border.

BLIND
boy escaping from the crude Korean stalemate,
sidewalk-bound with his fantasies, hoping
from Asia some Buddhist meditator may
float in scattering tranquil ghost-poems;

but traffic surging by honks *go for money*,
go for affluent loyalty, defeat all commie
colors of red and pink, blacklist all bums,
defend red, white and blue in blind color binge.

BLIND
ghosts sail uneasily over surging suburbs,
Indian peasant ghosts of the 1954 Guatemalan
invasion authorized by Eisenhower, the boy thinking.
after all, Ike may be another conquering Cortez.

Will fantastic ghosts help the boy rise from
sidewalk confusion, dance with sacrificial ancestors
in affluent years, where military clobberknockers
war against ghosts haunting their conquerors?

Wrecking for the Freeway

"Roadbuilding is really the American art."
A HIGHWAY CONTRACTOR
"A highway is a true index of our culture."
BERNARD DE VOTO

Day after day, commuting,
My office tie blowing in the breeze,

Wearing my hat in the rain
Dapper brim down, detective television style,
I ride with zing to my office destination
Bouncing past massive wreckage tombs.
The little stucco houses are boarded up,
Broken from their foundations,
Trucked away on thick beams, and pasted
Like postage stamps to another barren hill.

Bulldozers push up walls of dirt
Baking brown as flesh in morning sun.
    (Said Admiral Bull Halsey: "The bulldozer was one of four
    weapons that won World War II in the Pacific—along
    with the submarine, airplane, and radar.")
At night, on squares of jagged concrete,
Hammered apart by blast and drill,
Fervent, furtive precinct workers
Plaster election pleas:
        Vote for Shelley!
Adds a beatnik underneath:
        (The congressman, not the poet)
And a peacenik underneath:
        For Peace; Vote for Percy Bysshe Shelley!

Day after day in this freeway turmoil,
The arts are dead, theatre is dead,
Here is the Theatre of Cruelty—Artaud's
"Language of space, sounds, cries, lights . . ."
Enter the Theatre of Wrecking!

All of the neighborhood is hooded by ruins,
All of the neighbors are using the ruins
To walk their dogs, the dogs are pissing
On the ruins with their rivers of dreams.

Yesterday, a park of weeds grew from the wreckage.
Every weed that rain can grow broke through concrete,
Sparking and spiking up, a prison-park of growth.
Today it is gone, the park is gone . . .
I am driving, driving on a new curve.
This is all for the purpose of *flow*.
Our hearts must smoke and pound

In the flow: *we glow when we can flow,*
                    the flow is where we go,
                    we grow when we can flow.

An overpass rises! A Harnischfeger 35-ton unit
                    (tons of unity)
Pours concrete between high panels;
Foremen in jeeps hustle along the road
Talking on the radio with Field Headquarters.
                    My God this is a war!
I think the machines are winning . . .
The compacters with huge rubber wheels
And dozens of small, steel feet
Pack down the loose dirt of the roadbed.
Power shovels eat through the steep hills,
Agile graders pare shoulders and side slopes,
Ditchers with endless buckets scoop out trenches
For drainpipes, stone-crushers crush boulders to eggs.
After them, the pavers; finally, the finishing machines
And concrete saws cutting joints for expansion and contraction.
A Johnson Float Finisher smooths the surface
That everyone may finish and float.

(Last night I dreamt of the Universal Portable Crusher
That conveys, crunches, and screens up to
450 tons of gravel and sand in an hour.)

Through the fog this morning,
Socked in, I creep to work.
Peering, peering, reciting the litany:
   bulldozers
      scrapers
         graders
            compacters
               blast-hole drills
                  dump trucks
                     ditchers
                        stone-crushers
                           pavers
                              concrete saws
                                 finishing machines
A truck glares out of the furry mist:

140

DAWN FRESH PRODUCE
RUSHING TO
LITTLEMAN

Rushing, rushing, rushing—
we glow when we can flow
this flow is where we go
we grow when we can flow . . .

1960s
CHAOTIC CHANGES

Bashir Was My Name

In 1962 when Lyndon B. Johnson was Vice-President,
he met the Pakistani camel-driver, Bashir, and invited
him to the United States.

Years ago that Vice-President came,
Singled me out from a crowd in Karachi,
And invited me to visit the United States.
I arrived at a winged place called
Strangely Idlewild, flew to Texas
With my honorable host, rode his horses,
Sampled his barbecue, visited the Dallas State Fair.
A few days later in Washington, I met the President
And said, "Now I have seen the Man of the World!"
Returning to my home I asked, "Can you live
In the darkness when a star sits on your shoulder?"
My shoulder began to hurt and gleam in the dark,
My son took over my camel cart.
In a friend's garage glows the pick-up truck
I was given in America. I am taking driving lessons.
When I get my trucking permit, I will double
Our family income. I have been received by
President Ayub Khan, feted by the American Ambassador,
And had a standing ovation at the Lahore Horse Show.
Every night I go home to my house
Across the railroad tracks in Bashir Chowk.
The old woman who sells cattle fodder,
The milk man whose water buffalos squat
Outside my hut, and the betel nut vendor
Come together to see my privileged possessions.
From under the single rope-bed in the hut,
I pull out the bag I took to America and show them
The awards of my trip through the sky:
A transistor radio, a Polaroid camera,
A PT boat pin, the badge of a Texas Deputy Sheriff,
A medal showing the City Hall in Kansas City,
A doll, half a dozen ball-point pens marked
"Compliments of the Vice-President of the United States."
And then I can sleep, or rather I dream:

"Once we were chosen. Chance
Scratched, us with claws,
Marked us forever with a white
Shoulder glittering beyond laws.

Cursed, blessed with a white shoulder,
We dance into the dark,
And you can tell the dancers in the dance
By the gleam of that white mark."

The Executive and the Giveaway List

At the jagged age of fifty, I'm on every giveaway list—
WIN TWO BEAUTIFUL HOMES OR $77,777.00—
(If seven were my number I'd spin a seventy dream)
SAVE THE CHILDREN! I have two and a half to save
And a wife locked into my insurance security.
The mail floods in, third class, my name
Written on glittering, imaginary checks—
HOW WOULD YOU LIKE A TRIP TO THE MOON
OR SETTLE TEMPORARILY
FOR A WORLD GLAMOUR TOUR—
Still my life is on a rising track.
My wife is a formidable if complacent cook.
Nobody can tell me that a pecan pie
Ever did anything wrong in life even though
It's my dream more than my appetite.
When mail slaps in the box mornings
It's good to feel you've made the giveaway list.
Spend a tough life driving upward,
Lucky survivor in rough competition,
Commuting long distance, working out problems
Probing, pushing you into your shell.
You're on the edge, climbing up to the top,
You own a splitlevel house with a recreation room,
Appliances so bright they polish your eyes
In a suburb so neat the dirt can't get in—
And then the giveaway lists begin to arrive—
THE WORLD'S A WONDER IF YOU OWN YOUR PIECE
GET THE PERFECT PRIZE WITH THIS LITTLE COUPON—

146

My wife's got the pen. She's printing our coupons perfectly.
Through bi-focal glasses we scan the small print for clues.
One day we'll win! Then we'll be off!
Play it back again . . . The planet's a peerless place
If you spin through survival and hit the giveaway list.

Old Barry, the Balloon Seller

Two eyes twitching like flies
   in a waterfall of flesh
      Old Stubblecheeks sells balloons.

"Hey, buy my floating gas!"
   scuffed shoes prancing on gravel
      like a waltzing rat.

Five o'clock howls its pitch.
   Homeward cars in hot retreat
      pound through the sultry time.

With delicate puppet-string fingers
   he flitters his fool's gold—
      seven pink buxom balloons.

Behind him at Dead End,
   Tiger Tom, the alley cat
      also blossoms with pink color.

The Buddhist Car

> (A Buddhist, exiled in the United States, dies suddenly
> and finds himself reincarnated as a car.)

I
Slowly, I feel myself. Eyes squint at me
Through a long window. Across the glass is lettered
FURY. My skin grows hard, my bones hammered longer.

147

My veins flow in glistening wires, tubes.
Curious, glittering people glide in
To touch me. My face is etched in polished lines,
A metal beehive. Singular words sound against
My antique English, *throttle, mileage, accelerator.*
Suddenly, my heart explodes, sparks of energy
Shoot through my bowels. I hum, flow out
To hard streets. I glide on rubber circles.
Children call to me, smile, speak my title.
I know who I am . . . Across my rear puffing fumes
Curve the letters, F-U-R-Y . . .

II

"As the blade of a sword cannot cut itself,
As a finger-tip cannot touch itself,
So a thought cannot see itself . . ."
I cannot see what I think. Male fingers guide
My large-beamed eyes down the road,
A polished shoe presses my sex,
A woman stamps out her cigarette on my skin,
Children litter my body with candy wrappers, gum.
A man who liked the touch of silent women,
I echo with female flutes of gossip.
I flee from high, trilled syllables,
Devote myself to winds of motion,
Speed as vision . . . If *nirvana* is kin
To *moksha*, release, the liberating light,
I must learn to feather-float on metal parts.

III

An agony of sudden climbing . . . After learning
Stop and go in warm sun, I spring
Up mountains through ice and snow.
My family's name rolls with gutteral sound:
Mac-Pher-son, a candy manufacturer,
Wearing a cap and red-striped sportshirt,
His brown, jovial balloon of a face
Round over a clouded, blackstemmed pipe.
His wife, Raquel, wears a pleasant mongrel smile
From the melting pot, lined with anxieties,
Her grey hair washed and loaded with spring coils.
They create a friendly team of curiosity,
Poking at facts, investigating objects,

148

Eager to proclaim the wonder of natural views,
Their two tense, prancing children shaped
Tightly after the parents' investigating passion.
Since I am this family's walls of privacy,
I sense their fear of quicksand loneliness,
Their need to honor, obey the American verb, *to do*,
External action glitters fiercely in their eyes.
To them beauty is a fiery eyeball; it cannot
Sing from ancient unity of body with mind.
A child's voice shrills in my ear, *Sierra. Sierra!*
We search high places. I learn to curve, turn,
Climb on deceptive slopes that ache my parts.
I gasp for distant breath through lung-pumps
That press cooling air against my hot nerves.
Higher! Higher! If such a path wound through
The Himalayas of Wonder, what frenzied light
Could be seen. *Kanchenjunga! Makalu! Everest!*
MacPherson thrusts me into slower motion.
Every sinew strains. I force deep power.
What muscles! My water steams . . . *Sierra! Sierra!*

        IV
A slight pause on top of the world,
Intense light glittering on my body,
Then a sudden plunging down . . . My chest
Thaws out, expands in foaming desert heat.
My pores open like a fan. I sail along
Between sky and sand as if gliding on water.
Early wanderers here sailed in prairie schooners.
Are these extremes of sailing my immortality?
Whose graves are we passing? . . . Metal fields of death.
Old years, old shapes, lie hot in sun like cast-off
Withering snake-skins. A billboard shines blackly:
"Now Is The Time For Salvation. I. Cor."
A Christian country boils with urgency.
Is the time for salvation not eternal?
When the Buddha sat under the Bo Tree at Gaya
After seven years of meditation in the forests,
What he experienced was awakening, *Bodhi*,
But he spoke only the deep language of silence.
We are entering Lovelock . . . Love-lock . . .
The Americans even name an isolated town
After their pounding problems of the heart.

V

My long, flat nose is fixed to the wind.
I have become a savage hunter, destroying insects.
My speed creates a vacuum trap for little wings
That sucks them in, smashes them to spots.
Speed, speed, at what pace comes the final unity,
The God-Head merging, bringing endless peace?
A man's flesh is so light, so fanciful,
How can he feel my solid roots, my heavy surge
Through air, my skin printed with quick, changing images?
Near Fallon, prideful signs announce the sale of
Hearts of Gold Canteloupes and Bronze Turkeys.
I savor a dry hunger that feeds on liquid energy
From red towers in bright stations with flags
And prizes for my feeding. When I stop,
Servants hurry to greet me in white uniforms,
Pat or *Jim* lettered on their pockets.
At Elko, steaming in ninety degree heat,
I feed beneath urgent proclamations to visit
The polar bear, the ten thousand dollar
Cowboy boots with jewels and rich leather.
Money is forced into long-handled machines.
Cylinders fly in circles, flash images of fruit.
A tense legend forms in sticky air.
Perhaps the polar bear is chosen to assume
The burden of heat, wear the rich boots of wealth,
Work the levers until the rolling cylinders clank,
Shine with waterfalls and pristine mountain grace.

VI

Sizzling along through endless level salt,
The Great Salt Desert, a shimmering salt world . . .
At Wendover, the statue of a green cowboy
Swaggers over the white. His plaster hat is
An enormous mushroom shield against the sun.
His sweet cow face smiles a boy's innocence.
Weapon of loneliness strapped around his waist,
He dreams to be ancient warrior, not the youth of time.
My search through speed is like a jagged thunderbolt
As I pursue the white line to the horizon,
A line dividing the pursuer from his destiny.
What Karma might occur if I should swerve?
My bride may wait behind the spouting giants

That dominate our passage, as if whale-ghosts
Lose their oceanic spirit to haunt the road.
I limp to their pounding, long for
A liquid, flowing dolphin-leaping.
This whale-ghost society surges with frenzy
Splitting time into quick, noisy alarms
As the grace of Buddhist bells fades—
"The sound that frees us from
all agonies and sorrows . . ."
Desert and farmlands merge in evening glow.
MacPherson roars his exuberant laugh
As food images stare like tamed miracles.
"Look!" he shouts, "How's that for a slogan?"
"FOR US THE IMPOSSIBLE TAKES A LITTLE LONGER,"
Is written in arrogant gold across a factory breast.
America's genius tames miracles to placid facts.
As they devour MacPherson's chocolate candies,
The children ask the meaning of "impossible,"
As if it were an invisible eye
Shining through clouds into the visionary sun.

VII

Desert cactus, signs, reflect on my glass forehead:
"Watch for Sleepy Drivers." "Patrolled By Airplane."
I am being watched . . . If I could only look up steadily,
Look back . . . The desert at night is a brilliant
Wilderness of stars, sapphire, diamond distances;
My gaze locks straight into the singular beams
Illuminating rocky soil until we stop in buildings
Guarded by gigantic plaster animals. An electric legend
Shines: DINOSAUR MOTEL. My family chatters in to sleep.
I rest, my hot parts cool, begin to shiver
In cold night air. Above me colored lightning tubes
Flash on the dinosaur shapes. *"Terrrible lizards . . ."*
Those cold-blooded reptiles lived millions of years
Before the Buddha found his Noble Truths
Led to Nirvana. Some walked upright, some on
Four legs, some shaped wings for flying.
What died when their ponderous spirits disappeared?
Perhaps they too are changed to metal beings,
Their lumbering size and lost dreams of elegance
Forgotten memories smoldering in steel bodies
And glass eyes of speed. Around me, my chilled companions

151

Shine dully through dust in our waiting
Night positions. Hail, fellow Dinosaurs!

VIII

After fulfilling his private and public duties,
His obligations to family and the landscape of his birth,
The Buddha set forth on his task of contemplation:
To enter the spiritual world,
To find "unexcelled, complete awakening."
He said farewell to his family, gave up his sexual needs,
Forsook his worldly body and goods . . .
But I am in the world again, I serve my family,
Yet cannot know the river of their beings.
MacPherson dreams of manufacturing a new candy.
He speaks of a *Chocolate Tower* and a *Skyscraper Box*.
Manufacturing a candy . . . With what softness
His machines must shine . . . If communion with my family
Flickers, lost, we possess each other to insure communication.
The laughing children hurl their waste into the air;
Their father calls them fondly, litterbugs . . .
As for my sexuality, I still desire.
When I pass attractive metal beings,
I stare at knobs, curves, lamps, sniff their bodies.
In our swift world, a family vision swells;
I must not lose the sense of marriage
For steel bodies wake, like sleeping flesh,
To different joys. If we are born metallically,
That birth too can flare forth in a Star of Fire.

IX

My family and their servant wander on,
Pursuing faint trails of American pilgrims.
We pound into a National Monument—The Badlands.
Tormented, cracked towers of crumbling rock
Shine through red vistas of volcanic eruptions.
Such beautiful, lonely violence! Why must I pray for peace
When the eternal lesson is violent revelation,
Contemplative suffering. "Suffering alone exists,
Not he who suffers," said the Buddha . . . We sway on.
Suddenly, after bent, twisted desert forms,
The land climbs green again, The Black Hills;
Trees and granite mountains mix graciously.
Enormous stone faces push the sky away

From the horizon! Awe-struck, MacPherson's wife
Whispers, "Mount Rushmore!" Hundreds of travelers
And their metal companions stare at ancient memories,
Giant presidential heads; Washington, Lincoln, Jefferson . . .
The twitching, energetic children question loudly,
"Who's hiding in the back with his mustache?"
MacPherson chuckles forth his answer:
"The man with the Big Stick, Theodore Roosevelt!"
Oh blessed America, to reveal yourself so casually
In such gigantic images! You transform me
With your giant ways. This pilgrimage to size
Possesses me with sniffing power, the certainty
That I am an investigating FURY. We circle on
Through gentle-flowing Black Hills, bounce
Slowly up a dirt road. Whoa! My low stance
Attracts the rocky earth. I suffer intimate pangs.
I ring with clanging sounds, choke with dust.
We stop. A blast of light, shattered stone
Splinters the sky! Who is attacking?
Another giant mountain cracks, emasculated
By dynamite. MacPherson grins and shouts:
"Get a load of that Crazy Horse Memorial!"
They're blowing up the mountain to create an Indian Chief!
The Sphinx was only seventy feet high, the Pyramid
Of Gizeh a mere four hundred eighty-one feet;
Crazy Horse, his wild hair tossing in the wind,
Will conquer America from a record altitude
Of five hundred sixty-three feet! Redeem the rebel!
Carve the terrible story on the mountain
To reveal injustice in granite letters three feet tall,
Betrayal, rape, massacre of the Indians,
Crazy Horse murdered when he was only thirty-four:
"For us the past is in our hearts, the future never to be
fulfilled . . . My lands are where my dead lie buried."
Is this what resurrection means, great memories
Of desecrated pasts? Or do we change anonymously,
Shape gliding into stronger shape we cannot perceive
Until the pure balance of necessity is achieved
And every gracious form of existence honored
By acceptance of unique, changing individuality.
Oh Crazy Horse, your fate is that saintly martyrs
Are never buried. They burst from mountains in flames
And ride eternal roads until they earn their peace.

153

Blessed be the name of Buddha who has given me
A smaller torment, a lesser wandering through fate.
Look out, MacPherson, stupid man! This curse,
Can't you feel my stopping powers are tired?

          X
My aching soul revives . . . It is a long salvation . . .
I search on, I am changed again.
Cornered in the metal forest of an unknown city,
I crouch here gazing at fanciful, popular vistas,
Still seeking virtuous views. Around me circle
Alarming sirens searching through dim streets.
I am learning how to be a Buddhist car.
I yearn to move again, but my family has forsaken
My wounded body. MacPherson, MacPherson, where are you?
What happened to us? Why could not our family roots bloom?
Above me flashes a bright-colored, glittering banner:
      "SAM HAS EM! COME AND GET EM!"
A white series of numbers is painted on my glass.
$750 . . . Is that the value of my new flesh?
I have been altered, re-created, colored in red flames.
My old parts accept with expectation their new
Mechanical companions. As in the beginning
Strangers approach cautiously to touch me.
Yesterday a man liked me, felt me all over.
I shined at him. Perhaps we will wander together
And he will lead me to the fire of revelation:
      "Nirvana is, but no one seeking it:
      The path there is, but none who travel it . . ."

Huck Finn at Ninety, Dying in a Chicago Boarding House Room

Give up everything and
Float away under the sun!
The bliss of a bastard
Cut off from everyone!

Feel your Moms and Aunts
Pop their corsets like balloons,

And the breasts of love
Soar out in white moons

I sink back, a whiskey case,
Fondling the button I found—
"Make Love—Not War"—
In the park on the ground.

I've got the button, button—
Let me sleep in the gleam
Of that old raft floating down river
Through the frontier dream.

Joyrider

"For joy rides in stupendous coverings"
HART CRANE

Call from behind dark glasses,
Skin-tight jeans,
Joy riding in red, streamlined
Voyage at the curb,
Door unlocked, a gift of speed
Away from boredom into necessary night.
Fit a stolen key into electric pulse.
Go, find the end. Cruise for joy,
Race, corner, idle, listen
To the engine's luring hum . . .
    For joy rides in stupendous coverings . . .
Eat a chocolate bar, smoke a cigar,
Crumple the wrapper, crush out the butt
In the ashtray of leisure.
Lower the pushbutton top to uncover
The city's glittering neon lights
Striking dark glasses with colored lure.
Ride! Ride through joy's stupendous cover!
When the siren wails stop,
Slump in the cell, stare through bars
At the sky of fancy, mutter, "Joy, joy,
Who's the old rider wearing my face?"

155

The Images of Execution

On May 2, 1960, Caryl Chessman was executed in the green
gas chamber at San Quentin Prison in California.

"Neither in the hearts of men, nor in the manners of society,
will there be a lasting peace until we outlaw death."
ALBERT CAMUS

I

Force of fury in the sky,
Solar cosmic rays flare
From sun and stars

In deadly storms every few years—
So the force of murder, the state
Against man, man against state.

II

Black, the hearse speeds out of San Quentin, black,
Red glow the fires of cremation, red,
White lie the ashes of the end, white.
Sin and no redemption, sin and execution.
Redemption, the quality of new leaf
Bursting green through the green chamber,
Unswerving bird-flight through arching spring
As hands tend flowers for the grace of change.
Count years and lose; the ancient game of punishment
Tortures player as well as victim,
Racks us with endgame, ironic images of justice,
Iron of irony, the revel ends, word is flesh.
Death, the painkiller, tears off artificial clothes.
The skin, destroyed, burned, calcined,
Waits for spring growth, dies to be reborn.
Who mocks his naked father walks blindly
In another country, another exile, nameless end.
Who will discover the word for this country of exile?
In the beginning was the word, though the end be skin,
And shining skin the ashes of darkness.

A Woman Staring through a Telescope at Alcatraz

I

An eye staring through space and time
Creates the brush strokes of history,
An eye of fantasy, eye of fury.
From her head grows a clumpish hat,
Twined with imitation flower clusters
Above a freckled face, cherub of sentiment.
One hooked finger dangles a makeup bag,
Black case of possessions heavy at her side.
Trembling, she slides a coin into the telescope
Chained to a whitepainted stand with the slogan:
        VIEW OF ALCATRAZ 10 CENTS
Over the water where seagulls dive for crumbs
In an oily scum near the restaurant wharf,
Her thick legs braced slantwise on the ground,
        She stares at Alcatraz.

II

History is a clutter of islands remembered in time,
Islands of battles, dates, islands of creation and death,
Islands of inventions, rocks of exile, prisons of hate.
In 1775, a Spanish explorer, Don Juan Manuel de Ayala,
Saw an island in San Francisco bay battered with pelicans,
And named it for the flashing wings, *Isla de los Alcatraces*.
Democrats were the first political prisoners there,
Loud-voiced revolutionists stumping California in 1864,
Accusing the conduct of Republicans in the Civil War.
An Army post, it held at times Confederate privateers,
And Indian chiefs, wrapped in their blankets, summoning lost gods.
During the 20s, the rock jailed military prisoners,
Deserters, thieves, who were permitted newspapers,
A psychiatrist, and religious services twice weekly.
In 1934, the rock became The Rock, prison became Prison.
Razor-sharp cyclone fences speared the island,
Barbed wire entanglements, watchtowers, high catwalks,
Tear gas bombs suspended in the dining room,
Cell blocks tuned and fitted with tool-proofed steel.
At entrances electronic devices buzzed for metal.
Radios and newspapers were forbidden, calendars banned,

157

Time exiled, and the torture of silence enforced.
Half a mile from the silence hummed the city of Saint Francis.
As fog coiled in, The Rock shook with booming foghorns.
This was not brainwashing, this was for washed-out brains.

III

On an island in history, one day in Holland in 1608,
Hans Lippershey, a Middleburg spectacle maker,
Held a lens in his hand toward a church steeple,
And was surprised to see the weathercock,
Symbol of the dawn, loom nearer.
Two years later, after long experiments,
Galileo found a way to grind and polish lenses,
And discovered with his final instrument sun-spots,
Jupiter's satellites, Venus with her phases,
And the moon's cold hills and valleys.
The telescope became the eye that magnifies,
Dream of space, fantasy of Science Fiction,
Peeping Tom of spies, wonder of microbes,
Eye for the majesty of meteors or flaws of mice.

Through the lens with a feverish eye,
She sees only jutting walls, climbing towers,
Cutting wire, lashing waves, the outer depths,
But in her mind she creates inner depths,
Cold dungeons, chains, tormenting steel solitude.
This is her prison eye that sees.

IV

The prison eye sees
A vision of dead trees in the virginal forest.
The prison eye flees
Justice; makes frontiers creep
With war, the prison eye cannot sleep.

The prison eye never dies,
Justifying each cell and torture.
The prison eye spies
On freedom, mocks at love.
The prison eye cannot change or move.

V

The devil of islands lies in the fog,
Guarding our violence, eating our evil,
Punishing the fury of our sins.
The devil of islands lies in the prison eye,
Lipari, Shark Island, Solovetzky, Alcatraz,
Where tombs of exile are built for prisoners,
Where the conscience of exile is exiled by man.
Around these islands, swirls the water of separation
Over the primal ooze, rotted shells of dead animals,
Covering the bottom of the dark, separating sea,
The dividing water that reflects daily a simple boat,
A boat carrying prisoners to cells of exile.
The Navajos built the sweat house for purification,
But these island sweat houses celebrate the Black Mass,
Lust of the spirit's death and the body's torture,
Lust for the death of freedom and the blood's fury,
And the celebrant is the devil of islands who prays:
        "Lord, grant me more steel islands,
        Wind-lashed, wind-tormented,
        Surrounded by seas of sharks;
        There I shall build cages for my sins
        And create saints of solitude
        To serve me, oh devil of islands."

VI

An old man named Stroud, a withered seventy, is caged on Alcatraz,
Condemned to life imprisonment for murder.
Hunched shoulders below a green eyeshade cap,
Long face with blue eyes beneath metal-rimmed glasses,
He has been in solitary confinement, in deep lock,
For forty years at Alcatraz and other prisons.
A specialist in birds, author of a book on bird diseases,
His birds were taken away when he was sent to Alcatraz.
No one may visit him except his brother and the chaplain.
He sends and receives a letter once a month to a list of three.
He reads no papers, sees no television, hears no radio.
In his felt slippers, the prisoner pads his white room
And listens to the world of separation outside,
Dim echo of San Francisco traffic, bellowing foghorns.
He writes to his brother:

159

"I wish you could read French, Fred. I would have you read *Le Voyage* from *Fleurs de Mal* by Charles Baudelaire. The translation loses the flavor. This fellow was very bitter at life and he had reason to be, but it was that very bitterness that made him one of the greatest poets who ever lived. I have a bunch of his poems that I have copied and am learning by heart. In the one mentioned he says in one verse: 'It is bitter to know what one learns from travel; that the world is small and monotonous, that yesterday, today, tomorrow, and forever, it makes us see our own image: an oasis of horror in a desert of ennui.' Can you beat that for a figure of speech?"

The oasis of horror lies in the desert of the prison eye.
A scientist has said: "The rainbow is merely
An instrument for separating the colors of sunlight."
This is the mind of the desert of ennui:
"Prison is merely an instrument for separating the evil
In man from his good self." The logic is rainbow-absolute,
And the snail of conformity clings blindly to his shell.

Stroud writes:
"What keeps me in is that I am not a compromiser. I never condone what I think is wrong and I never forget anything . . . I have never turned back from a position once taken in my whole life and I never shall."

This dangerous mind, reformer in the quicksands of change,
Prisoner in the comforting climate of compromise
Where each servile hand must be shaken for advancement,
And the invisible, spiral staircases of the mind shattered.
Let the barren, functional mind lead boldly upward on
The worn steps of time where the rainbows are
Merely instruments of separation like the sea.

Pray for us, devil of islands, in our time of separation.

   VII
   Isla de los Alcatraces
The legend that the pelican
Feeds its young
With blood from its own breast
Is falsely sung

By the false singer,
Man, who seeks the word, *free,*

160

From blood of prisons
Suspended in the sea.

Devil of islands,
Birds are ghosts on this Rock;
Through grey mist
A foghorn wails as dawn's cock.

Only the name of pelican
In a foreign tongue
Remains, where freedom's dream
Once was young.

     VIII
Yesterday, today, tomorrow, forever,
She stares into the telescope
Caught in the horror of prison dreams.
She sees the Rock change,
The government give it up,
Indians occupy it
In memory of INDIAN POWER;
Tourists trooping through,
Hypnotized fantasy experts
Seeking Al Capone's syphilitic cell.
Devil of islands, saint of solitude,
Yours is the mocking eye in this lens,
The enigma of solitary punishment
Punishing for the community of men.

The Graffiti Fingers of
the Theology Student

As deadbeats pass from bar to can,
I read on the chipped wall
Deep in the skins of graffiti:
    "God Is Dead"—Nietzsche
Underneath, some cripple has scribbled:
    "Nietzsche Is Dead"—God
Another lost graffiti artist
Has drawn a picture of God naked,

161

Dirty hippie beard, long hair,
Drifting bell-like tongue
Where archaic wonders, Greek, Latin,
Hebrew, ring in silent majesty.
Two layers up, a rocket soars
In lift-off of space visions,
Overkill, afterburner, doomsday tape,
Escalation, go-reflex for megadeath . . .

I drew the hippie god. I drew the rocket.
I am the carver of pornographic signs
Celebrating the death of God.
Something is growing in me, roots
Cracking through the city's walled-in poverty.
Driven out by doubt, I walk at night
Seeking to lose the fog concealing sky.
I stumble over discarded drunks
Before they're tossed into the wagon
For their evening log-pile ride to jail.
I put my hand on thighs of whores.
I fight off cripples on crutches
Blocking my way, demanding money.
I end up at this drifter's bar
Where eyes stare looking for a fix.
"The enormity of evil is crushing me,"
Tolstoy said, "driving me to doubt everything."
But evil is still brilliant to me,
Floating in this haze like malignant diamonds.
When I learn to read everything in the graffiti,
My fingers will start their automatic writing,
Shoot through the roots of doubt in fire,
Write the great, sacrificial handwriting of blood
On walls to shine in new graffiti revelations.

A Fame for Marilyn Monroe

The pictures always laugh,
As your bust bursts
        out of its dress.
Fame strips you naked

And you cannot sleep;
     life is a peep-
Show; the psychiatrist
Gives you a new prescription;
     stronger sleeping pills
     need stronger wills.
     "Fame will go by
     and
        so long,
     I've had you,
        fame."

Coroner's Case 81,128,
Fame's number in a
     numbered time.
"A sex symbol becomes a thing
And I just hate to be a thing."
     A wedding ring
Is not for things; your agent
Bargains on with fame;
     on the lawn toy dogs
     guard you in the smogs.
     "Fame will go by
     and
        so long,
     I've had you,
        fame."

Studio executives say, "You're finished.
Always late." You get later.
     Exiles talk all night
On telephones, naked with fame.
"It's like grr do this, grr do that."
     When you're flat
In the morgue, fame snaps your photograph.
"It might be a relief to be finished."
     The lonely are always late,
     They have another date.
     "Fame will go by
     and
        so long
     I've had you,
        fame."

Specialty Barber in Beast-heads

I cut you to your natural face.
Deep in your hair lurks your animal look.
A barber just cuts your hair, but a real hair stylist
Like me plays the skin—hair—bone game
From all angles . . . If you're a dog man
I'll find your dog-face, your dog-fancies.
If you're a cat, I'll give you a cat-cut.
I find the hidden animals, fox, lynx, beaver.
Once in a balding gent I found a slick-skinned weasel
And he walked out of here into a new hunting world.
It's a real art searching for animal souls
In a city where people think animals are just pets.
When you climb out of my chair and your old identity
Lies cut on the floor, I want you to peer
In my big gold mirror, preen yourself
In your new Beast-Head, put a new prance
In your step as you scratch yourself
High with my motto—*Beast Does Best!*

The Violence and Glory of the American Spirit

(November 26, 1963. A ninety-year-old man, Barney Stetson, lies alone
in his disordered room in a small town on the coast in northern California.
Like everyone in the nation, he has been watching television, and lies now
restlessly in his iron bed with the lion-head knobs, staring into the dark.
In the room's chaos, yellowing newspapers, boxes, broken furniture, litter
the corners. Worn, faded clothes hang on a rope stretched across the room
at the foot of the bed. A bunch of bananas, which he finds easy to eat
because of his lack of teeth, hangs on the rope next to the clothes. His
thoughts run jagged, slow, remembering all the assassinations he has lived
through, as past and present seep together in his disconnected mind.)

I liked to slouch along looking at life easy.
When people think you're hunched over
Staring down at things, you peer up at them
And see through the walls of their skin.
What you see you can't tell anybody
Because they wouldn't believe it.
You have to live with it in a dead silence.
Not that I was so small as a kid . . . This hump

164

Didn't come till I got old . . . When you get old
You start hunching over, getting ready
For that last horizontal position in the coffin.
How old am I anyway? . . . Eighty-eight, ninety,
What difference does it make? . . . I got
A funny, old name too, Barney Stetson.
Everybody used to ask did my father steal
The name from the hat or the hat from my father.
Every time my dad got restless, he pulled on
That big, broad-brimmed hat, and we moved
Further west till we couldn't go no further—
The country had just run out of frontier land.

When I was a boy, Garfield was murdered by Guiteau,
That crazy lawyer and evangelist who called himself
An employee of "Jesus Christ and Company."
If there's ever going to be a kind of peace,
My father said, it'll have to be wrung
Out of violence. It'll take a long time, he said.
I never knew what he meant . . . All those guns he had.
He taught me to shoot when I was hardly out of the cradle.
He shot everything on his ranch, animals, birds,
Indians, for necessity and thrills . . . I liked to shoot too.
How are we going to wring peace out of violence anymore?
The President killed . . . Shot dead with a rifle
By some mad young fellow shooting into a Texas parade,
Trying to shoot into glory by killing glory,
Only to get shot himself by another murderer.

Murder for murder, a peaceful people always
Breaking out in civil violence, seeking glory
Until the violence and glory tangle
Tight together . . . When Guiteau was hanged,
People in the crowd paid three hundred dollars
A head to hear him yell, "Glory! Glory! Glory!
As he fell through the trap . . . *What'll we do*
With the body of this new crazy fellow?
Pour acid in his coffin like they did
With Garfield's assassin, a carboy of
Sulphuric acid to punish the murderer's bones?

I can't see or move quick enough to shoot
The side of a barn now . . . Lie here cracked

To the bone like those lobsters I caught
When I took people down the bay in my boats.
Wish I could do that again . . . Nets straining
From the water, shells bulging red against the cords.
High bonfire blazing against the sky as the sun
Fell into the western sea . . . *Pacific* . . . Strange name
For western violence . . . Drop the lobsters into
Hissing steam . . . Young people singing, shouting,
Violence is a young man's eye, a crazy eye
Pleading to belong . . . In old people the violence
Smolders deep inside like an old cooking pot.

It took a crazy young fellow to kill
A president . . . Like Booth, that frustrated actor,
Crying to his friends, "I must have fame, fame!"
Then shooting into the back of Lincoln's head
With his derringer, screaming "Sic semper tyrannis!"
The scream would have to be in Latin.
Breaking his leg in a mad leap to the stage,
The only place he felt at home, hobbling
Desperately into the night . . . Twelve days later,
Living like a wounded animal
Trapped in a Virginia farm and what happens?
He's shot by a crazy sergeant acting against orders.
The sergeant claims: *"Providence directed me!"*

How come we got so many cities and towns
Named after God's will, the whole country
Caught in its inner burning, wanting like
The old Puritans to be an ancient Israel, an eye
For an eye, wanting the murder as much as the murderer.
Tame the land . . . We've learned taming with machines.
We grew rifles like arms . . . Shoot down the Indians
At Wounded Knee, all those wild Indian names
Marking ghost lands we called "reservations."
Stop their "Ghost Dance"! . . . That's a laugh.
String up the outlaws! . . . Free and kill the niggers!
Ride the Frontier with a bottle of whiskey
Hanging from your teeth in the name of Christ!
Tomorrow I'll clean up some of this junky room
If I can get out of bed soon enough . . . Takes a
Long time to warm up these bones, but then
I always had it tough warming up to anyone.

Never had many friends, outlived the few I had.
Never think much of them anymore . . . People
Scraped over me like barnacles . . . I learned
To be a hull of my own like my boats.
When I couldn't clean my boats no more
I locked 'em all into the boat house
And left 'em there to rot . . . Why should it be
Any different with boats than with old people?
I used to visit all my rotting boats in the shed,
Watch the wood rot out in a kind of glory,
All those women's curves filling up the air
With the lost wonder of stinking wood.

When you're old you still have the desire,
You know the glory even if you can't touch it,
Can't see it again . . . Why do we live in
This strange kind of violent glory?
McKinley killed in the Temple of Music.
Who was the young killer of glory then?
Some crazy immigrant name like all our names
Tossed into the pot when we tried to melt a country.
Czolgoose, Czolgosz, something like that . . .
"I killed the President because he was the enemy
Of the good working people!" . . . And the good
Working people murdered him quick in a trial
That lasted some eight hours, shooting electricity
Through him forty-six days after McKinley's death.
That's quick revenge, that's glory for you.

Why did I let these boats rot? . . . I've seen
My murders real in life . . . Kill fish, birds,
Sheep, cattle, old people when their time's up.
That was the West . . . Better than this hanging on
Past your time . . . *Kill, kill, kill!*
Go out in a blaze of glory . . . That violence had
Meaning, kill to live . . . Better than lying
In the dark, dreaming violence inside.

I feel like that new murderer . . . I heard him
Screaming, "I never did anything!"
What kind of murderer is that? . . . We're turning
Into men with guns who can't shoot enemies outside,
So we blow ourselves up inside where

167

It's easier to hate . . . Go out in a blaze of glory!
That's a laugh here in this bed,
My mother's bed, surrounded by this junk.
Tomorrow is maybe Sunday.
I'll put on my suit and tie before I go
To my sister's house and see if those young punks
Are stealing my blackberries again . . . But then
It's winter . . . They'll be a few months yet.
That funeral is going on and on even though
The set's gone dead . . . Must have blown a fuse.
Or did I turn it off? . . . Can't remember.
The President's wife in black . . . Beautiful.
I never thought she was so real before.
She almost makes something out of this violence,
What'll she do now? . . . How can she live?
I should have married . . .
Afraid of a woman's touch, wanting it,
But I didn't want that kind of claim.
That riderless horse with the ghost on his back.
Who's riding there? Murdered or murderer?
A country ridden by ghosts of glory and violence . . .
These drums . . . That dirge . . . I wish I were dead.

The first time I came to this bay the silence was
So deep the water seemed bottomless . . . It rippled
Against the wilderness so wild we never recognized
It was ourselves . . . Deer waited for me to kill them,
Fish surged in the water at my hook . . . Trees
Loomed to be cut and burned . . . I walked down
To the still water lapping at the shore . . . I knew
I'd never leave . . . The gulls made whirlpools of
Gliding silence . . . A sandpiper waded in the
Low tide's mud on high, thin legs . . . All the mud
Glistened with moss-green rocks as if time were
Breathing up the stink of death, offering its own
Green resurrection, glory of the land,
Glory of spring shattering stiff branches with
New violence before we cut the land to our size.
Glory of the tides surging out of night and moon
Into the sun . . . Glory of sun and wind flickering
On boats . . . Flickering into the stable where
That horse munches under the ghost of its
Murdered rider . . . A face of hatred is all mad eyes . . .

Tomorrow when it's spring I'll catch those boys
Always stealing my blackberries and scream at them.

And: A Funeral Hymn for Ernest Hemingway

AND
    you used the hidden conjunction as a bridge,
    a wall between layers of short, syllabic meaning,
    marriage of simple clauses into a music of style:
      "The ugly, short infantry of the mind."

AND
    you built a century with the flesh of sensations
    facts of the body, of landscape, the hell with abstractions,
    and the words: "Sacred, glorious and sacrifice
      and the expression in vain."

AND
    many crossed the bridge of your prose, seeking
    a new simplicity of language and experience,
    until the sacrifices were like your stockyards
    in Chicago, where "nothing was done with the meat
      except to bury it."

AND
    you retreated to Idaho, the wild Sawtooth Mountains
    small frontier state, where your teacher, Pound, was born;
    and you searched for a final source of wilderness,
      a last camp, "in the good place."

AND
    before Idaho, your mother had sent you, as a gift,
    the Civil War pistol with which your father shot himself,
    and you could feel in humming veins the rising pressure
      of the age of hypertension.

AND
    "one of the simplest things of all, and the most
    fundamental, is violent death;" the last barrier,
    German soldiers climbing it; Italians clutching;

American expatriates wandering around the barrier;
Spaniards cutting into it, proud with dignity of death,
    that bull-torn, mutilated country.

AND

    you selected the silver-inlaid, twelve-gauge,
    double-barreled shotgun, specially made for your ceremony,
    placed the gun barrel in your mouth, and pulled
        both triggers to blow your head off.

AND

    the conjunction remained, the hidden link,
    arrow of connection, the shrewd, submerged sound
    which pulses on, running over the white-pebbled river bottom,
    where the water of simplicity flows "clear and swiftly moving
        and blue in the channels."

Last Words for Count No 'Count

They say you die in your own language.
The coffin and the lark of words read on
As your sentences wander remorselessly
Through the great Indian country, Yoknapatawpha:
    "William Faulkner, sole owner and proprietor."
Imponderable, immortal, immutable, immemorial,
The country lives in its legends of racial hate
And love, the odd, strained quality of endurance,
But you die in your language. The haunted run
Of your sentence dies in your flesh,
The clotted, frenzied adjectives,
    long still hot weary dead September afternoon,
A country and prose where
    "Everything, weather, all keep on too long."
Count No 'count some in your county called you,
Count for your dapper dress,
The undeniable coil of your achievement;
No 'count for the venomous, compassionate
Sting of your style into decaying manners,
The lost, bloody faces of nightmare
From the ancestral war in its futile stance of honor.

170

"There are not many dreams in the world
but there are a lot of human lives . . ."
Reading your dream, struggling to grasp
What one has read, slowly, the dream
Filters into consciousness—dim as emerging dawn—
Confusion of time and language,
Where bird-song is barely distinguished
From silence of the insect-ticking night.
So men go on dying for their dreams
As the summers of wisteria die,
Rich and smoldering as your prose,
        In the notseeing and the hardknowing as though in a cave . . .
Sentences with a long, growing pulse,
Roots twining, surging slowly through blind earth
Up the green vine until, one by many,
The glaring, purple blossoms burst
And fade with their illuminating light,
And Dilsey (*they endure*) cries out from
Her dark silence, staring at the cold stove:
        "Jason ain't comin' home, ise seed de first en de last."
Where you die in your own language.

The Scientist Surveys the Protozoa

To the achievements of Roman Vishniac

Under the moulding miracle of this microscope,
The commonplace curiously becomes magnificent.
Observe—here creeps a cautious litttle creature
Forever peering through the inch of his landscape;
There a second who searches fixedly for food
Like a fat man always in fancy of famine.
Look! This tiny animal is called a floscularia,
So beautiful I made her Queen of the Microcosmos.
Long, fine hairs stream singularly from her head,
Contracting, expanding through rays of radiance.
Hers is the eternal hair of Helen, the hanging
Harvest of a beauty that attracts only victims.
A sudden shock and twisting shakes her body
When some animal approaches to explore her hair.

171

The shining strands fire into a menacing corona
Pushing the prey delicately into her body.
In muddy waters, unseen, crawls an animal world
Outliving the fifty thousand years of man
By half a billion years. Before and beyond
The blasting age of atoms, they reproduce their world
Of miniature beauty, conquest, by radiant fission.

What Are the Most Unusual Things You Find in Garbage Cans?

*(A journalist questions members of the
Scavengers' Protective Association Inc.)*

BURRISTREZZI
After a wedding or baby shower
    I find
lots of gifts in the garbage.
What you don't like, you throw away,
    I guess.
Sell it, you're a cheapskate,
  Give it, you feel guilty,
    So you chuck it in the garbage.

DUCKMANN
Bikes, baby cribs, brand new coats.
Big hotels are the best for clothing.
Family districts you don't see nothing
Too unusual. Lots of little stuff
But hotels you hold your breath for
    chuck-offs.
People buy too much and stagger out,
    loaded.
They don't have no camels nowadays,
And planes don't carry all that stuff.
My dog sleeps in the baby crib.

BENSON
In the trash
behind the old Hall of Justice

once
    I found a wooden leg.

    JONES
Plenty of girly pictures
        you know, gals
        stacked up to the sky;
you see one of them
        comin' at you
            in real life,
you'd take off
        zoom
            like a rocket.
But in a garbage can
    they don't smell so real.

    FERRORE
I've found helmets, medals, a bayonet
For my World War I collection. The bayonet's
The first kind they made where you stick it in,
Twist, and it don't come out without
Bringing half a guy's insides with it.
I like to take a war in the past.
The uniforms were more colorful;
To wear those helmets you musta
Had a head as strong as a rock.
When you got a medal, they strung it
Real fruitcake on a rainbow ribbon.
You didn't just load your chest with
Little bars and flags like now.

    HANFORD
Picture frames. Pictures too, sometimes,
Landscapes mostly, cows, trees.
Once I found a picture of Jesus Christ.
I've got thirty picture frames at home,
All kinds of frames from plain to fancy.
I haven't bought one since I married.
Sometimes I just put 'em on the wall.
When there's nothing in the frame,
You can see the frame real good.

PAINTER
Cash
  wristwatches
    and a gold
      wedding ring

SWINTON
I've got about twenty radios I found
All around my house, on the floor,
    on the shelves, in closets,
      on the bureau.

That way I make my own stereo.
Maybe I turn on four at the same time,
    or listen to different shows
      in different rooms.

News for breakfast in the kitchen,
Music in the bathroom, baseball
    in the backyard with a beer,
      politicians in the basement.

Sometimes I just turn 'em all off
And walk around quiet through the rooms.
    That's a good feeling too,
      looking at all those radios.

HAMILTON
Old books
  you never saw
    so many
      goddamn
        old books
          with weird titles
        like
"Rebecca of Sunnybrook Farm."

BINDINI
The most unusual thing I ever found was
    an Espresso machine.
It worked and I still use it in my home.
    Every morning with that coffee

174

and you've got the stomach
    for a day with garbage.

On the Burning of Mingus's Bass

"Charles Mingus, virtuoso bass player and one of the giants of modern jazz,
was evicted from his studio in New York on Thanksgiving Eve in a hassle with
the city and the landlord . . . The city marshal shouted at Mingus, "I'll make
all your trash into garbage" and that is what was done. Mingus's piano was
shoved downstairs, his bass hauled off to the sanitation department and burned,
and most of his belongings have disappeared also . . ."
RALPH GLEASON, San Francisco Chronicle, December 7, 1966

When a wood mountain burns,
The high-level sense falls,
The tall, striding rhythm,
    thump-thump plucking
    of heat-strings,
That hot, holding tension,
    hearth-stone of sound,
    smolder into silence

In the crazy stillness, searchers
    hunt wild wood;
A scarred fear hides
    in sanitary fire;
The high joy,
    gut-peaks,
Fade, lost in garbage
    in sullen quiet.

The burned silence
    glows flat
with no thumping size.

Meditation on the New Space Language

(1)
Isolated in the American net,
The old frontier vision of possibilities,

175

Dream space language—
As Charles Olson wrote:
    "It is a geography
    at bottom,
    a hell of wide land
    from the beginning."

Wider, deeper, higher—
Caught in the struggle
Between a landlocked and
A seafaring people
Before the Civil War,
Fitz Hugh Lane painted
Ships in Gloucester Harbor,
Defining clear lines
From shore to horizon,
Distinctive loneliness of space
Sharpening earth geography.

    (2)
Moving, changing
From ships to railroads,
Planes, space ships—
A cycle of linguistic exploration
To break out of isolation?
Travel to satisfy the exploring will
While sleeping still
In superstitious homes?
In space confronting fifteen sunrises,
Fifteen sunsets every day,
Citizen-astronauts learn to gape
At light, keep hurtling
Into space against time.

    (3)
Language computerized
Into figurative complacency,
Dawn of incredible, speeding numbers:
Mach 6, 124,000 feet,
Space shuttle at re-entry fire:
    "Columbia, you're coming
    right around the hatch,
    what a way to come to California!"

Mach 1.3 at 58,000 feet:
>"Looking beautiful,
>right on the money,
>coming right down the chute!"

Mach 1 at 51,000 feet,
Sonic boom announces shuttle
Nearing landing site,
Powering down the computers,
Giants of impersonal calculation:
>"To clean up the spacecraft.
>This kind of excellence,
>You know, is absolute zero-flaw."

(4)
Zero, as the Mayans knew,
Can be drawn as peaceful seashell
On the shore's beginning.
> . . . *absolute zero-flaw.*
How do we draw zero
For the booster rocket
On the doomed space shuttle
With its sudden fatal leak?
So sentences explode into oblivion—

>"When the elevator gets stuck,
>I want out," says the astronaut.

Floating gravity-free,
Circling stars and planets
Faster than speed of light,
Can we voyage in space
Without verbal illumination,
Challenging metaphors of light?

(5)
Focused down, a spy satellite
Catches the earth's sensuous curve,
Spots a woman in an orange boa,
Her body swaying to the dance—
In Delmore Schwartz's jubilant words:
>*"The world is a wedding!"*

177

Who will attend the wedding unless
Language creates its shocking decision:
The world of space cannot be explored
By cold definitions of hardware and software;
Only by a new communal language
Linking together in lucid vision earth
To space as endless star community.

The City Planner:
Catherine Bauer Wurster

I

Where are the images of the ideal city?
We need many images competing with each other:
To free the imprisoned racial slums;
To build in mass structures
Admirable, private places;
To make from the gaping sprawl
A center of connection and community . . .
But we are haunted by images from the past:
Jefferson: "The mobs of great cities add just so much
To the support of pure government as
Sores do to the strength of the human body."
Whitman looking through his "moral microscope"
In 1871 and seeing cities "crowded with
Petty grotesques, malformations, phantoms."
Emerson thinking of the city as Understanding:
It "toils all the time, compares, continues,
Adds, argues, near-sighted but strong-sighted,
Dwelling in the present, the expedient, the customary";
The country as Reason:
"The highest quality of the soul
Which never reasons, never proves,
It simply perceives, it is vision."

Where is Emerson's 19th century city of Understanding?
Today we drive our cars as second houses
Searching for the happy, invisible place;
We drive through shapeless sprawls of real estate,

Great aggressive land-eaters unreal
In sullen, boring sameness, standardized tracts.
Understanding broods concealed in that sprawl,
Unable to win discovery of its confinement,
Desperately searching for strong judgments,
Fresh interpretations, desire for Reason.

II

As a planner, I sought to save the country
For the city, to save the source of wonder
For the sense of changing time. The city's
Power to achieve is the power of theatre,
Strong dramatic voices seeking a rhythm of connection.
Yet Reason's vision remains a solitary sight,
The Blue Herons and White Egrets I loved to watch
Glide in over the fog-dripping lagoon to their nests
High in silent redwoods piercing toward the sun;
Sound of coiling sea echoing not only
Searching wave, but wave wedding shore;
The mountain that we climb to discover the sky.
When will Understanding reason
And Reason understand?
When fact is married to vision,
And the city's restless motion
Finds its rest in harmony
Of sea, mountain, rooted tree;
In that marriage, death is no division,
But natural end, peace of balance.

III

Turning green hills brown
Is a legend of the sun,
Legend of death and resurrection,
The solitary change we learn.

Though we die alone,
We do not die in solitary accident.
A memory of tradition,
A vision of creation,
Sound through our isolation
Love's music marrying
Understanding to Reason:

179

In cities Understanding seeks
To change the speculator's lure.
Logic glows and cannot die
As long as mind exists to cure.

Yet only Reason lights mind
Beyond the time when fact falls
To the wonder of perception,
The music for a wedding pact:

Reason wed to Understanding
Strive for a unity, becoming one;
Their joyous unity of love
Alone endures the darkened sun.

Mississippi Sheriff at the Klan Initiation

to the memory of Mickey Schwerner,
Andrew Goodman, and James Chaney

Son, you don't know nothin' 'bout nigger,
It somethin' you gotta live with
To understand where it belong.
It somethin' like knowin' stones and trees
And woods and dark roots in the woods.
It somethin' animal part of the country
And you train an animal to its place.
If you don't hunt your dog or rein
Your horse in, where you goin'?
You got an animal top of you,
Ridin' you, your family ain't safe,
Your quiet town starts smokin'
And there's a fire burnin' your land.
You done that, son, you done set that fire,
You got the whole beautiful country
A-blazin' 'cause you don't want to
Tame black blood. Don't get me wrong,
I like black, I like ridin' wild things,
I like tamin' wild country to serve,
But time's come when you gotta
Keep that wilderness in place, son,

180

Kill for your white life, or you gonna
See a black world rapin' your white,
Animals in clothes pretendin' they're
Readin' books, walkin' into your store,
Eatin' at your table, leavin' your place
Covered with their dirt. One mornin'
You gonna look out your window and you
Won't see no white country anymore, they
Won't be no more white cotton to pick . . .
So you better learn, son, why we're settin' fire
To that cross. It's burnin' away the blackness,
It's lightin' up a new white day,
Blazin' against dark wilderness
In the killin' time so's we can see white again.

The "Vulgarians"

Many of the *"Vulgarians"* were mountaineers,
Turning to clarity of steep slopes
In the chaos of the demonstrating 1960s.
They knew speaking vulgar is a value,
You don't just curse in confusion.
The center of argument is often dark
Requiring sharp points of language.

By day they climbed developing their skills
And opened their packs at night
To philosophy and pot. Often you saw them
On mountains, laughing, plunging naked
Into deep, icy waters, then climbing doggedly,
Roped in brotherhood against inevitable falls.

Standing joyously on the summit
In a brief, blazing view of eternal distance,
Their commitment was to ambitious height.
They sang, and the echoes of their song
Plunged into the valleys of revolution
And lettered enigmatic, vulgar slogans
Searching for a ritualistic solidarity
In fading obscenities or graffiti walls.

181

In the Ginsberg Supermarket

In the Ginsberg Supermarket
a neon sense of frontier wilderness lingers,
    prairie schooners in the carts,
    outposts in the melons,
    refugees in the cereals,
    barbed wire in the detergents,
    t-shirts labeled INDUSTRIAL POETRY.

Flying into the Ginsberg Supermarket
supermen weave down zigzag corridors
    possessing things, transforming them
    instantly, packages into gaudy cans,
    cold mirrors of perfect freezers into
    security cameras blinking *hello*
    to faces trapped in the refining fire.

Superladies in the Ginsberg Supermarket
wheel families to triumph on their supercarts
    past invisible black poverty faces
    among refugees from CIA Laotian war,
    Mexican immigrants shouting "cousin"
    when the electronic cash register clicks
    and the sign of hearts never flashes up.

In the Ginsberg Supermarket
Make It New becomes a military slogan,
    eat newness, rape it if necessary,
    create fancy-name in search of fame,
    search for the small congenial corners
    where the community still gathers
    in the pitiless national light.

The Dance of Theodore Roethke

I

How he rolled down night streets
Like a barrel heaved from side to side;
How his heavy, high forehead,

Great chunk of a headstone,
Loomed over polished bars
In a frenzy of silent frowns
And pitch of glass-shaking laughter.

This was a master of witch-rhythms,
Gropings through the root;
A breeder in water
Floating light out of the depths;
A curious, waddling land-animal,
Air-fingered, at home by waves,
Who took from the whitecapped sea
A sense of skimming.

     II
He saw with his eye "close on the object,"
Staring at the disguises of God,
Stone, water, tree, elemental root,
Learning we need the catalogue
As well as the lyrical dance
To find a language
    "natural to the immediate thing,"
A language to seize from the self-trap
A time of communion, to sense beneath
Facile ornaments the simple drawing
That is the source of fire.

     III
Dance on! Dance on!
Through a country lost
In immigration fury,
Lost in the action,
Motion of disguise,
Burning of early angels,
Savagery of racial wars;
Through the long, tangled line of Whitman absorbing all
Down to your short line, end-stopped,
Paring everything away
To the final pause,
Breath that stops
As your song sings
Through death into
Time.

183

Chaotic Changes

Subjective again, my first person persona. The chaotic sixties are chang-
ing me too. I commute from Berkeley to teach at San Francisco State
University, where I also direct the Poetry Center. Commuting, the
American shadow. Like many Americans I commute two hours a day.
The blank time of enormous commuting hours shadows my life. Decep-
tive is the car's range of power and violence. Often it is joy; often it is
terror. Does it ease life? The new, hard word, *gridlock*, mounts, traffic
surging to a stop. Jammed in a line of smoking exhausts one hot day, a
defiant driver three cars ahead, throws up his arms, shouts: "Enough of
this shit! I'm leaving!"—departs to amazed stares. Like lumbering turtles
we creep around the stranded car, gaping at its sulking shell with won-
der. The driver vanishes in time, perhaps into a hermit's life.

Running a Poetry Center with my associate, poet-critic Mark Linen-
thal, is like tending an unusual cactus plant in a city favoring flowering
trees. Poetry grows protective spines amidst the decade's cinematic
frenzy. We put on many spiny poets, brave and timid voices, roarers and
squeakers, blazing egos, modest tormented souls, ascending female
voices tired of male dominance, dancing and rooted prophetic voices, for-
eign and domestic voices speaking passionate layers of history and myth,
voices speaking proudly of poetry's enduring mysteries. Around our
readings surge pulses of publicity labeled *Beat*, changing to *Hippie;* also
San Francisco Renaissance (ignoring the East Bay where many poets and art-
ists live). The sound of Beat conveys defiant or sneering tones; Beat is
beatific revolt; Beat is deadbeat druggie. Can drugs stimulate the imag-
ination, create new visions? Everyone is smoking pot, trying LSD. Mir-
acles are reported. Disasters erupt as drugs turn into addicts and thieves.
As Beats transform into Hippies and rock sounds louder and harder, is it
all a matter of hair, beards, clothes of revolt? No, poetry remains always
with outsiders whatever the name. The real revolt is inside against the
Vietnam War dividing the country. For Civil Rights and racial justice, the
release of the choking environment from exploitation and growing pollu-
tion. In these endeavors, poetic cliques finally unite, read together at
mass demonstrations.

One Sunday in May, 1964, a giant Civil Rights protest, some thirty
thousand strong, against the bombings, shootings, and police brutality
of blacks in Birmingham, parades down Market Street. Near the Civic
Center, even though it's Sunday, wreckers smash away with their "head-
ache ball" at the lavish baroque 1920s Fox theatre. The great golden in-
terior dome rises, shining, through shattered walls. Bits of angelic gold
crumple down. The parade moves past glowering movie theatres on
Market, *Mad Dog Coll, The Gambler Wore A Gun, Blaze Starr Goes Nudist.* A

fascination of signs wave in the air: "We March in Unity for Freedom in Birmingham and Equality in San Francisco," "To Fight Tyranny Is Obedience To God," "A Future Written In Blood?" A bearded poet carries a placard with large burlap letters reading *Love* and above it, imbedded in the intricate collage, *Eros*. "What else can you say?" he shrugs. A vast impression of youth, religious youth, bohemian youth, sceptical youth, youth searching for a faith. At the end of *The Rebel*, Camus writes:

> This is the end of romanticism. At this moment, when each of us must fit an arrow to his bow and enter the lists anew, to reconquer, within history and in spite of it, that which he owns already, the thin yield of his fields, the brief love of this earth, at this moment when at last a man is born, it is time to forsake our age and its adolescent furies.

Is it time? We Americans are materialist romantics. Romanticism dies hard in the United States. We feel we're beginning a new era if we can end the war and racial injustice, we find it hard to forsake our adolescent furies. An anti-militarist near me protests: "The thing to do is *walk*, not *march*. It's like the problem of *Peace Corps*. The name's too militaristic for peace."

At the Civic Center, the huge crowd sings: "We Shall Overcome." Reverend Bernard Lee, a Baptist minister and a leader of the black struggle in Birmingham, speaks passionately: "We want to be free, not tomorrow, not next week, but yesterday! They say the Negro in the South is not educated enough. That's all right, we're coming anyhow. They say he doesn't keep up his property, that he doesn't bathe often enough. We're coming stinking anyhow! We say to the nation, ready or not, here we come!" The issue is joined. Those who have faith and souls of any kind against the faithless, the indifferent, the selfish. Because the faith-seeker is the only one who asks "Why?" The faithless merely follow. The danger is that they may survive to populate the new parking lots the "headache ball" is creating and the new economically segregated, drab suburbs. And what then?

Teaching too fades into surreal demonstrations. In a 1967 playwriting class talking about Strindberg's *Dream Play*, I look out the window and dramatic practice erupts. The Marine Corps is recruiting again on campus. After their last visit, when anti-war students besieged them, they are prepared: four stiff-backed Marines in full-dress uniforms, medals gleaming, hands encased in white gloves. Racial equality and military justice represented by one black in dark glasses linked to his Marine pals. Formal power over the resisting territory. But here comes the opposition. *It* is a monstrous head of curly poodle hair covering deepset, fervent eyes. *It* is dressed in an immensely oversized mock uniform with

185

fantastic purple-striped pants, golden jacket decorated with tinsel stars, high priestlike collar covered with skull and bones insignia, paper medals cut out of cartoons covering the chest down to gut level. *It* begins to recruit, wailing, chanting: "Fellow id-i-ots. Enlissst in sal-vaa-shun war! Grrrowl with meee for freee-dumb! Kill Kong! Kill Kong! Grab your frontier gun! Be your own Kit, Kit, Kitty Carson! Learn how to blooow up yellow, pink, black peeepuls in ten eeeasy lessons. LBJaybird says Vietnumb is just another Ala-mo hell-low. Grooove with old Charlie Cong. Play tick-tack-toe with hell-i-cop-ter flights. Throw gren-ade toys with gleee-ful fingerings. Learn how to fuck native gooks in jungle bushes. Get your free, shitproof pants. Kill Kong! Kill Kong! Kill Kong!" End of inside class. Beginning of outside class. *It* is joined by other glittering, improvised uniforms, against which the Marines square off rigidly. This growing civil war will not cease until the war ends.

Education turns into dramatic battle. End of spring term, 1968, the first student sit-in over curriculum changes and student minority issues occurs in the Administration Building. Friday night, final exams start next week, the sit-in is peaceful, students are policing the halls. For momentary relaxation I am home, on my way to the movies. Suddenly the President calls. As a Ford Foundation consultant, he is on his way to Ethiopia! He says he is asking several faculty to go to the Administration Building and make sure nothing happens. He has negotiated with sit-in leaders and is confident of a peaceful end in a day or two. When I reach the Administration Building, I learn that the Board of Trustees dominated by Governor Reagan has ordered that, if the students do not disperse, they will be arrested by the Tac Squad at midnight! Assisted by turncoat faculty administrators, this mad resolution has been arranged behind the President's back. The Board has decided to get rid of a liberal President whom they consider "wishy-washy." Whitefaced, the turncoats try to convince me they had no other choice. I argue futilely that the students are well-organized throughout the bay area. A midnight bust is absurdist and will provoke endless trouble. At ridiculous, melodramatic midnight, a hell of publicity erupts as the solemnly dressed, helmeted and goggled Tac Squad enters in full riot gear, spectre of the future. The media invade with flashing cameras, TV, and radio equipment. The writer, Kay Boyle, appears with her invited guest, the astonished Italian novelist, Alberto Moravia. So much for absent trustees who conceive midnight as conquering pliable students with invisible publicity. Through megaphones everyone is ordered out of the building, threatened with arrest for trespassing. Students do not move and are led out one by one to cheers from a gathering crowd of fellow students. Me, trespasser, requested by the President to assure peace in a building where I work? With several faculty colleagues I am led out too. Booked and jailed, smell of urine proves I'm in a real cage. A stinking urine world is prison. Nothing has been accomplished. I am in King Lear's world, "Nothing, nothing, nothing . . ." Yet out of nothing, everything will continue its disastrous course. The university will suffer an agonizing, debilitating strike in the coming year as the Nixon-Reagan era of deceit gains power. In 1970 during Nixon's Cambodian invasion, universities will be shut down throughout the country. Two anxious colleagues help to release me on my own recognizance in the morning and I walk into freedom charged as *trespasser*.

During these turbulent years, passion changes my secure family life in Berkeley. Security is dangerous, subject to complacency, impossible to my poet's faith. Commissioned by singer, James Schwabacher, to translate Hugo Wolf's *Italian Song Book*, I join with him and mezzo, Margot Blum, in a dramatic performance. I read the poems in my English version, while they sing their romantic conflict in the original German of Paul Heyse. A new kind of multi-lingual chamber opera that audiences can appreciate on several different levels! Successfully received, we perform the work throughout the bay area, then in New York. I fall into a web of passion with Margot, leave my family in Berkeley. She is married too. I move into a cheap apartment in San Francisco. What have I lost? Will this passion consume me or save me from the trap of security? The clash between Passion and Divorce begins.

Passion and Divorce

(1)

Passion flows like a river past blocking shore
    erupting in a saturnine storm,
        creating an impetuous, blazing landscape.

Enter this landscape of luxurious flowering,
    a beautiful, tormenting garden,
        roses towering to demonic heights;

Consuming power of eternal change
    beyond impossible levels of caution,
        creating thorns sharp with desire.

Passion requires a different cooling,
    a silent composure in the shade,
        departure from previous time patterns.

187

You cannot see passion in the distance;
    its vision is close-up astonishment,
    forceful veins, furious devotion.

Passion has no clear beginning or end,
    surges through invisible time
    fusing the beautiful to the dangerous.

In my life I have experienced Passion twice
    moving my life to another place,
    entangled with another body of force.

Passion is the dreaded god seizing you,
    demanding change in your life,
    Passion the conquest of reason.

Passion is the target requiring peace
    and security be attacked
    if Dionysus is an eternal god.

(2)

Divorce looms when rational law
    denies Dionysian passion.
Divorce demands you leave everything
    suffering memories from the first Passion.
The first Passion was youthful,
    a wartime dream of salvation,
But that dream endured for many years
    and produced two loved children.
During the bitter necessity of Divorce
    I live in poverty for a year
In a San Francisco slum surrounded
    by agonies of black/white conflicts.
In Divorce the past struggles to prevent
    the future, a promise yet to be revealed.
Divorce is hangtime of waiting when
    time runs slow and has no stop.
Divorce is a bestiary of law and lawyers
    creating a zoo of climbing conflicts.
Divorce is a bridge which children often
    fail to cross, a bridge of sacrificial children.
Divorce is the infection of miserable nights
    when memories return, children cry.

Divorce is a contract for agonizing failure,
    admission of guilt, recipe for blame.
When Divorce and Passion appear in court,
    Passion hovers as invisible ghost.
Every judge is struck dumb by separation,
    unable to judge Passion, the absent force.
Irrational Passion is never declared victor,
    all spoils go to Divorce's triumph.
Passion flies, invisible bird of mythology,
    creating dangerous crossings in illuminated air.

Kristallnacht

In my mid-forties, ruled by the curves and
Angles of experience, straight lines fading,
I sit in a cheap, dirty apartment
In San Francisco's Fillmore District,
Separated from my wife and children,
And listen to bottles tossed, tinkling
On the street, drunken escapes from poverty,
Street of grey pigeons and dogshit,
Newspapers sodden in the gutters.
Tomorrow I will walk carefully
Through shattered glass, remembering
A cool fall day in Germany, November, 1938,
When I visited a friend in Freiburg,
Small, proper intellectual town, where
Citizens cleaned their front walks
Carefully, even in rain. Ancient Gothic
Cathedral and famous university,
Heidegger, the philosopher-professor there,
Das Nichts nichtet—Nothing nothingizes,
A philosopher mute amidst Nazi power . . .
Kristallnacht, all over Germany that night
The Nazis smashed, looted Jewish stores.
In Freiburg they burned the synagogue and
Built a fence in darkness to hide destruction.
A naive, young American music student,
I wrote my first poem about that burning;
I spent that night in a cheap hotel,

189

Turning, turning on a lumpy mattress
Beneath the soft cloud of the featherbed,
Listening through the thin partition
To a German stormtrooper screw a whore
On percussion springs . . . Since then,
In many foreign rooms, I have heard
Lives tinkle on cracked pavements:
A childhood friend in fast cars
Smashing ruthlessly and smashed;
A teacher, intellectual suicide,
Crazed between the tension of ideas;
A mother, proud, crippled, blind
In the rolling wheelchair of age;
Friends, relatives, summoned to mystery
And violence when the peaceful air
Splits with fragments of suffering.
Nights, I wake, sweating,
Kristallnacht splinters in the cutting air,
Glass lives shatter from unnatural trees.

Place

I *The Roots of Place*

I wander, dragging the roots of place
    behind me,
an animal of memory.

Across the night city,
the Hamms beer sign
drinks glass after glass
    of neon-foaming light
above the lofty freeway cars
riding cold in their white stare
    through metal blackness.
In the Bank of America,
    blazing, empty offices
signal the money is being cleaned
    for tomorrow's sale.

If everything moves, searches,
    where is place?

Place withers behind the Victorian facades,
    dead carpenters fading
    in fantasies of wooden ornaments.
Place freezes behind the massive bulk
    of Federal buildings, gang-built,
    ponderous weight of group-thought.
Place shines green nostalgia from the City Hall,
    search-lit with white longing
    for classical mastery
    under winking planes.

Is hell always to move,
    flee the struggle of roots?
The roots never answer, never depart,
    yet they are strange travelers.
At night they spread their tentacles
    through dreams; the foggy air
    fills with their distant, fiery points.

The roots of place are like
    the lithographic limestone,
        soft, porous,
    when portions of an old drawing
    seep back to the wiped surface—
        the stone's "memory."

II *The Murder of Place*

When we kill place, leave, wander,
we murder ourselves for redemption.
Place enters the peril of memory;
    ancient pride threatens us,
    gilds the dark horizon of the past
    to a golden, ironic tomb
    for sanctuary of remembered parents.
Poor sanctuary . . . You exist only in lost time,
    in monuments of regret we build
    to commemorate our deaths.
How can we assume the essence of rebellion
    without its saturating, destructive rage?

191

Choosing a place is always to kill another place,
    kill, kill the roar of ourselves
      we cannot face in relatives, friends.
Each new place invites a luring death,
    treacherous meeting, waiting woman
      with whom we kill time, kill place.
Our murdering veins flow with violent joy
    into lust of flesh,
      conquering of place.

III *The Wandering Place*

Along the road everything sells;
the chunky waitresses in faded dresses
beckon sullenly. Their men bury your garbage,
    caress your thirsty gas tank.

Place is a billboard pledging rest,
motels, restaurants where selling fancies
decorate glass windows, vacant hours
    cool the speed of vanishing flesh.

To live in place that always disappears,
to see a haze of faces always fading,
to hear laughter echo on the lost horizon,
    learn that love is always left,

a glitter on the road of memory,
the Evening Star over your hunched shoulder
luring all lingering wanderers
    in search of the lost place.

IV *The Next Place*

In the morning color of the new place,
sun blinds us with illumination,
    a brilliance concealing all shadows.
Curved like a woman's breast
for the lost dead to caress,
the mountain called Diablo
    quickens over the coast range.
Oh Spanish devil's mountain,
your ancient curse of place looms over

sprawling thrust of new suburbia,
places shaped by steel appliances.

Appliance! Shrewd, colorless word
pointed like a hypodermic needle:
    "A device or machine for household use."
Caught in the paradox of living in places
to which we must commute, we seek to tune
ourselves to comfortable buildings without style
or texture but "exploration of the latest materials."

The isolation of the next place!
        To confront in the shadows
        hidden feelings of lost tenants;
        to sleep disturbed by their dreams;
        to wake twitching to other movements.
Over the next place always hover
        restless lives that cannot rest,
        lonely spirits that cannot leave.
        Through a conspiracy of memories,
        wandering spirits seek their place.

    V *The Sexual Place*

After raging thoughts and memories,
endless puzzles of parables,
futile balancing of words, excuses,
to come to the sexual place . . .
To see her wandering, puzzled in the light,
reflecting a myriad of colors in sunlight;
to see her turn and run to meet me,
her eyes luring in the search of all legends.
Every violent motion seeks a quiet place.
I pull her to rest; we begin the upward search,
legs, thighs, breasts, mouth, hair;
        we turn to similar flesh.
What I taste is mine, what she tastes is hers,
        as changing place rises,
        fills inside her.
We possess place to float in peace.
She sleeps, content . . . I watch her.
Love is sacred promise of renewal;
in sleep her body breathes with an odor

193

transfixing night, smell of fulfillment,
the room transformed with lust of search,
proud sense of place that changes always—
the sexual place as eternal entrance,
her flesh my harmony,
      her flesh my only fame.

    VI *Celebration of Place*

Wild disasters of place,
ruined walls, tombs,
shattered idols who pray
for a religion of place
while the gods move!
Lost places! Lost loves!
Lost cities, civilizations!
Wood, metal die beneath
moving flesh as body dances
in the walls of its life.

Sing the blessing of place
that is discovery of flesh,
duality, not trinity,
mounted union of desire
and need, true source.

Sing the blessing of place
that contains love's revelation,
spirit in the wall of flesh
flowing through solidity,
    discovering
the settled river of place.

The Shapes our Searching Arms

The shapes our searching arms
    make in the empty air
    are women's bodies
that when the wind and rain
    possess our sight

194

we have that grace to touch,
those white shapes to know,
    and keep a sanity for love.

Green Frog at Roadstead, Wisconsin

Consider the way of a pleasant path,
Walking through white birch, fir,
And spruce on a limestone trail
Through quiet, complacent time of summer
When, suddenly, the frog jumps!
And you jump after him, laughing,
Hopping, frog and woman, to show
The stationary world its flat ways.
Love is a frog, I grin that greenly
To your green eyes and they leap
At me. Up, I will enter the Frog World
With you and try the leaping ways
Of the heart that we do not fail to find
The sunlit air full of leaping chances!

At Frank Lloyd Wright's Taliesin, Wisconsin

Seeing the architecture of joy is
Feeling the materials of love,
Sensing that flesh is stone,
    water, glass, wood.

What are hand, foot, breast and hair,
If not an arrangement of flesh,
An architecture of space creating
    a sensuous symmetry?

Feel, touch, smell, learn to see
The house you build is like your body,
Fixing the unique materials of love
    for endless entrance.

195

At Packer Lake

Delicate dragonflies
Float in their thin blue-veined search,
Fasten themselves to my skin and eyes.
Shapes of natural desire, their spirits
Reach from the past to assert
A pride of flesh, dancing motion
Against immovable pines, lucid lake.
Over the great solid, stationary
Shores of time, the dragonflies
Dance above the liquid skin that flows
With grace along your arms, love.
Swimming in the lake, you reach
And reach again in the lovely gestures
We make against distance and place
To open the hard, motionless shores
Of discovery with flickering music,
Blue wings, churning body, white arms.

Alone, in another Lost Room

Alone, in another lost room,
Staring out at the dark
Foaming in its desire of storm,
Where separating night
Blows up wild births of mud and mire,
I dreamt you undressed as dawnbreaker
And came to me in flesh of fire.

Love, Do Not Shun the Dark Gargoyle

That lost time which celebrated beauty
Of the Virgin beyond corruption of flesh;
Which awarded to loyal, sheltered ladies
Heroic knights and legends of purity,
Built carefully into the light of grace

196

These dark gargoyles, demonic rainspouts
Protecting walls, saving worship
By drinking storms with bestial ferocity.
When salvation lights fade at evening,
Beauty of flesh is swift to die
Unless we feel the terror of weight,
The ugly endurance that anchors us
In drifting time. Love, in our celebration,
Do not shun the dark gargoyle,
Weird face glowing in proud perception,
Wings chained to high walls,
Who carries rain, like love,
Free from the cold stones of time.

Where We Were

Awake at night, I watch the Japanese blossoming trees
Shine like tiny illuminated fish swimming in moonlight.
February in California, 1968. The tulips from Amsterdam
Soar leafy tall, sprayed against bugs. The night is green with song.
Electric sound rocks the night alive in all Palaces of pleasure.
Imagine beginning a poem with:
        "What makes the cornfields happy, under what constellation
        It's best to turn the soil, my friend . . . all this
        I'll now begin to relate . . ."
Today they'd publish Virgil's *Georgics* in sober blue
And call it *The Care and Operation of Profitable Farms.*
This morning I saw a man, thick-bearded, with walled-in eyes,
Wearing a button reading, RELAX . . . We compared buttons,
Mine pleading CELEBRATE LIFE. He twitched
Nervously with a lake's massive wind-ripples;
I twitched with him in the American dream of relaxation
Knowing that the frontier is still our invisible goal.
Who is hiding our inexhaustible American fathers?
Jet planes dive over Vietnam against peasant rifles.
Why can't machines conquer Asian agriculture?
Kill all the water buffaloes and we'll win.
Winning is a game after all, the highest body count.
Practice Rimbaud . . . "To whom shall I hire myself?
Which beast must be worshipped?"

197

I imagine that bench to be an angel.
Somehow it remains a bench carved with the slogan,
MAKE LOVE NOT WAR. I agree, but which is which?
My pleasure . . . Everyone is writing subjective poems.
I stare at myself naked in the mirror with ecstasy.
Well, ecstasy is maybe too un-American like Rimbaud.
My navel doesn't seem like a real circle anyway.
It's kind of square. Maybe that's my hang-up . . . I like breasts.
Inspired, I write poems on the back of envelopes.
I stop to scribble lines in lighted doorways in the rain.
How subjective can you get? Free time, I go to art galleries.
A Peruvian is painting envelopes. The stamps are nude.
That is he puts a nude where the postage stamp should be.
Maybe the message is, Liberate the Post Office!
      Free the International Mail!
Gaping, I crack off a tooth and flee to my dentist.
He fills up the hole with acrylic filling material
And smiles a warning: "Don't bite down too hard
On your lamb chops—150 pounds of pressure you know."
What am I to do? I like lamb chops. I like women.
A dedicated man, the dentist reconstructs my mouth
With classical precision: "Your teeth are like crumbling
Greek columns. The arch is gone and the columns stand alone
Struggling against the force of time. Without the arch's support,
The column, your tooth, falls." I feel like an archaeologist
Struggling to keep my Greek teeth on guard
Against the pressures of time. I walk into the rain,
The acrylic filling material proud in my mouth.
Now I am part of the synthetic materials
That occupy my country. I walk through the rain
Imagining what would happen if Rimbaud were alive.
Would he feel again, "the disordering of all the senses,"
Win the Latin Poetry Prize, chalk
GOD IS DEAD on the park bench,
Feel his shoes hurt walking through the Tenderloin District
Accosted by all the male hustlers and whores on the make?
The notice says Sister Divine has just arrived from Bombay, India,
"Land of Miracles," and is located in her own home:
      "Do not classify her as a gypsy.
      She has the God given power to heal you by Prayer.
      The touch of her hand will heal you.
      No problem is too great for her to solve.
      There is not pity for those knowing they are in hard luck

198

Sick, in need of help, and do not come for it.
Free Luck Charms and Lucky Days with each reading.
All Readings Confidential and Private."
I'm going to her and cure myself of this goddamn Vietnam War.
"Poetry is the breath and spirit of all knowledge."
My breath stinks. A wounded American, my spirit is sick
With complacency from machines I use and cannot know.
The Wash Palace down the street is washing me
With the contradictory voices of our time.
In the bombed cities, American officers cry:
    "It's a terrible thing to do, but we have to do it.
    We had to destroy the city to save it."
In Berlin, after a peace demonstration, the German mayor says:
    "We will not allow anyone to spit on American shoes."
Why can't I sleep if the Germans are protecting me?
How will I ever sleep with nature blooming around me
When it should be snowing in February? Kill those water buffalo.
Black people are saying, "Mr. Charlie, we'd rather do it."
What have I done to earn the name of Charlie?
The rain has a curious, foreign sound.
Probably my immigrant guilt is haunting me.
In the living room my step-son is always playing
Some kind of Jewish chant. Why not? The old Puritans
Sought to establish a New Israel in the wilderness . . .
It's not I who am at war. It's my machines.
"The mob in the heart the police cannot suppress . . ."
The trouble is they've got us confined in the heart.

1970s

Vietnam and
the Splintered Aftermath

On the Photographs
of Torture in Vietnam

I believe in the poem's
    fierce, ironic silence . . .
Feats of absence . . .
Festivals of silent presence . . .
The space that speaks
    of nothingness . . .
The void that fills
    between words
    to create
    the invisible presence of chance . . .
A silence different from
    this silent nihilism,
    the torture of identity,
    the use of terror for interrogation,
    as propaganda, punishment, or revenge,
    where death comes for prisoners
    tied under the tracks of armored vehicles,
    decapitated,
    hands chopped off bleeding to death,
    kicked and stomped by military boots,
    water choking nostrils and mouth,
    a bullet shot through the head,
    impossible silence of torture.
Slowly, in the arts, in life,
    man and object disappear;
The painter cries, "Each object is unreal!"
    and dreams his nightmare abstractions.
I seek my own silent flesh
    lost in photographs of torture.
Speak, I will not be heard.
"Nothing is unreal in the poem."
I cannot live in the silence of the poem
Which slowly fills up the world with silence.

The Game-master Explains
the Rules of the Game for Bombings

"The signal is the thing."
A Pentagon Official

(1)

Begin in cockpit darkness,
the aim of secret instruments.
Security is locked space, walls nameless indoors,
a panel of superior pointers . . .
Begin with the shining of engineered rules.
Team-players, our radium-bright, clockwork fingers,
alter the sky to shine with brilliance
at key terminals, decisive points,
as the automated battlefield sparkles, blinks . . .

(2)

The enemy must be reminded
what the rules of the game are,
whether he understands them or not.

(3)

Whether he understands them
is not particularly important.
The signal is the thing.

(4)

When the grid sparkles, lights flash,
the bomb-bay opens like a metal eye
glinting with computed knowledge.
No player sees the earth any more.
The signal starts the run and drop.

(5)

After the clouds color with flame,
reconnaissance planes snap pinpoint photographs.
The specialist interpreters study
how to wind up the war
without nuclear escalation.
New signals are discovered
on the photographs protecting
sanctity of the demilitarized zone.

Estimates are made to
fill up the credibility gap,
verify the body count.

(6)
On the ground, in the flesh,
The signal is the thing.

The Terrorist

"The ratonnade [the hunting down of rats, a French epithet for Moslems] are
necessary to save Algeria for France."

"In a time of violence, you are either a patriot or a traitor, a lover of your country
or a rat to be hunted down and extinguished."
AN AMERICAN IN VIETNAM

I walk my hate and let it harden there,
A plastic bomb to blast his hiding high.
My time to purify the glowing air.

Search out that traitor with his injured stare
Whose terror causes innocence to die.
I walk my hate and let it harden there.

Answer his terror with the terror
Of my bomb, explosion answers every *why*.
My time to purify the glowing air.

Often nights I hear him scuttling to scare
Us from our longing dream of liberty.
I walk my hate and let it harden there.

Blow up his secret holes, strip him bare
Until his silence breaks into a cry.
My time to purify the glowing air.

We'll meet in rat-hunts in one burning glare,
Traitor and patriot fused in the bursting sky.
I walk my hate and let it harden there.
My time to purify the glowing air.

205

In the Theater of the Absurd

In the Theater of the Absurd,
    the Pacific coral stage
    where we practice bombs,
    fish swim on land,
    birds burrow
    deep into earth,
and the cold, withered character,
      the sea turtle
      lays sterile eggs,
    then flapping slowly
    like a clown beneath
the weight of archaic armor,
    turns toward the quiet sea,
sense of direction killed by radiation;
    wanders in comic circles
    around around around
watched by staring birds
    crawling finally
    into an illusion of water,
      flippers swimming
      blissfully on sand,
      the natural anti-hero.

In 1970 in Madrid, President Nixon Presents General Franco with a Red, White, and Blue Golf Bag, Clubs, and Twelve Autographed Golf Balls

With this bag, General, it'll be like
Driving an American flag. Colors to make you blink,
Everything will glow so clear, so bright,
Down the fairway you'll go, straight down the middle,
Staying free from the rough to left and right . . .
When you bend over that ball, you'll find
A perfect lie, my name beaming up at you,

Shining whitely, an American president's name.
Maybe you dance a little Flamenco on it with your heel,
Maybe you cut it with your sword—that's all right too.
Your power's an old Spanish thing I learned about
As a boy in Southern California, where your Spanish Fathers
Converted all of us Indians with tobacco, cross, and guns.

It's great to see you still playing, a gamester at 77.
Golf is good for that old walk of authority,
Slice, hook, cut, blast out of the sandtrap,
Any trouble we drive into it's only a game
To conquer waterholes, a little smaller
Than the Mediterranean, right, but the same gleaming water
Over which our jets whiten your clear Spanish sky.

Here's to you, General, to our long international friendship.
I toast you striding sturdily on green grass,
Your Red, White, and Blue bag blazing beside you,
A General of Games sparkling with pleasure's power!

At the White House, Washington, D.C. 1973

Camelot was a romance. We're not here for that.
I want the facts, charts, graphs,
One page memos, deductive reasoning.
Maybe we are a sort of middle-class
Fifties generation, lacking style,
But we try to make it work for the nation.
We try to *think*, not intellectual loose-thinking.
When I'm wrong, it's *my* mistake, not the Chief's,
When I go to a film, *Patton*, not *Last Tango*,
When I read a book, *Six Crises*, not *The Prince*.
Organize right and you don't worry about innovation.
A little tennis, some chess, keep me in shape.
My crew cut, white shirt, suit, are merely functional.
Washing long hair, dressing mod, require more time.
The people voted that success depends on hard work.
The tide's changed. People think bland is beautiful.
What we have in abundance is a straight face.

Around me I hear the absence of laughter
And then I know everything is working right.

The Money Man

Come buy, come sell with the Money Man!
Learn American language—balance of payments,
Deficit spending, bull markets, net and gross figures.
Live American style with loans, easy budget payments,
Credit cards shining green and gold in white snow.
Stock Market quotes you learn to read as metaphors
For Rising, Falling, anxiety leaping to joy.
The Defense Secretary claims this is no time
For a Bugout Shuttle. He says if we reduce
The Defense Budget by thirty billion dollars
We'll have to spend at least a billion dollars
On white surrender flags. Money Men understand
Money's made for power, not surrender.
It's a visible art now in bank ingots.
They started in 1970 when The Franklin Mint
Produced solid 1000-grain sterling silver ingots
With a special design for each issuing bank.
Fifty new bank ingots are issued each year
From a prestige bank in each of the fifty states.
Buy and show a glow for your favorite bank!
A deluxe walnut chest holds the complete set.
Your home or office will sparkle with silver.
They'll know that you're a Money Man,
An Investment Banker, a merger maker
Who moves through the Stock Exchange,
The corporate board room, overseeing fortunes
Of private clients. They'll know you've learned
The pleasure of interlocks between partners
And fertile, expanding companies you merge with.
They'll see how your day of satisfaction dawns
When you've implanted development banks
In developing countries. Don't listen when they say
"Get the deal done, take the fee, walk on."
Walking on may make you rich, but to live money
You have to love the Money Man, show only

The tip of your iceberg. If someone bumps you,
Utilize the tap line, turn on the money faucets
Of corporate information, submerge them with cash-flow,
Lovely green securities flowing like ocean waves.

Purchasing New Bicentennial Stamps, 1975

At Christmas time
I go to the Post Office,
Stand in a long, slow line
To buy illuminating stamps.
"Give me forty tens," I ask,
"Ten of Emily Dickinson,
Ten of John Greenleaf Whittier,
Ten of D.W. Griffith,
Ten of any artist you have."
"No artists left. They're gone,"
Mutters the Post Office clerk
Pulling out a thick wad of stamps.
"These are all we got."
This Christmas I celebrate
BANKING, coins and wheels of progress.
Looking carefully at the stamp
I see in the upper righthand corner
A Roman-nosed Indian in a headdress
On a penny dated 1875.

Song of the Little Official of Maybe

The Little Official of Maybe
Who never says "Yes" or "No,"
Has a head the size of a peppermint,
A stare as blank as snow.

He wears a prim, anonymous suit
Of neutral, washed-out grey,

And strings around his thin, pale neck
A tie the color of hay.

Baskets like fences rise in his office,
Marked *File* and *Hold*, *Out* and *In;*
Over his desk hangs the needlepoint motto:
"If You Don't Act, You Cannnot Sin."

At night he prays to his wife, *"Perhaps . . ."*
Then she tucks him in bed like a baby,
Where he tosses and teases the tickling thought,
"I am the Little Official of Maybe."

In Praise of a Diane Arbus Photograph: "A Jewish Giant at Home with his Parents in the Bronx, 1970."

My vision is everyday normal,
Yet I see a grotesque out there, above me,
A hero of legendary size
Who lives in the bizarre altitude.
So enormous he cannot move,
He leans bent over a cane,
While his normal parents
Stare up at him with wonder,
Embarassed, impressed
With their son's heroic size.
To bury him will require
The largest coffin ever made.
The coffin exists only in my mind;
In their minds the grotesque giant
Can never find a suitable coffin
For their mythical son.
The grotesque is our secret desire
Dreaming always of ascending space.

210

Illumination: Martha Graham

By dedicated practice
to become an athlete of God,
dance as the "performance of living,"
magical feet upon which
the whole weight rests,
miracle of thrust that permits
the body to dance out
its sexual and soul attacks
through contraction, release,
the earth-sun relationship.
At eighty-three, after her company
has demonstrated life's performance,
she takes one curtain call, alone,
hooded, draped in priestess robes
to reveal for dancers and audience
how dark legends endure into light.

The Commuter in Car Tunnels

Before sunrise, suspended in rising
light, I wake to orange glare
of the breaking dawn,
hear on the lower freeway
beneath the trembling apartment house,
metal tunnels shake with
surge of endless, unknown destination.
I think of the evening before,
commuting, accelerating along
tight in white lanes
through the quiet park
when, suddenly, a broken squirrel
still half alive in his panic,
cowers from spurting cars
in the middle of the freeway.
To swerve would be a danger,
so kill, kill the smaller life.
But when I stop, when I wake,

a drop of sweat, a glaze of memory,
hangs on the tunneled roads I travel,
surrounds the safe walls I live in,
shakes out lives to die against my
               speed.

The Jovial Mortician

When I met the jovial mortician
And asked his profession, he only grinned
And handed me a card with the inscription:
"I'm the last man to let you down."
Club-time, fraternal luncheon meeting,
Hour of buttonhole flowers, civic speeches,
Southern Fried Chicken, Mashed Potatoes,
Hot Rolls, Rocquefort Cheese Salad,
Vanilla Ice Cream, Cookies, and Coffee.
Gradually, during the election of officers,
Just after the Merit Awards and charity
Exhortations, he loaded me with gifts:
Fountain pen, clubpin with a girl
Climbing out of a casket, floral bouquet
For my secretary's help with his mailing lists.
Enthusiastically, I undressed for the grave.
Lying there in my plush satin coffin,
My best suit radiantly pressed, white carnation
In my buttonhole, handkerchief correctly
Triangled from my lapel pocket, I smiled up
Through my painted, cosmetic face,
And saw him looking down, nodding reassurance
That he was the last man to let me down.

Apple, the Family Love and Asshole

As they construct an old tire-swing over the river,
The working class family on vacation
Strikes with hatchet words,

Enigmatic salvos of belonging.
"Don't tell anyone in camp we've got this swing,"
The young, heavyset father yells to his kids,
"If you don't have anything to sell
You don't have any goddamn life
And we're here to live. Look, Apple,
You've got the tire stuck behind the tree!
Put it over there, dummy,
And there's no way it won't work."
But she can't do it to his satisfaction
And her two older brothers grin at her efforts.
"Apple, you're the biggest fucking asshole
I've met all week," he shouts at her.
"All you have to do is put the rope
Around the backside of the tree
And let it hang straight down!"
Frustrated, she hits him with a fist of mud.
"You bitch! You're going to get it, Apple,
One on one, nobody is on nobody else's side."
Afraid, Apple retreats as he advances:
"Do you like my rosy cheeks, Pa,
Do you like me, raise your hands."
"Bullshit, Apple, you're going to get it."
"Apple go home, Apple go under water."
"Apple, don't start it if you can't take
What's coming back. All you've got to do
Really is sit on the knot and you screw up."
"Apple, you're the fucking lowdown of this situation!"
They are all calling Apple in unison.

The Broken-field Runner through Age

The newspaper says he's dead,
He made it, the world record age of 168—
Shirali Mislimov, an Azerbijani farmer
In some unpronouncable Caucasus village,
Lived there every day of his life.
Who can imagine such a wrinkled Russian
Observing only what he knows intimately,
Never traveling to find something new?

213

Probably his birthdate is a phoney
And he's much closer to a hundred.
The old buzzard even left a life formula
  Get up early, work in the garden,
  Go to bed just after ten in the evening,
  Never sleep in the daytime,
  Take daily walks of one kilometer.
There's boredom for you, a death-schedule.
I get up early, jog, drive one hour to work,
Travel every chance I get to see new things,
Catch at them, their blurring television speed.
I dodge the silent, staring shapes of age
With dazzling American broken-field running.

The No-name Woman in San Francisco

Bulging in a faded orange dress
From her window over hot-black asphalt
Like an anonymous Halloween pumpkin,
The No-Name Woman stares with a puzzled frown
At the street theatre playing *The Three Penny Opera.*
Beneath a sleepless tangle of grey hair,
She gapes down at these satirical actors of joy.
Who are these stylish whores, crooks wearing spats,
Beggars threatening the coronation of a Queen?
"Who the hell are you?" she shouts, "Who's that
Stupid Queen? What the hell is this about?"
Jenny the Pirate sings about the Black Freighter
Coming to rescue her . . . In the harbor shine
Tankers, freighters of multi-national corporations.
A mass of unknown visitors sit on Mrs. No-Name's street,
Watching, drinking, laughing, children wandering in sun.
After the play a printer passes out a broadside:
Brecht's poem to the actors, "Masters of imitation—
Do not step too far from the everyday theatre,
The theatre whose stage is the street . . ."
Police remove barriers to let traffic surge again,
While echoes of Brecht's Ballad Singer resound:
"We see those who live in the light
And we don't see those who live in the night."

The No-Name Woman bangs her dusty window down,
Continuing her voyage through oblivion's dark identity.

Dumb Love

Desperate with dumb love,
Dick H. pours a glass of beer
Over his girl's hair, fizzing it;
Rams her car into a wreck;
Then, for emphasis, opens
Fire on the wreck with his rifle.
Shuddering with sudden conviction,
His girl cries to the Judge:
"He's just full of dumb love,
Your Honor, all he wants to do
Is smash me into my senses.
Now I know I loved him all the time.
Please, Sir, dumb love is enough trial."

The Motorcycle Gang Honors
the Newsboy's Seventieth Birthday

Light the cake on the littered street,
Thirty-nine candles red in the white icing!
Swaggering to the birthday in skull helmets,
Leather jackets bragging DAREDEVILS,
The motorcycle gang roars up to the party.
The newsboy, two sunken eyes in skeleton skin,
Leans against his stand under a sign:
        THE DADDY OF LUCK
Newsboy . . . American age permits grotesque youth.
Mouth full of false teeth, grey hair stiff
As a paint brush hardening alone in a can,
He blows his halitosis over the chocolate.
Candles flicker like his hardening veins.
Another breath explosion, great surge of spit.

215

The candles wink out. With a grimy hand
He cuts a piece of cake for each Daredevil.
Clutching the crumbling cake in their hands,
They begin to sell the Daddy of Luck's papers,
Improvising headlines, wild, dirty, lost:
    Impeach the Cox Sacker!
      Resign You Dented Pres!
        All Power To The Daredevils!
Gang of night, their headlines hammer passing ears
Like artists tatooing obscenities in flesh.

A Screamer Discusses Methods of Screaming

We all scream, most of us inside.
Outside is another world.
A neighbor fills her television dinner
With too much pepper and screams.
One woman stabs her door with a sword.
Another, overweight, steps in the shower
And screams, "Fat! Fat! Fat!"
A man who takes flying lessons
Soars high in the clouds to scream.
Another dives to the bottom of his pool
Where his screams bubble away underwater.
A friend cleans his gun, screaming "Assassin!"
I like an interior, smiling scream.
When you walk past me on the street
I nod my head to you and, smiling, scream.
You never hear me through the smile.
The inside scream has no echo.

Gambling in Las Vegas

Business backlashes style, white spot on the crap tables,
Watch the whip shot, "Up jumped the Devil!" cries the stickman.

Each night the house bank roll is a million dollars.
Spinning roulette rolls placid as a paddle wheel,
While paternal managers caution the credit limit,
Build for the gambling widows a bleachers gallery,
Where they loll in a fire of filtered cigarettes.
Swang go the slot machines, jingle the jackpots,
And silver cartwheels roll from the blonde cashier.
A hundred hunting eyes in the house case the chiselers:
Floormen focus on droning dealers and cardsharpers;
Pit bosses, bulky bulldogs, peer at the floormen,
While the housemen, intent from their high ladders,
Devour the air with their sucking mouths like hagfish.

The T-Shirt Phenomenon in Minnesota on the Fourth of July

A happy confusion scribbles through hot air
The wistful, latent sense of American poetry:
"I planted 26,000 Trees. Thank God I'm done."
"This is the 204th Birthday of the United States—
Young Again!" I feel two hundred years of youth
On my aging shoulders. Hundreds of parents, kids,
March in T-shirts, go-carts, bikes, wagons,
Toy tractors, eternal sense of American motion.
I stare at each T-shirt passing by,
Analyzing the alliteration, assonance, the images.
"If It's Physical, It's Therapy." "White Elephant."
"Chicken Shirt." A world of Joycean punishment,
Wild identities flowering in groping metaphors.
Behold the American version of Mexican Wall-Art
Or French *Art Mobilier*, Art On The Move.
"Norwegians Have More Fun." Well, it's a
Scandinavian community even if Vietnamese and Laotian
Refugees are watching, near some Chinese Communists
Studying Engineering at the local university.
"Sña. Theresa de Jesus Avila." "Sgt. Pickles Deli & Saloon."
Religious drama confronts the advertising world.
"Jesus Is The Pride Of The Morning Star."
"The Minnesota State Bird Is The Mosquito."

217

I feel caught between startling light and tiny bites.
"Librarians Are Novel Lovers." I always knew
Poetry was Fiction. All of the Asian watchers
Are gaping with culture shock. American humor
Translates like glue. The wife of a Chinese Communist
Tells me, "Your writers we know are Mark Twain
And Jack London. I'm reading *Life On The Mississippi*
And I love to see the Mississippi, like our Yangste,
But I don't understand his river talk and jokes.
Can you tell me how to translate American?"
"Sorry," I say, "I can't even translate these T-shirts."
Suddenly I notice the American flag I'm waving
Reads in small print in a corner, "Made in Taiwan."
I start to laugh and everyone looks at me.
Quickly I expose my T-shirt; "Someone Went To
New York and All They Got Is This Lousy T-Shirt."
Now the crowd laughs back. Is poetry an isolated art
Where the shaman symbol operates magically to cure
Individual wounds, or is it a communal song of praise
Celebrating a ceremonial time? Can both ever unite?
In a park corner two teenagers in dark glasses imitate
A television fantasy, sell illegal firecrackers to kids.
As the firecrackers explode, I ask my Lady Communist:
"You Chinese invented firecrackers, didn't you?"
With a smile she answers, "Yes, we have fireworks
For everything, promotions, birthdays, graduations."
We laugh together. When I retreat from laughter
Into my isolated search for community again,
I'll think of our desire for poetry, how we
Don't know what to do with it despite Whitman
And so we try to display it on our chests.

The Quiet Man of Simplicity:
Robert Francis

When I met the quiet man of simplicity,
I found him retired from material things,
No car, no machines, not even a telephone,
In a plain wooden shack on the edge of town,

Growing his vegetables, cooking simple foods,
Making dandelion wine, playing an old upright piano,
Burning juniper against bloodsucking mosquitoes,
Writing short poems that pierce our time humorously,
Never glorify the brutal obsessive ego.

Escaped from a Roman boyhood, "all duty and observance,"
The Pursuit of Happiness has ceased in his eyes,
A time for contemplation shines in his face.
Evil is a natural thing to be felt and shared,
Hidden from the old American E for Excellence.
Compassion is a search for rest, not movement.
Returning to my city job, I think of him
As I visit monumental malls and Supermarkets,
Greet my family with tense recreation plans,
Practice my vision for the dawn of simplicity.

The Flower-washer in New York

"You might in this city become a flower-washer."
SAUL BELLOW, *Mr. Sammler's Planet*

Please read the invisible writing on my card:
"Flower-Washer—the purest, most dangerous profession."
It's like cleaning a car's windshield with razorblades.
In fact, scraping carefully at flower-grime,
I often use razorblades with a delicate hand.
Most of the time I use a variable water-spray,
My herbal mixture for sensuous compatibility.
I regulate the spray from butter-soft to drill-hard
Depending on the petal's strength and endurance,
The calyx's ability to absorb symbiotic relationships.
One day I'm going to patent my water-spray
Before crooks steal my secret flower-nozzle.
I think of my profession as any good professional,
A craftsman who invents, masters his techniques
To defeat amateurs who force colors without grace.
Sometimes, in my obsession to wed plants to sunlight,
I feel like a transparent technologist,
Climbing and hanging by a strap from glass walls.
Every aging year I feel the light is higher,

219

Yet every time I wash a plant in pure light,
I feel the power of a saint probing space.

Looking at Wealth in Newport

Dream American, look at wealth through
Warm, misty rain; wander waterfront drives
Staring at mansions of visionary marble,
Renaissance villas oriented east in tribute
Toward the Madonna, Italy; the mistress, France.
Gape with rebellious nostalgia at English
Country estates, fixed rational order
Where servants serve the idea of service.
Here tennis was invented for the right sports clothes
And Cole Porter composed "Night and Day"
While summer socialites dreamed perfect entertainment,
Money pursuing happiness in prosperous summers.
Now in these grotesque, vacant mansions
The ghost of Henry James speculates about
The Jolly Corner, where you're haunted
By yourself, the puzzled, enigmatic observer,
As James's Newport family home flickers
Transformed into a Funeral Parlor.

If God Does Not See You

If God does not see you
Try to become music
As in the desperate slum church,
Where burned-out cars
Slump before broken houses,
The minister grabs for customers
With billboard prescription:
BECOME AN ALLELUJAH
    FROM HEAD TO FOOT.

220

At Whitman's House in Camden

Correction, Walt, has becme a new American word.
Across the street from your memorial home,
The only house you owned in your restless life,
They've built a prison, a *correctional facility*.
In the old days they stuck you in the hoosegow
Or slammer, you knew you were deep in shadows.

Now, the experts pretend they're going to correct
Dead souls, and the jails grow larger, anonymous,
Like this ponderous steel and cement tomb,
Bloated metal cancer across from your shack.
How can an American sing of "correction"?
They've taken your language, set it in prison,
But you're still here confronting this atrocity:
"The open air I sing, freedom, toleration."

A few days ago, Jorge Luis Borges, the blind man
Who writes of mazes, wastelands, enigmatic histories,
Visited your memory here, his white cane tapping
The floor while television cameras clicked, whirred.
The two of you laughed and muttered *"correction"*—
How the correct go wrong, the wrong transform correctly
In Houses of Correction to which we're all condemned.

Dog-pack

Mornings in the Sangre de Cristo Mountains,
Sun rising over Santa Fe below,
Desert glowing red and green in dawnlight,
The dog-pack arrives to accompany us
Through juniper and pine trees.
My dog expects them, waits eagerly,
Barking at them in frenzied dog-language.
They put up a huge brown jackrabbit,
And race with spectacular failure
After his hopping body into a meadow
Fragrant with yellow and white wildflowers.

221

Panting with frustration and satisfaction,
The great dog-pack returns slowly
After chasing the ardent American dream,
Eyes shining with the pursuit of happiness
That is the central meaning of dog-pack.
Dog-pack knows how the natural community
Decides finally how a civilization
Leaves its individual traces on time,
Not the isolated heart which dies alone.

The Mathematician Thinking
of Ghost Numbers

People count themselves into oblivion
Where names lie numberless in death.
Old, they count backwards with every breath.
Young, they rock the walls toward twenty-one.
Numbers cannot tell the names of time.

Favorite numbers fade in meaning
As Buddha's father summoned forty thousand
Dancing girls to keep his son's great spirit
Attached to the world. Why forty thousand?
Numbers cannot tell the names of time.

Beyond three hundred lurks the world of chaos.
Two is comfortable, four summons
Wild winds to attack easy success.
Climbing to thirteen is a laughing risk.
Numbers cannot tell the names of time.

Men of power invent fanatic numbers
That march and kill in hidden camps.
The trinity reminds us of a living hell
While the Maya zero puzzles as peaceful shell.
Numbers cannot tell the names of time.

The Mailman and *Das Ewig Weibliche*

Through a dark drizzle of rain,
Plodding to work on mountain-heavy shoes,
The jumping thing is to see
The old mailman as sudden nun
    float up to the door
    in black-draped raincoat,
    hooded helmet
    flare like a wimple,
    and deliver the mail
    through a driven,
    coffee-tense scatter
    of masculine commuters,
    as if it were
    sealed with quietude,
      a female gift.

Living in a Boxcar in San Francisco

When you get older you kind of settle like a house,
Except in my case it's a boxcar . . . Smoke down
The doubledeck freeway, take a quick look out your window
Before you hit the distance—you'll see me sticking up,
My boxcar solid in backyard sun, challenging the freeway,
Fresh brown paint, big white-lettered name on the side:
EL CABALLO, Spanish for horse, we used to go
From ranch to ranch, endless grazing land, proud horses
Kicking against the boxcar walls, waiting to run . . .
When they started building the freeway, it took a lot of
Stubborn persuasion to get my boxcar left smack at the track's
End when they retired me and the railroad same time.
Along came what they call development, bulldozing
Everything for the freeway, trees, hills, houses
Smashed down . . . You bet they didn't expect a boxcar!
Looking down from their surveying gadgets,
You should have seen their eyes frost up
When they saw this silent old witness watching them!
How they screamed before they decided to go around
And leave me tight against the noise and smoke,

Those damn cars smashing along all day and night.
So we go on. Not that it's a war. No one pays me
Any attention except they got to slow down for the curve.
I've had her fitted with lights and I sleep in her now.
I'm kind of deaf, so those cars pounding up there,
Going where they have to go, don't bother me.
I pull into my boxcar, my lights shining at the
End of the line, maybe the last brakeman of the old,
Clicking western rails, train whistling to the western stars,
Slow puff over tough mountains to the waiting sea . . .
When there's a frontier to remember, you got to live in it.

Song of Aeterna 27 over Los Angeles

Aeterna 27, the new face cream that eliminates
wrinkles and makes you eternally 27
A BILLBOARD SIGN

Racing on freeways over Los Angeles
In lanes of poured, white liberty
I see the sails of billboards flare
Through smog the golden letters
      AETERNA 27

In the smoggy, rear-view mirror,
My sagging lines of 40 fade,
I sail homeward in my fancy
A Flying Dutchman to my wrinkle-free girl
      AETERNA 27

Hog's Elegy to the Butchers

(1)
Hog, 'cause when I lean over my guitar
My bulk clamps on the strings, man,
A savage weight, it's a hog playing!
My left hand finds princess fingers to free chords
While my right hand drums hog-weight in the wood,

224

And here I come, Hog, the guitarist, to Chicago.
"Hog-Butcher to the world" it's called,
But it's oldtime country music they want to hear;
The Big City eats high on hogs like me,
They know I can play them out of their drinks and chatter.

(2)

My hotel says it's the biggest in the world,
But the rooms are so small with my guitar so tight
Together in the bed I feel like I'm living in sin.
No matter, the convention folks got to pay,
So I phone room service any time I want
To feed my guitar the corn-whiskey it likes.
People are running around the corridors
With badges from music stores all over the country.
This convention I'm playing is Holiday Time!
Talk to any drunken stranger and find out
What simple music fits the climate of money—
Play 'em the old, mournful country tunes
They like to think was played around the stove,
Then go back home my string tie sailing in the breeze.

(3)

Late afternoon with another rough guitar player
We come out of the hotel on our way to a drink.
Sudden shots crack out across the street in Grant Park.
Half the city police, dressed and undressed,
Roar into the park hell-bent for some target,
Furious energy criss-crossing in a demon maze
Like a nightmare. Things happen under your nose
And you never know them. They whistle past your skin
Like a vulture cutting into some invisible mouse.
You wonder, "How come I missed that cutting beak?"
This time the mouse is a crazy West Virginia guy
Out of World War II into mental hospitals.
Why he comes to Chicago from his country cave
Is a guess of guns that he hides in his coat.
One policeman says he came to kill the President
Who's scheduled to speak here tomorrow morning.
Another police official says there's no evidence
And maybe he was just going to kill himself.
Assassination or suicide! it's all about death.
An idiot hider of too many guns, he drops one,

225

Clattering, glittering on the crowded sidewalk.
Police chase him into the park, gun him down
With a fierce, eager volley of shots—you don't play
With Chicago police, they believe in that
Old frontier vision of odd man out.
In the pockets of the guy they shoot they find
Three pennies, a Bible, and a pack of chewing gum.

(4)

That night I sing my Hog-elegy to the
Crazy god-power shining in the spotlight.
I hear myself improvising words while ghost-music
Plays, clamping on that wood I can't let go.
Ladies sit listening politely in their badges
And perfume from some lost world of manners
That's like a breached dam trying to hold back
Furious water; they stop their gabbing suddenly
Listening to Hog-power play this city out of
My blood 'cause my blood rejoices in those wild guns.
Listen . . . It's better I kill with music when I want to kill . . .
You hear a man die . . . My guitar smokes with wild sounds,
My fingers ache from slashing gut, pounding wood,
And they love me for that. They clap, yell,
Out of their minds for Hog-music. All right,
I'll play again . . . I'm gonna bust your ears.
Hear that rhythm driving hard? *Who's playing?*
A man with a Bible, three cents, a pack of gum.

The Columnist Listening to "You Know" in the Park

Listening, you know, to voices in the park,
I hear the great American gesture,
"You know," weaving through wandering words
Like the roots, you know, of a tree;
And I think, what is it, you know,
In twining words groping for meaning
That makes, you know, a connection,
You know, a spark, a surge of green,
Sometimes, you know, a kind of branching

And flowering, a tree of language,
And the whole damn tree stands there,
You know, like a sentinel, warning
The hell with communication! You know,
Say what you mean, but the meaning,
You know, is how you see and hear the tree.

William Carlos Williams and T.S. Eliot Dancing over London Bridge in the Arizona Desert at Lake Havasu

Come dance with me, Tom,
The ghost of William Carlos Williams,
Doctor and dancer of the measured line.
Come dance with me, Tom Eliot,
Give up the formal British crust of your T.S.
Come dance with me naked
In front of the mocking American mirror
As I danced naked, lonely, joyous, in my room.
We dance over your Mississippi together
Toward Arizona to see your London Bridge.
It isn't falling down into your Wasteland.
We numbered the huge blocks of Victorian stone,
Dismantled the green Art Nouveau lamps,
Eliminated the foggy Thames River atmosphere,
Engineered every detail to dry Arizona desert
And resurrected her over a man-made lake.
Even your British mayor came to dedicate her anew,
American and British flags flying in unity,
Drooping a little in one hundred and ten degrees
While Tudor buildings loomed as facades of desert shacks.

All of the spectres you fled, Tom,
Applaud this real estate promotion:
P.T. Barnum, Melville's Confidence Man,
The Lost Tycoons, Anderson's Winesburg grotesques,
Mark Twain's rubes and hicks, your mother
Trapped in St. Louis, dedicated to Savonarola,
They all burst clapping out of their graves

To celebrate this bold, new grotesque frontier.
Listen, how they applaud culture for the cactus!

Come dance with me along the burning bridge, Tom,
As the hot pavement burns our naked feet
And we hop, singing, "Tom's home again!"
Our new community will cook us a barbeque
To celebrate the struggle for its desert identity.
Let's sit down and have a drink, Tom,
And relish our American concept of *grotesque*,
This town crying with evangelical fervor,
Writhing with desire for lost historical connections.

Sit down, Tom, and revel in our American Grotesque,
Our hidden voices cracking against your British tongue:
"Grotesque is the vulnerable, pathetic fantasy
We distort in our joyous pursuit of love and property.
Grotesque is the mystery we eliminate to create
The revolt of simple things, goods, that desire mystery.
Grotesque is what we become when we seclude ourselves
In the suburban community closed to awe and wonder.
American Grotesque, sad, searching patron of beauty,
Struggles to balance the comic weight of our fantasies
That glow in the sky with their singular distortions."

The Suicide Runner

"A good elbow shot broke my nose in Chicago.
Another guy rammed his fist in my neck for the hell of it.
You might as well get out of town if you worry
About breakin' your nose . . ." Cowboy boots
Propped on a chair, phone pressed to a scarred ear,
The suicide runner grins into the plastic:
"Look, darlin', don't say you'll call me Monday
After the game. Lord, don't ever say you'll call
After a game. I'll be drunk, bettin' at the race track,
Or lookin' for bail. When you're on a suicide team,
You don't wait till next week to start livin'.
Just get me those ringside seats, will ya, love?

Don't promise me nothin' you can't produce."
Banging down the phone with a joyous "Yippee!"
He turns to the long-legged girl holding a fur coat.
"Put it on me, Babe! I earned that! Hundred percent
Timber wolf and cost me 750 bones. Great to go
Struttin' in the snow. Wanta know somethin', sweetie?
Next punt I run back I'm gonna get *you* a coat!
I had to prove I was no rookie on the suicide team.
After my first game, we're in this bar, see,
And they send me for drinks 'cause I'm a greenie
In the suicide business. I go get six martinis.
Before I swing back to the table, I drink two.
Then I wait till the old guys drain their drinks;
I grab their glasses-and chew 'em up without
Spittin' out a piece. 'Course I didn't eat
The real big pieces of glass or the long stems.
That's lookin' for trouble. But they kinda got
The idea I ain't afraid to be a suicide runner . . ."

Putting on his fur coat, he parades before her mini-dress.
"That's some thick wolf, honey. You know I dreamt
Of runnin' back a kickoff through the snow in this fur.
Wouldn't that be great? Those bastards see a damn fur coat
Comin' at them, suddenly they think they're chasin' a wolf! . . .
When I'm goin' full steam, you know, it's like bein' hit
By a motorcycle travelin' forty miles an hour.
Those white lines shake like a buffalo stampede
As a thousand pounds of trouble come crazy-doggin' you
To mess you up. See, dearies, why I dream of runnin'
In my fur coat, closin' my eyes, steppin' high like a bitch?"
He runs in his fur coat through the mirror.
"Let's get it straight, sweetie. You want a suicide runner,
You got me. I gotta live against all those tackles
Who get named Cannibal of the Week . . .
Before I hit camp last summer, I worked for free
On a garbage truck as a swamp rat. That's the sharp tooth
Jumps out and picks up all those heavy cans.
But I didn't just pick up that stinkin' garbage.
I *threw* it on the truck like I was flamin' mad!
I spent six weeks as a swamp rat and three days in jail,
Some eyeglasses lecturin' me on drunk drivin' and stuff . . .
When you're a suicide runner, love, you're in the wilderness.
You've gotta yell, 'I'm gone!' and go for free out of the trap."

229

Report to the Moving Company

WAS VAN CREW COURTEOUS?
>The mover walked out singing
>"I never knew how much I loved you,
>I never knew how much I care,"
>Carrying a sofa on his head.

DID VAN CREW PRESENT A CREDITABLE APPEARANCE?
>The packers wore white coveralls
>Blazing your company's name stitched in Gothic red,
>A uniform appearance glowing with incredibility.
>The mover and two helpers loomed seven feet tall
>Like football giants. Because of their muscle
>I could not discern unique identities
>Beneath the mountains of rippling flesh.
>Credibility vanished in tribute to moving.

ARE YOU PLEASED WITH SERVICE RENDERED?
>By evening, after they had moved
>The fifteen hundred pound marble table,
>The mover and his helpers dripped sweat.
>They were so tired they could only stagger,
>Curse at each other, they seemed hardly
>To understand the spirit of four-letter words.
>My furniture was smothered in green blankets
>Which the mover unfolded from a weary distance
>As if he had forgotten the still roots of sitting.
>The service rendered was beyond pleasure.

WERE THERE ANY WORRIES IN CONNECTION
 WITH YOUR MOVE?
>I remain a little worried about Reno and Ohio.
>Moving is a different space. The mover said, "No one
>Can stand me more than a few days at a time.
>My wife cut out on me. I go it alone now.
>I don't even like a helper to drive my truck.
>It's too tough to try and get along with him.
>Together, you have to take care of people.
>Alone, steaming east, I can stop in Reno,
>Park my truck in an alley, hit the fast clubs
>For a couple of days. Then I keep steaming east,
>Around Ohio, though . . . Last summer, speeding through,
>I lost my sticker for that corn country."

WHAT SUGGESTIONS WOULD YOU OFFER
 TO IMPROVE THE SERVICE?

Dear Sirs, The question of improvement
Has, I'm afraid, no stationary solution.
I go on moving in the wind,
Watching the wind move
The insanity from moving.
May the morning
Discover a silent destination
Free from movement.

At the Sin and Flesh Pond

Must we always be ruled by language and names?
James Shrewsbury Erwin Schevill I was named.
How could I walk to school in that rhetorical decoration?
This eastern pond seems only water, an average polluted shore,
But Puritan heritage called it the Sin and Flesh Pond.
How can we picnic at such a haunted place?
Never mind. Americans believe in the instant bypass of history.
Across the road, that hamburger stand boasts:
"1,548,286 burgers served . . ."
Flesh eaten near the Sin and Flesh Pond
Sets some kind of amazing record.
In China restaurants are called in modesty,
"The Second-Class Establishment of Mr. Hsiang,"
"That Trifling Place in the West Market," or
"The Restaurant Into Which You Would Not Take A Dog."
Down the road a sign advertises Frito-Lay.
What penetrating names America creates near
The Sin and Flesh Pond! Are you ready, my darling?
Flesh is the joy in which we lose our names.
Here at the peculiar Sin and Flesh Pond,
I reduce my name to James Schevill and make love,
Make love against the grotesque names of my country.

231

Theatre in Providence and Washington

(1)

Theatre is a dangerous discovery of community,
a public gathering revealing sins and triumphs,
a weapon against hypocrisy, a revelation of spirit.
Every time I walk backstage in an empty theatre,
my skin bristles, the air is full of spectres
waiting to appear, to manifest their presences.
Theatre is an arena of opposites, despair and hope,
joy and skepticism, incarnation of roses through
thorny weed gardens struggling for dominance.
Theatre is a rare environment, existing as in Greece
in a spiritual, therapeutic valley to cure
mythical illnesses, conflicts between god and man.
No wonder theatre is often suspect in official society;
theatre is a temple of power, director demanding,
actors yielding, risking the darkest display of self.
Where else is it better to illuminate themes of power?

(2)

In 1968 I accept an offer to teach at Brown University; my wife and I
move east to Providence, Rhode Island. Astonishing, revolutionary ar-
chitecture floating in time. Striding uphill from the old harbor, I walk
from 18th century through 19th century into 20th century, powerful
trespass of architectural styles. Thrust and feel of history; in so many
American cities history is eliminated. Brown, poorest of Ivy League uni-
versities, faces a challenge; how to create a New Curriculum for the
20th century. Give students more freedom to pick their own classes and
create their own programs, cut across specialized education that threat-
ens disaster to the humanistic mind. At Brown the performing arts are
curiously under English Department jurisdiction. This gives me a chance
to bring poetry and theatre together. Marvelous to find Shakespeare
under one roof instead of the false separation between literary Shake-
speare and dramatic Shakespeare in most university English and theatre
departments. With Brown theatre colleagues I have a chance to write
and produce many short and full-length plays. In Providence, too, is one
of the best regional theatres, Adrian Hall and his Trinity Repertory
Company, and I work with Hall as dramaturg and playwright. In 1970
Hall commissions and produces *Lovecraft's Follies*. In my play, a disillusioned
physicist, Stanley Millsage, has worked on the Manhattan Project and is
haunted by security problems. Millsage is based on the experiences of
Bern Porter, a physicist-artist-publisher who quit the Manhattan Project

when the nuclear bomb exploded on Hiroshima. On leave from his nu-
clear research, Millsage experiences a series of nightmare visions, imag-
ining H.P. Lovecraft, Providence master of weird tales, narrating various
"follies" about the perils of American power. After the 1960s, weird
tales seem appropriate aspects of American Grotesque events. In weird
tales the dead question the living. Glory is the sunshine of the dead, as
Balzac wrote. The dead of Hiroshima, Nagasaki, Korean and Vietnam
wars will not be appeased. They continue asking questions about the na-
ture of power in my play. Hall works with a remarkable designer, Eugene
Lee, and an experienced composer, Richard Cumming. Lee designs a fes-
tive circus atmosphere appropriate for the different "follies." Space to
Hall and Lee has a revolutionary theatrical meaning, the ability to move
through time with speed of a film, to confront the audience directly
without the intervention of a proscenium arch and curtain. No huge,
solid sets, instead remarkable set pieces and props blend with unusual,
timeless costumes in which the actors transform openly into various
characters as needed. One actor, Ronald Frazer, plays Adolf Hitler, Tar-
zan's ape, Cheetah, in a Pop Art "folly" based on Tarzan's legend, and,
finally, J. Robert Oppenheimer as an Indian shaman (at Los Alamos in
Indian territory Oppenheimer was often called a "shaman" for his mysti-
cal powers of leadership). Characters are delineated in their environmen-
tal space, not merely through traditional plot sequences. In one scene,
based on Lovecraft's "Rats in the Wall," partly a parody of T.S. Eliot"s
"The Wasteland," actors behind the audience draw a long string with
feathers on it down over the audience's backs to simulate the terror of
feeling rats in the wall. Experimenting with unusual space relationships,
Hall and Lee bring to Trinity an exciting sense of the new space age. One
scene in *Lovecraft's Follies* even depicts the moon landing, and astronauts
hopping across the moon's surface on pogo sticks to the audience's de-
light. Hall's production is invited to New York, the Tel Aviv Festival, and
the Edinburgh Festival. In New York, the set waits backstage at the
ANTA Theatre, which Lee has boldly remodeled, but never opens, never
travels abroad, due to sudden cut-off of promised funds. Weird tales of
theatre, a constant menace.

(3)

Cathedral of Ice, my play that Hall directs and Lee designs in 1975, takes
actors and audience on a search through space and time into Hitler's
fantasies of power that still haunt us today. I wanted to display aspects
of Hitler's banal, commonplace personality that caused the frustrations
behind his obsessive drive for power. For example, in their addiction for
Hollywood films, Eva Braun once performed in blackface for Hitler a
comic imitation of Al Jolson singing "Sonny Boy." Unmentionable in pres-

tigious biographies that want to show Hitler as the epitome of mystical power—tyrant rather than the product of what Hannah Arendt calls "the banality of evil." The play's basic set is a huge arena like a football stadium or a political hall, but audience does not sit down in seats and relax. During the first part, they follow events in various "sideshows," including assassination games, a skit on Hitler's youth as a young, would-be artist in Vienna, and a scene on his American western fantasies derived from his readings of the popular German writer, Karl May (Hitler liked to call Russian soldiers "redskins" as if recalling May's vivid descriptions of Indians being slaughtered). In the first preview, a riot almost occurs; audience stampedes through ropes barring entrance, claiming arena seats defiantly with the ironic result that no one can see the opening scenes. By the next night, Hall and his staff instruct ushers on the way to advise and lead audience into following the scenes on foot as if in a carnival. The play's title reflects Albert Speer's use of anti-aircraft searchlights to dramatize Hitler's Nuremberg Nazi Party rally. Shafts of cold white light probe the sky to create a freezing "cathedral of ice," as the British ambassador called the Nazi spectacle. In Hall's production Hitler strides to power across high platforms rolled in and slammed together by actors intermingling with audience. A huge swastika flag drops from the ceiling to celebrate Hitler. Actors standing along the platforms like sentinels flick on Bic cigarette lighters (remember the popular advertising slogan "Flick my Bic" with its sensuous poses). Tiny flames of light lining Hitler's nightmare passage to power flicker eerily in the dark in mocking imitation of the frozen searchlights. Financed partly by a grant from the state Humanities Committee that I was awarded, the play creates a program of talks and discussions before and after each performance. Lee erects a Chautauqua-like tent in the alley next to the theatre. Every evening free beer and soft drinks are available while the cast sings songs and two different, prominent community leaders each night speak on problems of power they have witnessed (amazing how some politicians do their homework on the play's theme and some sugarcoat the issues of power, which has a decided effect on audience reaction to the performance). Then audience and cast wind up the stairs to witness and perform the play; afterward passionate discussion erupts from a sizable number of people who stay every night. This production marks the beginning of the use of theatre as a forum for Humanities discussions throughout the country.

Only in the last part does audience sit down around a boxing ring, which Hall stages with giant puppet figures wielding plastic bats (actors riding on the shoulders of other actors), showing the brutal murder of their opponents by the Nazis. This is followed by a huge tap-dancing scene, "The Big Lie," depicting Nazi-like manipulations of propaganda

234

and advertising, toward which Hall aims from the beginning of rehearsals. A week before opening there is still no trace of the redemptive ending in my original text to frame the horror of the concentration camps. Suddenly, Lee traps the ceiling with a multitude of lifesize dummies that plummet down over the audience to darken the bright carnival lights of previous scenes. This permits the elegiac lament of two concentration camp victims whom I call "Night" and "Fog" after "Nacht und Nebel," Nazi names for their secret concentration camp world. But the ending of the play cuts a great deal from the script and never fulfils my purpose. Still, Hall has presented his remarkable, theatrical interpretation. A young publisher, Peter Kaplan, prints my original script, which is later reprinted in the international anthology, *Plays of the Holocaust*. The invisible greatness of theatre lies in its paradoxical disappearing and appearing forms. As a playwright, I cling to my visions; as a director Hall clings to his. We both know that behind the vanishing performance lies the promise of redemptive theatre.

(4)

Taped Watergate Dreams of Success

We could go
Through the crowd
Like a cannon-ball—
Shoot down passive people
And stand over them
In a Killer Shadow
Like Balzac's Vautrin.
We've got the power
And the secret Intelligence.

But this is a democracy
With a Christian center,
And it's better to
Creep into the Crowd
Like a benign force—
Feel them up,
Inject them slowly,
Stain them with success.

(5)

The ivory tower of learning vanishes; campus blends into community. No more Ivy League separation of town and gown. The 1970 invasion of Cambodia enlarges the Vietnam War, shuts down campuses all over the

235

country. Youth in spontaneous revolt, strike posters everywhere, student centers full with anti-war meetings, petitions circulating, public marches, continuous street theatre. A committee of Brown faculty, students, and administrators travels to Washington to meet with government officials, and I am one of the faculty selected. Washington offices reflect defensive walls alarmed by the youthful uprising. Saving face in Vietnam is a whispered necessity. How do we get out "with honor"? The United States can't be defeated by Vietcong "gooks." Blacks in our delegation say maybe "gooks" are just regarded as "niggers." In the sprawling, five-sided Pentagon, that curious bulk of military supremacy that an anti-war demonstration attempted recently "to levitate" in protest of its excessive might, we meet with Navy Secretary, John Chafee from Rhode Island, and his top Marine Corps and Naval advisors. In our delegation, which includes various minority groups, I hear myself asking how the Navy handles the racist label, "gooks." Split America answers suddenly as a passionate dispute erupts between top-ranking officers. One says he banned the word "gooks" with his men; the other says it's a democracy of free speech and you can't prevent the use of labels and swear words among fighting men. As we visit other offices, contradictions continue. Every high official states we must get out of the war as soon as possible. The Solicitor General pats a drawer in his desk and says, "I have my protest ready to send to the President." Time barriers loom before our eyes, distant time, time of false pride struggling to defeat time of reality.

Our most revealing visit is to the White House's awesome theatre of history. Power here means penetrating formidable, impersonal security corridor after corridor. Communication is by private secret talk on top of the pyramid of power or by public telephone access through legions of polite bureaucratic masks. Too much public veneration of power concentrated in the presidency. We have an appointment with Charles Colson, Nixon's Special Counsel and a Brown graduate. Colson is a stocky, jovial Marine Corps veteran, reputed to have the unofficial Marine Corps slogan over his bar at home, "Get 'Em By The Balls And Their Hearts Will Follow." Youthful, carefully groomed appearance, eyes sparkling pleasant greetings behind his glasses, waves us to seats in his large impressive office. White House bureaucracy is not like other government offices. The mountain's peak reflects the sun. Even the huge, old brass doorknobs shine impressively. Ceilings soar, lavish power requires lavish space. Each clock ticks with urgency. Our appointment is for forty minutes, plenty of time for questions. Colson starts off reading a list of weapons we have captured during the initial days of the Cambodian invasion. An impressive, quick-thrusting action, American troops in and out as fast as possible, of course. Looking around I see my companions

236

ready a barrage of questions. If questions fly, maybe answers, like Delphi, will emerge with truthful, prophetic weight. But secret power remains enigmatic. Colson drones through his triumphant list, page after page of captured weaponry, stopping only when a few minutes remain of our allotted visit. By this time we wink at each other incredulously, realizing there is no end to this surrealistic weapon list. When Colson finishes, time remains for only a few questions which he brushes off, and we are ushered out politely muttering to ourselves. Later, during Watergate, Colson is revealed as Master of Dirty Tricks, the zealot who said he would walk over his grandmother for the President if necessary. After serving a brief prison sentence, he becomes a Born Again Christian, working for prison reform, sinner turned into savior of sinners, evangelist speaking against abortion and homosexuality. In a television interview, he will plead for "a moral order to the universe. It's there, and it's absolute. And the job of scholarship has been to try and find that truth. That's where the word *university* comes from: unity of truth, diversity of approach." Clever Power: reading a diverse list of weapons against a unified university. An absolute moral order he proclaims, extreme fundamentalist of power, no matter what he does. The Japanese poet, Basho, writes: "Poetry is a fireplace in summer or a fan in winter." In the contradicting, ambiguous metaphors of life, the ruthless literal search for American Power and money confronts the democratic vision of reconciling opposing forces, a theatrical war staged in the White House's historical anguish.

Death of a Teacher

(1)

Lying on a couch in late winter afternoon,
I stare at light fading high in the Japanese plum tree.
Sun glitters sharply on high-peaked ice.
For a moment the radiance is like death.
Dark closes slowly over suspended light,
The way of illumination through agonizing times,
To perceive light as it defines and dies.

(2)

Thirty-five years ago in college
We got drunk together one afternoon,
Dedicated to the vision of how many poems

237

We could write in one ecstatic burst.
As each poem slashed, jiggling with excitement
And booze, across blank white pages,
We praised Blake, Rimbaud, Hart Crane,
Their mystical powers of liquid language.
I wrote fourteen poems into oblivion.
Waving, our fists full of scribbled poems,
We saluted joy before we passed out.

(3)
Only once after college, I saw my close friend,
Teaching at a private school in Connecticut,
Writing poems only for private moments.
I returned west to live, he remained until,
Magnetic opposites, I settled in the east
And he moved west to teach in Seattle.
Yesterday I read of his death at fifty-four,
Diabetes defeating his daily insulin shots.
Of his life teaching the young he wrote:
"I understand the young. Like me, they are human;
Like me, sloppy; like me, idealistic;
Like me, responsive; like me, searching;
Like me, confused; like me, unself-realized."
Was he referring to his missing poems?

(4)
Does a teacher spring up like a tree,
Rilke's singing Orpheus? Immigrant America's
Challenge to unite turned into public school conformity,
Grades and sports essential for college admission,
Test scores to "mainline it" into the "right track,"
Kids escaping into hard rock, drugs, television fantasies,
So he disappeared to teach in private schools,
Teaching the sloppy, vigorous few like himself.
Watching, he saw the ideal of public schools fade.
Into the special rooms of the imagination,
Factual Skills marched into corners, secret closets.

(5)
Fifty percent of Americans don't read books anymore.
"It's a media country." Why bother with teachers praising literature?
Batter eyes with advertisements, violent action films.
Teachers, who survive five to eight hours of discipline per day,

238

Will be awarded Honorable Certificates of Endurance;
Never mind the scattered flesh of Orpheus singing
In another climate, the Greek longing for metaphor.

(6)
In his north-west corner he worked silently,
Lost poems charging his students with magical words.
In absent letters we should have written, I write,
"Teaching is only another word for electricity,
Light and experience sparking from age to youth
Creating students who will illuminate the world.
Farewell, friend, master teacher of electricity."

Obsessive American Sight

In sudden spring,
blazing white dogwood
is too white
for my Polish visitor.
"Flowers are not so bright
in Poland," shading his eyes,
"Here in America
your burning flowers
make obsessive images."
Hot accusations!
I ask, "Why do foreigners
always think America is full
of bright colors of violence?"
He laughs, "The answer glows
in your advertising signs.
Everything you Americans see
is full of singular energy,
obsessive American sight."

The Last New England Transcendentalist

In pure spring, dry wind, high clouds,
The last New England Transcendentalist
Runs to fly, renew his soul as a kite.

His kite soars, a blue organic circle
Searching through space data for the form
To find a meter-making argument in the sky.

In the cemetery park he sees his comic maneuver
As a defiant personal way to soar into heaven;
The astronauts only discovered "Magnificent Desolation."

He knows the earthbound, animal-digging soul
Must ascend, fly in weightless joy to release
The dead from their lost marble memorials.

He thinks, "How can one ascend apart from the community?
Emersonian *self-reliance* is gone with the Over-Soul,
Shrouded in principles of chaos and indeterminacy.

"Back in their lunar module, the astronauts thought
The moon-dust on their suits smelled strangely
Like gunpowder to Aldrin, like wet ashes to Armstrong.

"Heaven no longer walks among us in triple disguises
Deceiving the wise, we stare into the electron microscope
To see an invisible world create its own beauty."

Flying his kite alone in the cemetery, or in the park
To Jefferson Starship, old grotesque American choice,
Isolated communicants seeking the Puritan memory of Israel,

His blue kite tangles on a humming telephone wire,
His damned soul lights up with electricity and nuclear fire.
Like Ben Franklin he discovers lightning haunts his spirit.

How American to be trapped proudly in the power lines,
To perceive glory flashing, sparking in the sky,
Fouled in electric metaphors of the divine mind.

From his pocket he pulls out the new Theology of Liberation:
"Do not thin out the Gospel into pale, bland letters.
You must read the Bible with the eyes of the poor."

"With infinite frontier space, how can we ever be poor?
"Property keeps the accounts of the world, is always moral."
As long as we soar, no pure malignity can ever exist.

"Yes, it is still the age of the first person singular.
Let me fly free in my own American fancy.
The sun shall be witness to my floating soul.

"If we whittle our minds to one point
Can we ever know God? Does God smile
Seeing a forest of sharp points below him?

"In America meditation has become big business.
Meditation owns thousands of acres, buildings;
Meditation publishes best-sellers, performs on television.

"Once we sought God in nature, only to lose him in space;
Jet trails mark geometrical angles of our ignorance—
And still the community of God is our soaring dream.

"America blazes in the night with evangelical fervor
That in my kite's blue circle I may catch God's glaring vision
And the mad, lonely salvation of the Prince of Peace burn my eye.'

The Boilerman

Heavy-bodied, furry-fleshed,
he prowls into the damp cellar
like a suspicious bear
lusting after fire.
Eyes squinting fiercely
through thick glasses,
bald head glowing with summer radiance,
he plugs in his torch-light
illuminating moldy darkness.
"Condensation," he spits his verdict
in a wave of fan-like consonants
over his dead cigar-stub,
"Look at that damn moisture
rotting out your good old furnace.
The nipples on those pipes are gone.
Enough rust there to fill Yankee Stadium.
They'll have to smash 'em out
with a hammer if you don't watch out.

You've gotta take care of this moisture.
Water's a real killer of fire."
Exactly, he plunges hands into the furnace
like a doctor poking into a surgical incision,
scrapes, cleans, seals with cement.
"Now we gotta get a fire going,
a good fire to clean this baby dry.
How would you like to rust out your life?"
As the fire grows, he turns silent,
his eyes glitter, his mouth moves with words
burned away by flame, burning language.

The Forgotten Wall

(1)
Solo,
        saturated with himself,
        stung with economic valor,
my neighbor begins his repair dance—
his grey, sagging Victorian house
        will soar in commercial value
            "if maintained . . ."

(2)
"God damn ridiculous these market values,
inflation is some kind of humpbacked elephant!
Can you believe she's worth $100,000
        if I paint her up
        and I'm worth zero?"

(3)
"Commercial painters want $5000 for the job.
You could take twenty high-class vacations
        or hire yourself a Bionic Woman for that,
so I'm starting my dogged high ladder dance
to paint her high parts. She's all I've got,
        she's what I have to paint."

(4)
Dancer as retired naval officer,
"How can I fall off,

me built like a fire plug?"
Golfhat, peering, square-edged glasses,
unlit cigar stub clamped in mouth,
        "helps me with the angles—
you just keep looking up for birds in the sky."

        (5)
Chip, scrape with electric sander,
dig into moldy, infested holes,
clean out dead mice, spiderwebs,
        decayed leaf-mold, larvae,
"It's like putting your hand in blind
into a hundred year-old grave."

        (6)
Done for the day, he dawdles below,
hypnotized by the arduous, high task,
kneading a beer can in stubby fingers,
contemplating the thirty-foot heights,
"You know those old Victorians
        liked to float up to God.
They were sure the original High-Risers."

        (7)
Six months of work
        "like a prison sentence."
When the stark grey and white job
        finishes/is finished,
an unfinished side wall remains
        like an action painting,
slashes of white primer unsubdued
        by furious, attacking streaks of grey.

        (8)
"You missed that hidden wall
        up against my property,"
        I joke with him.
"You left it for me to look at."
"That's my Forgotten Wall," he grins.
"You get to look at it all winter.
If you don't like it,
        next summer I'll finish it,
But it'll linger on to haunt you."

243

(9)
Snow falls over his grey house
whitening my eyes to lucid points,
trapped observer caught like a crab.
Never mind museum action paintings.
Active house, resurrection ablaze
with exact prim, grey-white Victorian tones
against the turbulent Forgotten Wall.

(10)
Kissed by snowflakes he stands triumphant,
beer can upraised like a tributary lamp,
        beer-body foaming with achievement:
"How do you like
        your Forgotten Wall, neighbor?"

(11)
Now it's my Forgotten Wall.
I give it to you, viewer of walls,
television reader, sleepwalker
        in an age of visual dreams.
The act of contemplation contains always
        a nagging hangnail
tormenting the dreamer with
        dreams unfinished,
the audience with finished dreams.

Fabulous Debris

"Anything fabulous you want to keep?"
With a glint in her green eyes,
My wife spills the latest debris
From my wandering life
Over a yellow paper napkin—
Rubber bands, thumb-tacks,
Crossed-out notes, bills, letters,
A curious blue pencil, ticket stubs,
A broken hammer, a dog-chewed book . . .
"Throw it all out," I mutter quickly,
Afraid of litter that exhausts the heart.

After my garbage toss, return to order,
A crazy renewal dream hovers in cleaned space—
Resurrected wonder lurking deep
In the exhaustion of fabulous debris.

On the Beach Watched by a Seagull

December storm briefly suspended,
Ice melting, still air alert for sound,
I burn papers on the lonely beach
Strewn with oil-soaked stones and garbage,
Oil companies leaking money on the shore.
Behind me, a watcher is watching me,
A fat, tough sea gull, a strutter,
Mouth clamped on a long silver fish.
Refusing to release his greed, he can't take off,
So he glares at me. Teasing him, I move closer,
Curiosity down the slide to scorn.
Clutching his fish, he waddles indignantly away,
Paddles through greasy water to a rock
Ten yards offshore to show his scorn
And preserve his meal, frustrated that he
Can't fly, eat, mock me from the air
At the same time. I almost throw a rock to scare him,
But restrain myself, spectator to his greed.
Forced to eat, he sucks the big fish down his throat
Like a vacuum pump turned high to emergency;
Then takes off, ringing the air with shrill anger,
Flying around me in a fury of joyous delight
At eating his fish and having his flight too.
After the burning, I tell my wife about the gull's rage;
She shrugs: "You gave him indigestion. Was that nice?"
Eye-driven are the ways of compulsive watchers,
Who stare and find in visionary questions,
Enigmatic answers disguised as burning action.

The Duck Watcher

(1)

Slowly, through fading leaves of the autumn Copper Beech,
a white ship appears . . . the visionary opera commences.
Lohengrin riding his swan triumphantly!
No, a plain oil tanker in a polluted bay . . . Ducks floating . . .
What references can I summon magically
to become a T.S. Eliot of metaphysical insight?
Was there a duck somewhere in the Grail legend?
You are too small and squat to be a swan.
The gull easily outsoars you in power of flight.
I must learn how to see without legends.

(2)

They have taken to catching light!
Tricks of the sun, perhaps,
or is it that they turn and turn
        toward the light?

(3)

Winter stupidities . . . Hundreds of black ducks,
floating stoics in the cold wind,
ducking for invisible food,
their asses up in the air like comic flags.
This is what it means to endure.
I too am looking for invisible food,
my ass to the rear of time like any beast.

(4)

Ducks scrape the water, surface-precision.
Do not ignore the metaphor, they have a razor quality
of sharpness in their slash for food.
They open up inches of surface depth as they . . .
My god, that is why they are called *duck!*

(5)

Duck in the snow is like cork in a bottle,
pressed tight into the bay's wet force . . .
Inaccurate vision. The cork is a cold agent
of tight preservation, duck is a warm spirit
of survival; bouncing, twisting, gliding

246

with the wind, absorbing the force of chance.
Duck is only like a cork, floating elements,
light forces in a world of heavy weights,
bobbing, weaving, Ariel touch on solid earth.
Look, I am weaving too, but I cannot duck.

(6)
So many of them, are they ever lonely?
They surround loneliness
as if it were the center of a circle,
always moving tighter together
until the invisible center of loneliness
is obscured, shifted to the shore
where my house, my species, watch, alone.

(7)
Incredible how they veer and swerve in wind patterns.
Arrows, lines, squares, even a cross!
All too symbolic, their patterns mock me with symbols.
A symbol is what a duck hoists you by.

(8)
"See ducks, Common Black . . ." *Anas rubripes tristis* . . .
How sad the sound of science, particularly lost Latin.
To be called Common Black is also dangerous,
a classification failing as blood identity.
Who is that Common Black Duck drifting there?

(9)
Storm! Blizzard! Fronting the rising wind,
they face the waves like Nevsky's troops
facing the rigid line of Teutonic Knights,
but without uniform disguise, this is no film;
They are only floating feathers against nature,
natural huddle of defense . . . How my duck-poem
goes from aggressive warfare to football
is an American sequence of power.
I salute you, defensive American ducks!

(10)
God damn, a grey day, they are gone.
From my high house, I look out on a glaze.

The Glaze! It may be my mind.
The levels of water confuse me with their emptiness.
I cannot see the invisible life, hunted and hunter.
The Glaze has abolished depth.
I want to navigate backwards, forwards,
escape this dead center of the Glaze
that fixes the picture, kills time,
stops the heartbeat, pacifies even death.

(11)
Through winter trees, a tanker approaches
as wind whips up the spindrift. Vacation boys,
full of assassin blood, fire beebie guns.
The ducks fly away. The tanker lingers,
green forecastle bulging over a gut of oil,
steaming slowly away for heat and money.

(12)
They are floating in the juice of spring,
Black dots of memory . . .
I must leave this rented house
and my duck observations
before my vision dips completely duck.
Anas rubripes tristis . . .
The ducks are gone, they're changing
into common black dots of memory
as spring shatters earth with old forms.
I am what is around me, said Stevens,
skin-possession, separation inside,
the observer struggling for an eye of wonder
to create from those lost black ducks
The Uncommon Black Dots of Memory.

1980s

THEORY OF AMERICAN GROTESQUE

Theory of American Grotesque

(1)
Conforming to community standards,
    something twists by in shadows.
    Blinking our eyes, we don't recognize
the grotesque element woven into our behavior.

Grotesque flares from bizarre characters
    featured in a carnival sideshow;
    Fat Lady and Sword Swallower
loom grotesque and we delight in them.

But what if normal standards turn grotesque?
    If multi-million dollar salaries are fantastic realities?
    If movie stars reveal grotesque tantrums?
If the Stock Market is a quotesque, frenzied institution?

Carved in a memorial gate at West Point,
    where Poe attended briefly as cadet,
    is a quote from his Ligeia: "There is no
exquisite beauty without some strangeness in its proportions."

In the 1980s exquisite has vanished from beauty
    and curious strangeness peers from the proportions;
    trains are questioned by spy satellites
and the landscape of forests is lured away by freeways.

(2)
At Brown University in the 1980s, I invented a new course, *Theory of American Grotesque*. The university's New Curriculum created a series of Freshman Seminars called "Modes of Thought," permitting small groups of twenty students to investigate unusual, broadscale concepts with interested faculty. Through research and reading, my purpose was to examine the grotesque side of what passes as normal from politics, sports, and education to advertising, television, movies, and rock. Long reading list from Poe's *Tales of the Arabesque and Grotesque* through Melville, Hawthorne, Whitman and Emily Dickinson to Anderson, Faulkner, Hemingway, W.C. Williams, Nathaniel West, Flannery O'Connor, and my Brown

colleagues, John Hawkes and Robert Coover, whom I invited to sit in when time came to discuss their work.

Is grotesque merely dictionary definition: "Fantastically extravagant, bizarre—from *grotessco*, grotto—a kind of decorative painting or sculpture in which portions of human and animal forms are fantastically interwoven with foliage and flowers." Has not the European origin of grotesque suffered a sea-change in American transformations?

In the early years of Jeffersonian agricultural democracy, a country of vast space and open western frontier, grotesque in the 18th and early 19th centuries was visible distortion, conflict between immigrant cultures with different religions, dehumanization of native American groups portrayed and killed as "savages."

For his Indian raids, native Americans gave George Washington the name "Burner of Villages." The Civil War sought to resolve the grotesque issue of slavery by asserting the simultaneous paradox of national union, states rights, and civil rights. After the Civil War, the sense of grotesque as European abnormal distortions of man and nature was transformed by an industrial surge of supposed urban normalcy. A twelve-hour workday was considered normal and penny ante salaries lucrative. Long workdays six days a week and religious Sundays set normal life patterns for destitute immigrants seeking opportunities for new secure homes and jobs.

Grotesque in the 19th century was tragic distortions from religious and social pressures, reflected from Poe's, Melville's, Hawthorne's broodings over manic forces in characters such as Usher, Ahab, and Dimmesdale. By the twentieth century American Grotesque was subdued behind normalcy's masks of power, money, and fame.

Corporate Executive Officers became the highest paid officials in the world while public schools and health systems foundered. Disillusioned with politicians, increasingly controlled by money interests, fewer and fewer people voted. Suburban developments, mainly designed for the isolation of affluent life-styles, devastated urban centers. A grotesque term, "safety net," labeled a difficult welfare program for millions of poor Americans. What invisible chaos lurked beneath the sinister "safety net"? In 1982 a full page *Fortune* ad in the *New York Times* counseled how "to succeed with the fast-track people," proclaimed that "you don't have to hide your ambition anymore—if you've got it, go and get it. That's what society is telling you these days."

(3)

In *Winesburg, Ohio*, Sherwood Anderson defined grotesque as "the moment one of the people took one of the truths to himself, called it his truth, and tried to live his life by it, he became a grotesque and the truth he embraced became a falsehood."

Truth by relativity? Are not truth and falsehood clear opposites? Why should we have to live by compromise? Liberalism was labeled a false ideal because it tried to balance the opposites. How can a society devoted to absolutes, to fundamentals, materialistic and spiritual, become grotesque, successful, and powerful at the same time?

Emily Dickinson wrote:

I'm Nobody! Who are you?
Are you—Nobody—Too?
Then there's a pair of us?
Don't tell they'd advertise—you know!

They did tell and advertised Nobodies into brief prominence and then cast Nobodies back into shadows. Somebody advanced into instant, quickly disappearing fame, as he and she struggled for new identities in a rapidly changing world. The feminist revolution burgeoned, women advancing and retreating in the new age of technology. Nobodies struggling to be Somebodies in a "downsizing" computer time, machines shaping "lean corporate structures" as more and more people became unemployed or reduced to menial "service jobs."

(4)

Grotesque language of AIDS: "A savage God to be appeased."

"We need to love each other
as much as the microorganisms love us.
I don't fear death, but I feel
abandoned by the bureaucracy."
When the system of community fails,
the illusion of safety fades
like the absurd defensive
Great Wall of China.
That death comes to youth
so suddenly and mercilessly
makes us wanderers
in a space no longer free.

Sometimes people with AIDS
will simply walk away into oblivion
as though formalities
are no longer possible.
A man wears a cape
full of photographs
of the missing dead.

253

Can one still break through
the staring mask of disease,
reach out, and take the hand
of an anonymous dying man?
	Beware of fear and ignorance.
	Grotesque does not always
	grimace with menacing looks;
	Grotesque learns from pain,
	dances with courage brashly
	into death invisible to your eyes.

	(5)
Why study fantasies, American grotesque theories?
	To confront painfully life's agonies and distortions?
		No, grotesque heals too if we can balance conflicting dreams.

Grotesque begins with language, invisible children
	who have seen and heard too much to be children.
		In a new school an eight-year-old girl is accosted
			by an eight-year-old boy who says "I'm going to rape you!"

Confusing language masquerades often as violent roots,
	fundamental words, television force, America Wild Master
		seeking one God amidst a thousand splintered sects,
			countless Messiahs dominating their cults with
				television personalities proclaiming fire and redemption.

Move out of the river of conditioning.
	The grotesque looks to bewitch our senses.
		"We're just legends, myths, sacred stories," say
			Native Americans seeking their lost heritage.
				If we do not illuminate our grotesque fractions,
					our divided nature may dance us into shadows.

At Frost's Farm in Derry, New Hampshire

In October, rain darkens the glacial stones
Looming out of the woods on the mending-wall—
"Something there is that doesn't love a wall."

The neighbor is dead who argued,
"Good fences make good neighbors."
In the bleak woods I feel the fantasy
Of "an old-stone savage armed."
The simple frame house is now a monument,
But the real spectre haunting this place is
A colloquial war; how to shape plainness.
Here he saw hard lives warped by the land
And shaped them into deceptively simple speech:
What could be reduced would suggest more.
I imagine Flaubert sitting here and writing;
"Let us strum our guitars and clash our cymbals,
And whirl like dervishes in the eternal hubub
Of Forms and Ideas." The eternal hubub fails.
I try vainly to whirl like a dervish, my guitar
Falls, lost cymbals clash only for communal dances.
As a solitary man I write to overcome my solitude,
Where exaltation is in the shape of isolation,
The way stone rises to anchor the air.

A Game against Age

Slowly the old men, bald, bearded, white-haired,
Enter the towering brick warehouse, crumbling
In the industrial district like the Colosseum.
Factories around stand darkly in the evening,
Only the rented warehouse is lit against loneliness.
The old men present official membership cards
And greet each other with challenging glee.
Eagerly, they walk into the huge, gaping space
And switch on a thousand, blinking lights.
Each has his own electric trains and track
Running through a festive glare of space.
Immaculate with spats and cane, flower
Yellow in his buttonhole, a retired engineer
Has conquered a deep ravine with a bridge
And roars his train across into a tunnel.
These are no temporary trains for boys.
The oldster in his sweatshirt has discovered Africa;
Through lions and elephants by the tracks,
His train chugs to the edge of a diamond mine.

A Russian Jew rides fervently away from Siberia,
An Italian reconstructs The Brenner Pass,
The son of a frontiersman puffs past Indians,
Real wood burning in the furnace of his cab.
Tall and stoop-shouldered, a gleaming bald head
Builds a grandiose station for The Eternal City,
Rome, where all trains arrive and never depart.
For hours they work over beer, coffee, and cigars,
Twenty old men cackling at their projects.
Late at night they abandon the warehouse,
Lock up their game against time, drive home
Slowly under the blinking lights of planes.

Remedial

It's a crippled society.
The only jobs left
Are in remedial work.
I study my defects
And learn how to perfect them.

Sitting on the Porch at Dawn

All light is extraordinary,
But dawnlight is
The source of wonder.
As dark silence
Becomes illumination,
Trees sparkle with
Lucid green information.

A Blue Heron glides
Along the river,
Perfect natural flight,
No question mark in space.
As the river mist
Burns away slowly,

All questions of darkness
Are clarified
By answers of light.

The Search and Discovery of Rodin's Nude

Rodin loved the dance of naked bodies
Which "charm force and translate it into grace."
Always he moved living models before his eyes,
"Men and women walking about in my studio
To fill my mind with their forms and movements . . .
To my contemporaries the nude is an exceptional vision."
To be sure, his vision was French, not American.
Not that we don't have a naked vision, the topless;
From magazines and papers, the stare of defiant flesh
Offers a display of bought bodies. Nakedness
Wanders our cities, a lewd threat, while the nude
Stands concealed in mysterious, lost desire.
"Any attitude that is imposed is unnatural
And useless to study . . ." Perhaps our tragedy is
That we believe in studying the imposition
Of unnatural attitudes; with crazed faith
We believe in the power of correction, the ability
To replace the infinite by the finite,
"To interrupt and isolate the secret laws of our being."
Why let an old voyeur teach us about nature?
Analyze, dissect, destroy to create, a concern
With detailed flesh will permit us to embrace nakedness.
Yet I hear that old voice those old eyes warning:
"The body loses its charm, becomes absurd, ridiculous."
I turn to your body walking around in my head,
Claiming my eyes, charming the force of sexuality,
Translating naked violence into the graceful nude.

The Moon and the Beautiful Woman

In ancient Chinese poetry,
The moon and the beautiful woman

Flow whitely together.
How shall I sing these images today?
Through weightless space
The moon is a spectre
And the beautiful woman a billboard image
Advertising film seductions.
Time for the simpleton again,
The Old Fool singing in Space Centers
Of the moon as love's sensuous eye—
Moon-Woman whose arching white skin
Flares out to calm the beasts of earth.
The astronauts must bring home
Your flesh, not their glassy rocks.

Bouncing Vision of the Commuter

Far away from the threat of foreign countries
That we supervise intimately on television,
We let the Old Stone Bank buy our homes,
Rise to solve the fast car we must drive slowly
On the maze of roads marked with gas stations,
Shopping malls, bars of our daily commuting.
Along the throughway, dedicated advertisements
Shine their miracles of goods and bads.
An advertisement reader with a dreaming mind,
I travel daily to a job growing more remote.
Tense at my destination, I drive underground
Into a huge concrete monument for parking
Where my car sits all day like a silent snail.
As I am taught the puzzling role of commuter,
I hum, rehearse my rock songs on the journey—
How to shout, sing, chirp, in my comfortable cage.

The Elizabethan Fool Applies
for a Corporate Position

What melody hides in these instructions?
I have filled out all the application forms,

But there seems to be no category for Fool.
Do they not recognize savage singing ghosts?
If I can persuade them of my abilities
In my lost, wide-ranging, entertainment job,
How will I learn to sing, dance, on a team?
Can I disguise myself as Corporate Secretary?
Can I joke about pornography instead of sex?
They have said don't call, they'll notify me.
I shall wait singing into the land of statistics.

The Real Parader

If you're a Real Parader you follow Main Streets,
Breezy waterfront routes, an eye for spectacles.
You search for the glowing line of march to get away
From bugs in back alley rooms. You live for parades.
A parade never ends, it just dribbles off.
You study starts, memorize who walks where.
You're going to be first, out there alone,
Ahead of young, eagle-fierce girls
Waving their banners high in rigid lines.
Someday they'll be Eagle Mothers of America.
To be a Real Parader you've gotta have color
Shining above all the smooth-talking politicians
Dapper in their suits showing cool money power.
You've gotta wear a really smashing uniform,
Hit 'em in the eyes with their secret fantasies.
I like two points of color on my jacket,
Shoulders and heart, so I've got bright cords
For flying epaulettes, flowing ribbons to float me,
A power of medals brightening the air with pride.
A real medal shines boldly with its own mystery,
Nothing too warlike or too sentimental crap.
You gotta see it's shining for life, not death.
For pants I've got the best Indian buckskin
Covered with hundreds of little gold stars,
A strong pair of jumping pants to walk free in.

I'm a Real Parader, no Chamber of Commerce bigwig
With iron-grip hands, glowing teeth-smiles.

259

I love greeting people, make 'em enjoy parades,
How to break out in public without bragging,
How to leave off trouble and tickle some fun.
I set my top hat high for the right look,
Tall red, white and blue stovepipe with two birds,
A fierce eagle facing an enigmatic dove to keep
Folks guessing who I am, what their country is.
That way I keep 'em laughing, screaming at me,
Dancing along behind me, the Real Parader,
Marching to liberate the old spirit of July Fourth.

Lookin' for Gas at the Youth Guidance Center

What kind of gas are you goin' to give me?
I like the sweet-smellin' kind don't burn.
I want to go on a trip, man.
I smelled it once when I lived in
One of them ten foster homes
Where you paid the owners to keep me.
You paid 'em with those checks
Got holes in 'em. Some smart-assed machine
Punches holes in hard green paper.
They used to show me those checks
When they bought me. When I goofed off
They shipped me back to your Youth Guidance Center.
You're the guide, man. I guess I'm the youth,
But I got no age. You won't let me wear no mascara
Till I'm eighteen. I think I'm sixteen.
It's a date on some lost paper. At night you lock me
In my room the way you lock your gas tanks
When I try to drain out some of that good gas.
I don't know if I'm a boy or girl,
Though my breasts are big and I've got a cunt.
You don't want me to fool with the blinds
On the window. You watch me goin' to the bathroom.
I can't spell or read good
But I know what I say most of the time.
I can't seem to do nothin' right.

I want to fill up my mind with good gas
And take off . . . Zoom, man!
Guide the youth to the good gas!

The Listener to Rock above the Pain Level

Believing in the power of silence,
I'm forced to a recognition of noise
When electric music eats me alive,
Hits my ears with ecstatic sound
Piercing above the pain level.
Is noise inevitable to create silence?
High above, the whining blast of jet planes
Sears the sky with fiery white paths.
The Space Shuttle soars in a cloud of flame.
I imagine Saint Francis bouncing along
These white trails in the sky,
Bare feet dangling, bells jingling
Softly from his ankles
To warn crickets away
From his noisy passage.

Street Corner Signals

Punctually, every evening in commuter traffic,
The broad-hipped Mexican boy sways on the corner,
Eyes closed, dancing feet churning in tennis shoes,
Ears tuned to joyous, invisible signals.
Bored commuters call him "mentally defective,"
Cagey drivers, media-minded, say he's a Martian.
If the intense signals can never be decoded,
They transform his fat, placid flesh
Into some heart-sucking, frenzied magnet
Pulling steel filings through his skin.
No, the traffic's magnetized, not the boy,
Who hears his chest full of singing birds.

261

The Search for a Subject

If we could abstract the squirrel from the snow,
Only white would remain in the pattern,
Beautiful abstraction, absolute wonder of the world.
But the search for a humanistic subject continues—
To build from the red-flowing animal heart
A feeling for the frenzied community of error,
Where human eyes retain perceptive vision
Penetrating time and space, promising visionary days—
As in Hopper's *Sunlight in a Cafeteria*,
The buxom, red-haired woman sits alone,
Head down, brooding in a shaft of sunlight,
While a lonely man at another table
Sits, staring at her, or out the window
At the empty building across the street,
Both meditating on doubtful possibilities,
Neither willing to forsake lost dreams,
Sorrow's blood flowing into redemptive power.

The Strange Names of America

Canajoherie—the strange names of America
Pass on the highway, wander through
A confused linguistic daze of lost time,
Americans haunted, blessed by wild blood,
Crossbreeds of a violent melting pot
That scrapes and changes if it rarely melts,
Native cries translated into
    WHITE MOP WRINGER COMPANY,
Recreation vehicles with the banner:
    THIS IS OUR PLAYPEN—
As if we're really creating a new travel language
Absorbing every ethnic name—but the names change
Relentlessly, assuming new writhing meanings,
Attaching themselves to trucks, billboards,
Neon motel signs, America's strange names
Shedding highway skins in snakelike resurrection.

Uncertain Messages across the Country

1 Packing

Come, see how we're container-packed,
Cased in huge, bold rectangles
Out of which we have to make
Anonymous, hard-edged poetry,
No compromise, only a touch of
Soft color to control hard space.

2 Note on the Vacant door

Here is some stuff
To lure you for a visit.
When and if you appear
I hope that I will not be gone.

3 Bottle Rockets

Speeding across country,
You encounter *Bottle Rockets*—
Language as tough container
With concealed, violent tongues.

4 Artist's Farewell to His Studio

I have been working
On this project
For forty years.
Try not to look
At the simple surface,
But at the suggestive layers.

The American Dream on Superbowl Sunday

The American Dream unfolds on the high plateaus
Where ultimate bigness veers off into luring blue sky,
Headbutting, the Superbowl Kiss, aggressive action

Speeding down every highway to the invisible horizon.
Transforming, we all become bears and eagles in stance
And speed, running in black shoes to become supreme,
Eggbeater energy avoiding the necessity of roots.
Everything whirling in motion, go, people, run,
Never stop, decay is when we're forced to rest,
The modern rusts in our body. Our dream is dedicated
To the future, today is only where worn-out people die.
What we desire is the greatest spectacle of all time:
Eternal youth in the spotlight, and the light endures
As if glorious wings create angelic territory.

Driving through Clyde, Ohio, 1985

Driving through Clyde, Ohio, I am welcomed
By a sign, Sherwood Anderson's Winesburg, Ohio,
Where he was born in 1876 to study grotesque life.
In his small wooden house, transformed for winter,
New owners live with ghosts they don't acknowledge,
Kate Smith, sexually frustrated schoolteacher,
Jesse Bentley, dogged farmer and Bible fanatic,
Dr. Reefy crumpling woes into little paper pills,
George Willard, hometown boy determined
Like Anderson to leave Winesburg for larger horizons.

If books at times can change our destinies, small towns
Often live on, unchanging, large old Victorian houses
Still promise neighborly talk on screened porches,
While small backstreet homes measure shrinking hopes.
If Winesburg spoke uneasily of industrial change,
The grotesque torments that condition our lives
Causing us to flee smallness for exciting cities,
Clyde still survives despite vast urban migrations,
A backwater puzzle with a certain calm knowledge:
Remaining small shines as the survival paradox.

The Gold Salvation of
Oral Roberts in Tulsa, Oklahoma

Nine hundred feet tall,
Jesus came to me in his true height,
Commanding me to raise
An unfinished tower
Six hundred feet high:
"You must find a way,
Oral, my son, to finish it."
He inspired me to erect
A Golden University
With luxuriant gardens
In Tulsa's boiling petroleum world.

At the center of the campus
I built a spaceship to celebrate God,
A futuristic prayer tower
Depicting my astonished, blessed life.
In the first room, visitors approach
A poor, struggling farmhouse shack.
In the big sky overhead, white clouds
Float with sacred, glowing promise.
Suddenly, the house blazes intensely
With divine light, a baby squeals,
And my mother's proud, worn-out voice
Says softly, "I'm going to call you Oral."

After my magical birth, you visit
My fervent rise from tent minister
To television healer, my guided hands
Curing with passionate prayer, directed will.
In the last room of my salvation,
Dazzling mirrors twine together
Reflecting God's divine power,
And God speaks through Oral Roberts
Praying for your sinful soul,
My international prayer
For the world's salvation.

How many Americans has
Jesus spoken to personally:

"Build me a University
And a Golden Skyscraper Hospital—
I teach and I heal."
Come to my University, my Hospital
Flickering with lucid gold crosses,
And pray with me that
The Devil's shark will die in the ocean,
And the desert flower in prayers
As this Golden Campus helps
Release us from our sins.

Out of the City into Miracle Valley

All I'm doing is move my old, battered trailer
Out of the corrupt city into a quiet, holy place.
Sure, sacred names here are a bit spectacular
Like Chariot of Fire Drive, but that's just
Because this is a place where God lives.
In every desert there's a Miracle Valley
Where the cactus wren pecks through thorns,
And Holy Water flows out in sweetness.

Sitting on my trailer steps, reading my Bible,
I know we read word into true world,
Real Hell-Fire shines out of God's syllables,
His breath so powerful it singes His beard.
America's the land where we move on
In search of God's fiery eye. It's all
Writ down by His moving finger, and read
By us trailer folk moving into His fire.

All you need to create your own Miracle Valley
Is learn the faith to read God's blazing ways.
If we was meant to live stationary in big cities,
He wouldn't write no sunsets to move us on.

Singing Madly

At night she returns often to counsel me,
Broken-hipped, blind in her wheelchair,
My mother grins at me, "I am immortal!"
Escaping from her Irish blarney, I drive
Frantically into foreign cities
Swollen in time with anonymous ghosts.
"Can't you hear me, son, singing madly
In the desert house I designed for my
Poems soaring up to the Sangre de Cristo mountains?"
I can hear your life-songs, Mother,
Though your house is lost in time,
The fireplace you tiled with Navajo designs
Vanished in growing suburban sprawl.

"Drive on, my son, killing time is
Curing time when death discovers memory
And mad singers sing on forever:
Though love be a chancy thing—
          The Irish in me said—
I'll let it have its glory fling,
And sing and cling
Till I be good and dead."

I'll drive on, Mother, search that place
When I can live, calm and peaceful,
But your blind ghost sings sharp to me:
"You hear the sharpness of knowledge,
Son, a keen-edged song cutting at you,
Singing how houses die, build your own
Dream home, singing to you with an Irish lilt,
Singing madly is our redemptive guilt."

Wander

1984 Indiana
license plates
      say

267

WANDER
   proudly
as if American wandering
      is a
      spiritual
      surge,
         a curse
         or crossing
            into
                invisible
                    eternity

Island Time of Animal Sensibilities

   (1)
As we kiss and fall
Into the natural flow
Of summer time,
We take off clothes, grow hair,
Explore anew love's flesh.
When two bodies dance free,
The world dances by analogy.

   (2)
Everything half-fixed!
How pleasant to give up
Mechanical Perfection—
Unhook our watches
From superficial speed
Hammering the world of need.

   (3)
A quarrel of children and parents
Erupts outside the window,
Passes quickly like a thunderstorm.
Indifferent trees, water, birds,
Absorb the red veins of anger.

   (4)
Far off in the underbrush
Our dog is missing. As we search,

268

My wife calls across the field,
Addressing feminine perceptions:
"Keep going! She can hear you crunch along.
Animals have greater sensibilities."

(5)
So we crunch along in life
Searching for greater sensibilities.
Our dog returns panting in glee,
As this island against the sea
Isolates the tide of love
In losses, enormous victories.

The Muscle Memories
of Ancestral Houses

Like ancient musicians, old houses
                ripple muscle memories,
sing stories of time's tactile changes,
knowing plain houses breed plain loves.

Without women houses harden
                in rigid lines,
lose wonder of feminine curves
flowing in lucid moon-tides.

Lovers live forever in their houses,
                pause, embracing
the historical flow of enduring walls,
turning time's slow pace to racing.

Winter Peace

Through lashing winter of the soul—
        clouds like clawing animals in the sky,
        rigid ambitions of national power

separating the white world from
the attainment of just compassion—
we must turn from the frenzied pursuit of happiness
and find a winter peace.

As the Chinese use bamboo completely—
the pulp to make paper,
the stems are split and woven
or serve as baskets,
the leaves are used for
thatching and raincoats,
brews are made from the seeds,
leaves, sap, and roots
have medicinal application—
let us explore the forces of winter peace:
To gain from ice the shape of necessity,
from snow to take the blessing of cover
as we learn life's ambiguous layers,
always in the soul's blizzard weather
to feel hunger's Hydra-headed power
when poverty is exiled to dark privacy—

To find in winter peace how "light and shadow
never stand still," as painter Benjamin West said,
how menacing skies disclose freedom's real meaning:
liberation of our frozen creative forces

from false persuasion of weapons
masquerading romantically as Star Wars
or bureaucratically as Strategic Defense Initiative,
to find the celebration of communal needs
instead of the arrogant aggression
of commercial pride and wealth;

in winter peace to feel
through stagnant minds and bodies
that we do not belong merely
to the age of statistics and methods
grinding us into vanity numbers,
but to the flowing stream
of the world which is ours.

Madness

Madness, as Foucault defines it, is
Delirium, derived from lira, a furrow.
Moving out of the furrow, away from reason,
Is madness. With Pound locked in St. Elizabeth's,
Williams dreamt of his friend wearing the beast face
In Cocteau's film *Bauty and the Beast.*

If I find myself stuck in the furrow
How do I wear the hairy beast face?
At night I practice before the mirror.
See, beauty, are you coming to rescue me?
Beware of the electric landscape vibrating
In my mad eyes. I will kill to see.

Indian Dawn in Gallup

After rain the sweetest smells
Flow from cactus and mesquite,
Mountains glow with rising sun-gods.
At dawn the world seems wise
As a pale three-quarter moon
Calms the soaring sun into a
Lucid natural balance with earth.
Incredible rose and quicksilver light
Quicken the sky from shadow sources.

Stationary in his sun-worship,
A Navajo stares at the turquoise sky-dome,
Praising silently his sacred gods
That strike with their doubleness,
Twin spirits of the gods luring
The soul to its unified grace
When two ambiguous eyes,
Like sun and moon,
Shine in one dedicated face.

Pasadena Museum

Staring at old masters in the museum,
I hear a little girl say, "The pictures are
Lonely here," and her parents laugh.
They tell her Van Gogh's red-eyed portrait
Of a peasant is "worth a million dollars.
That's not loneliness, honey."
The little girl keeps on looking uneasily,
Skipping around security guards, peeking,
As if loneliness is an invisible leak in the museum.

Reading Creeley's Collected Poems

Pursuit is perfect
in the short hop,

leaves us gaping,
hopping to the voice

in jagged rhythm,
precision accents—

How to go, Jazz,
sweet syncopation—

create a mold,
eccentric American invention,

break out of it with
true black and blue tone.

Donkey at the Door

In Los Angeles, my doorbell wired
To play Gershwin's *Rhapsody in Blue,*

A small, thin Chicano appears
Leading a donkey
Decorated with brass bells.
"My donkey's got a beautiful sound.
You got any children you want
Photographed on my donkey?"

"Sorry, no children live here."

"That's bad fortune for me,"
He grins, plodding down the long street
With his donkey performing bell-music
Through wealthy suburbs
Buzzing shrill spasms
Of false and true burglar alarms.

The Maestro Pickpockets in New York

Trained in a superior pickpocket school
On a dummy with carefully stuffed pockets,
The maestro pickpockets come from South America.
They cultivate tender fishhook fingers,
Probing with grace into pants, purses.
In every pocket on the dummy, a hidden bell
Jangles abrupt failure of the course.
When all bells are silent praise, you graduate.

Every triumphant graduate earns a ticket
To the pushing battlefields of New York,
Pays his fare on the Madison Avenue bus
And the standing, crowded subway trains.
As he hooks his hand into bags and wallets,
A sudden smile suffuses his face as he
Trespasses beyond mercy into the realm
Where lions of passion claw at crooked praise.

In a Bar at Las Vegas, New Mexico

Hunching down over the polished wood,
I order a beer and remember a friend,
Walter Van Tilburg Clark, who loved bars:
    "A bar is where you discover people
    and dream their natural visions."
In Ireland, another friend instructed me:
    "An Irish pub is where real fantasies begin."
American bars are usually more furtive,
A place for sudden meetings, dangerous encounters,
Searching for a lost neighborhood community.
Still, as Walter liked to repeat happily,
Boilermaker clutched tightly in his hands,
    "A real bar exists only to breed natural vision."

Maybe that's why the man sitting next to me
Dreams aloud hunting myths of this Indian country,
"The deer is the image of the hunter's desire for grace."
I wait patiently with him, questioning the
Approach of natural visions. His woman arrives;
Deer-like she runs to him with graceful laughter,
Arms enclosing him in a world radiantly discoverable.

How Language Spells Us: A Sequence for Josephine Miles

    (1)
I see her sitting, talking, laughing,
    books piled on the lapboard
    over her body crippled by arthritis
(no one laughs harder amidst
    a puzzling pyramid of knowledge).
Holding my poem she points:
    Cut this, it wanders.
I end with an invisible poem
    and we laugh.
America is full of invisible poems, we say.
Invisible poems roll off the production line

disguised as sports cars, cigarette ads,
    artificial flowers, band-aids.
In the shimmer of an eyebrow
    poetry flickers invisible.
We teach, she says, by frantic gestures,
    teaching as invisible translation,
    poetry as translations of the invisible.

    (2)
How can you teach writing, Josephine?
You can knock someone's teeth out, she grins,
    why can't you knock out a poem?
Or rather knock at a poem, knock into it.
    Poetry is a decisive knock.
Knock and enter—the door opens
    into a room with students, teacher,
    tumbling, turning comically.
You must listen for a mysterious tone,
    cut out phoney symbols,
    cut down for starker things
    as knife cuts into wood
    in search of a carving—
Words on paper, she says, are never white,
and what you write must kindle with light.

    (3)
She writes in a sacred search for compression,
    hiding pain behind her grin,
and we learn about irony and compassion,
    how to balance anguish with laughter.
She writes a flow of wicked postcards:
    "What a curious abstractness you have."

    "From Idle Names
    you make the framing
    of a world with naming."

    "Just celebrated our birthday
    by getting through thousands of papers."

    "Here the grit of dogged resistance
    is being enlivened by a closing of all
    college campuses, in order, as Gov says,

to rebuild Camelot in Cambodia. Nothing
worse than the dull shame of past months."

"He ran sorority dinners and made pledges
sing Star Spangled Banner backward.
Something is wrong."

"I wish it could be true, but anyway
it was good."

"Welcome home from heaven!"
"The 'public' sat and laughed in the
most hearty way while friends sat
frozen-faced."

"Well, anyway, if you still feel cross
I owe you a sessson of listening."

    (4)
Dear Jo: Yesterday I heard a lecture here at Brown by the
sculptor, George Rickey, and he was talking really
about your poems:
    The sculpture of space
        to cut it, squeeze it
            with simple lines
pendulum balances,
        knife edges;
Surfaces are responsive to movement of air,
movements through a plane
        (we are conditioned to it).
Important to have the friction kept low,
        the poem should move,
            dance to a twelve cent fan
                (demonstration to applause!)
After several years of working with the line
        I began with the surfaces,
            then the depths;
        problems of mounting, timing,
        adjustments of posture at rest—
Sometimes I have to install shock absorbers;
        my reason in doing this
        is unexpected movement,
            images to catch the light.

276

The Sound Magician

After a talk by the composer, Darrell De Vore

Wearing a wool-knitted cap, Guatemalan shirt,
He says, "I consider myself a primitive composer
Because I live close to nature. I want Sound Magic,
A term I take from composer, Harry Partch, who said:
'Primitive man found sound magic in works around him.'
Listen to this part where a hummingbird landed
On my lap in Petaluma." On the difficult upright piano
He plays the fluttering bird landing on his lap.
Then he takes out a cymbal: "There's quite a little bit
Of magic in this cymbal from Tibet. In this piece I use
Four bowls of water, four cymbals, and four candles;
The candles are just to set up a magical sound mood
Like the way you use candles at your dinner table."

He strikes the cymbals gently over the water
And a tinkling, gentle sound flows softly out
Into the air-conditioned room as if a whisper
Reminds us that we often speak too loudly.
"These lights," he muses, "are good for
Stark reality, but not for spiritual searchings."
Everyone stares at the classroom's fluorescent lights.

"Now listen to this gourd I grew in my garden,
A new technique of mine—singing through gourds."
We listen to muffled, mysterious, syllabic wails
As he plays a live gourd to a dead tape,
The electronic world meeting in enigmatic clash
With vegetable sounds of the natural world.
"This is a children's buzzing bee, an
Outer Air instrument. Listen how it clears
Unnatural spirits out of the air . . ." A woman asks,
"Mr. De Vore, is there a future for Western music?"
In his silent, meditative smile, for a moment,
I see unnatural spirits flee from despairing lands
Over which the bomb hovers. "There's a great future,"
He answers finally with a spreading grin,
"If Western civilization is around to hear it."

The Hippie Shack under the Redwood Tree

(1) "Thou art an Eater of Words."
After the sixties, I painted my motto
Into a god damn mural of my life,
Covering the walls of my western shack,
High on dope, spattering paint
Under a mile-high redwood tree,
Painting the holy and profane
Devouring my life like junk food.

After twenty years of wandering,
I still keep working on that mural,
Revelation of motorcycle voyages,
My rage roaring into cities and bars,
Searching for green country peace—
And how I hung on past my time
Eaten by electric numbers, ghost names.

(2)
Living in my shack under this redwood tree
(It ignores me and wears my shack away),
I shrink into my mind, or sail up in fancy.
In my public time for sale, I painted
Tree portraits, how tall tree personalities
Marry the sun and settle down eventually,
But many loving women taught me
I got a moving solitary nature
Good only to penetrate lost spaces,
Sing against lonely walls like the wind.

(3)
My art is like my fucking words,
Burnt-out layers of dripping images,
So many deaths I can't even remember
Like carving strange ghost names
Into some massive highway cliff.

Today I tried to carve my name
Into this watching bastard redwood tree,
But a widowmaker branch broke off,
Nearly speared me to my shack,
As if telling me to take my long hair and beard

And paste 'em on my naked birth certificate;
Maybe then I'll know who I really am.

(4)
Nights, lying out in my sleeping bag,
I try to practice telescopic night eyes,
Staring high to see if the vanished sun
Leaves any star lessons in the sky.

Too many years I've tried to live on the run
As though the end is infinite and sacred,
A final peak of song, or marvelous disaster.

But night's infinities of time tell me
The endgame tangles back into the means,
And how in holy hell can you find
A quiet end when you force yourself
To move, change numbers and jobs,
The way terminal flames flicker out
Changing the enduring nature of fire?

(5)
A curious, if phoney, space philosopher,
I have seen the luring spectres of space
Arise beyond this ancient redwood tree,
And they are damnable and glorious.

I painted that swastika in my mural,
Lucid bones of ghost names telling how
History kills, and you live and die alone.

When you paint myths living ghostly in time,
This blessed, ignorant redwood sings and sings.

(6)
To croak at any moment, is that God's fate?
Hello is shock of voices on impersonal telephones.
Old is wilderness knowledge, age against vanishing youth.
Universe dances to master fire, wind, and space.

A is adjective of force, perception of redwood vision.
Romance is the frenzied dancer who never stops.
Time is how we die for something or nothing.

279

Ronald Reagan and the American Soul

"Nixon was to Reagan as Theodore Roosevelt had been to
Woodrow Wilson. Like Roosevelt, Nixon had a far better
understanding of the workings of international relations;
like Wilson, Reagan had a much surer grasp of the workings of
the American soul."
HENRY KISSINGER, *Diplomacy*

The American soul is like a fiery football.
You have to grasp it firmly, throw it out of the pocket
Like a meteor into distant end zones of glory.

Strong as steel, from those brilliant touchdowns, emerges
A bright, singleminded soul, radiant in winning
For the coach, resolute in developing a strong defense.

No more mushy liberalism, trapped in opposing views;
Heroic acts from films make the invisible soul visible.
See the American soul fly free, true eagle of Star Wars.

They Call Me "Football"

Look how they nudge me, call me Football
Because I'm attached to the President.
In the White House and the Pentagon,
They laugh at my sober black box shape,
My somber case with the nuclear codes.
A nickname works like a grating metal tag,
You get used finally to its tickling itch.
Watch out, Football, learn how to play . . .

Don't worry. I've weaved through crowd-frenzies
Into the white, sterile operating room
Where my President lay unconscious
Shot by a mad young assassin.
Suddenly, I, Football, was in charge,
Master of the soaring aerial game,
The long, pinpoint throw through space.

I know how to protect the country
And continue the old pursuit of happiness.

No one can throw the football
Farther, swifter than I can
To score the magical touchdown.

The New England Island Handyman

A handyman is made for unhandy people.
Call it a water job, learning how to live
On a small piece of land surrounded by surf.
Your mainland handyman's got a world of junk,
Dump-heaps, secondhand stores, Salvation Armies.
An island handyman waits for natural disasters,
Walks the beach every morning looking for wash-ups,
Keeps his eyes sharp in the village for handouts,
Knows how to fit broken things together for use.
You discover anything fits. It's just a matter
Of working it around, letting it sag a little
If necessary. Only thing my shack's so full of litter
My wife couldn't stand it. She cut out for the mainland.
"I want a little comfort," she yelled at me.

A man can take a lot of talk, but I couldn't stand
Her yelling comfort, as if that were my job in life.
She didn't ever understand what handyman means.
How can you make comfort out of old doors,
Windowframes, tires, buoys, electric wiring?
What you make is a temporary deal with time,
A door against wind and rain, a few rusty wires
For a patch of light. Not too strong a light
'Cause you can't look at yourself much in winter.
Your beard's too thick, face wrinkled against the cold.
Maybe, if you're lucky, you find an old stove.
You fix it up, sell it to people who like
Old things better. Or you find enough fancy driftwood
For a fence to keep deer off someone's vegetables.
That's no comfort. That's a real handyman showing
You his skill—"A patched thing is my signature."

Yeah, I take worn-out stuff and give it new life.
Why these mainland doctors with their transplants,

281

They only steal handyman's language.
I been transplanting dead things for years.
You wouldn't believe stuff I resurrect.
I squeeze an island glow out of every leftover.
To make odd ends fit, I use my bottle vision.
You know that burial joke about "pushing up daisies"?
When they find me, I'll be pushing up bottles.
Preacher'll read the roll-call: Cutty Sark,
Jim Beam, Spanish Burgundy, Old Forrester.
Good whiskey when I can get it, mostly rotgut.
Sonoma Red . . . Like a mouth full of puke.
I like the best that's available, but on islands
Unless you're a pirate, you can't choose much.
So-no-ma Re-e-e-ed . . . Look at that lightning!

Comes a storm, thunderclaps closing your ears,
You don't run for shelter to some mainland cage.
You sink yourself in like a ship in a bottle.
It's a way to know people, know a lot of bottles.
One good Scotch is a big, big property man
With a fifty room house, a stable full of horses,
And two hundred mistresses in all the bedrooms!
My old lady can come and yell comfort at me then.

Son-o-ma Red . . . What bullshit . . . A jug of cheap wine
Is nothing but an old man staring at broken
Furniture stacked in a dark room in a crumbling shack.
Cut-ty Sark . . . That's one of them old clipper ships,
White sails taut in the sun, racing clouds in the sky.
When Preacher reads the roll-call of bottles
And prays for my soul, don't you believe I'm gone.
An island handyman lives on in broken things.
All my bottles are gonna rise from the dump heap
And make a picture-window for some island house.
You hear me, Lady Comfort? My bottles are gonna smash
Into a new mirror for you to see my grinning island face!

The Dynamite Artist

I plant dynamite sticks in big, open fields
Free of trees and boulders that sit tight,

Run the fuse to safety down the hill . . .
Blow things up, blow them free!
It's not just a search for new forms.
I change the landscape by design
The way you change your personality.
I move earth, I don't destroy it.
You can't just shatter nature,
You have to release it where it's tight,
Blast it high, let it fall free.
That's the real meaning of chance—
Underlining power of natural force.
Let the dynamite of perception operate
And mountains will soar up, fall
In flying forms of glory and doom.
Some day I'm going to blast a real mountain,
Tumble it into a shrine like Mount Rushmore.
Jumbled, peaceful shreds of that mountain
Will transform the sky with my signature
So large they'll never be able to fence it.
If you have to charge admission afterwards
All you've got is a slick museum piece.

Postmodern Mixed Media

Meditating about the marvel of mixed media,
I turn on the television set, twist off the sound-buzz,
Tune in the radio, stereophonic FM station,
Stare at baseball as Brahm's Fourth Symphony blazes.
Mix media, scramble eggs, bacon, beans and toast
To discover romantic texture of American sport.
Baseball rhythm is pastoral, not pounding like Rock.
The pitcher's grace is confident-allegro,
Smoking the ball hard to exuberant strings.
The centerfielder dances floating to the wall
As strings climax in the green, soaring world.
Andante, Boomer booms one over the leftfield fence,
Homerun as high, circular rhythm of discovery!
Sudden, explosive hits, hammering chords, records broken
To the Scherzo's jagged sensuous scattering!
Look! Our hero is thrown out at home plate
To jolting music, frenzied strings, bleating woodwinds!

283

On the edge of jaunty triumph, players trot out
For the ninth as the brass begins mysterious summons . . .
Wait! The finale fails, game called by thunder and rain.
Tomorrow I'll try again this crazy world of mixed media
To find the right mixture curing my specialized life.

The Refugee Jewish Grocer
and the Vegetable Forest

When his wife sleeps with him
She dreams of sleeping with a porcupine.
He is all wild hair, a busted mattress
Of steel wool jutting from head and body.
Every day he stoops a little more,
Bending to push and lift the crates
Into an impossible symmetry of form
Announcing the capture of nature.
Yesterday he came with a broken arm,
Waving his cast high, stance of an
Old-fashioned actor in the semaphore school
Signalling historical knowledge of disaster,
Selling madly through his grinning, brown teeth.
To me, entering alone, he accuses
The store of being "a forest of vegetables."
"Stupid God," he smiles, hands and arms
Whirling like lost, dead branches,
"Stupid God has created
A forest of vegetables in cement!
You ever hear of a cement vegetable forest?
A forest is trees you get lost in!
Stupid God, what have I done
To get a cement forest in a grocery store?"

Looking at Old Tombstones
in a New England Graveyard

Descartes had an epitaph from Horace inscribed on his grave:
"Who has hidden himself well has lived well."

To hide yourself well.
In the grave. Beneath winter.
Is it the same as hiding in life?
To conquer death
Through metaphysial miracles
"I think therefore I am."
How long have I been thinking?
How long have you been
Hiding yourself well?
I drop a key into your well
And hear it echo eternally
In your hidden depths.
Are you living well?
Did you die well?
Your well sparkles
Blankly in the sun.

At Writer's End: For William Goyen

When writers begin early
Their obsession with words,
Young ears feel language
More romantic than life,
Apocalyptic paper revelations
Reflect body's rage for sex,
Mind grappling with injustice.

At writer's end, language shines as
Paradox of life-in-death—
Our daily resurrection: words that speak
How we lived and how we died.
For you, fantastic words shaped a
Difficult, loving life. Goodbye, friend.
When words are earned, they never end.

285

Love as a Cubist Landscape

Daily your life changes like a Cubist landscape,
    a constant naming of nature.
One morning I look down at you
    sparkling in the depths like a canyon
with light trembling on your pinnacles and spires.

The next morning I look up at your towering cliffs,
    your pink skin like Navajo sandstone;
suddenly I am staring at a mirage of sea
    with enigmatic, ceaseless murmurings.

A Cubist landscape begins to dominate
    and I embrace your three noses,
four cheeks, seven smiles, ten pairs of legs,
    the landscape of love
        as compulsive, changing space.

Love Song in Summer's Furnace Heat

Let the white blossoms blow,
My love is away on a journey
And summer's furnace heat rolls on.

Let the white blossoms blow.
Hell's breath lines the streets
With fumes of foul days.

Let the white blossoms blow
Telling when my love returns,
Love learns when it burns.

Masks in 1980 for Age 60

"We are inseparable from our fictions—our features.
We are condemned to inventing a mask for ourselves and
afterward to discover that the mask is our true face."
Octavio Paz, 1970

(1)

To create a fixed expression, immortal in time,
    my withering face set conclusively in magical wisdom,
power of identity shaped by fury of experience,
    stationary mask admitting youth flows in lyrical movement,
while age is perception of spirit against changing landscapes,
    a mask that is finally serious with a slight smile.

(2)

To be serious sixty! The smile broadens into a comic mask
    as if trying to fix itself on a telephone pole,
anonymous age anchoring speeding messages stubbornly,
    an old wooden mask sparking new technology,
Old Transformer! Take the gabble of loose language
    and anchor language in silence of comic dignity.

(3)

Stuck in technology, growing the American media mask,
    remembering I am child of lavish baroque film theatres,
accustomed to spectacular, lonely masks, grotesque seductions,
    more powerful ghosts than Hamlet ever saw,
I wear satellite masks, moon-mask, my red Mars face,
    white clouds spin around me with missile heads.

(4)

I put on my Gemini twin masks. Which is the weaker vessel?
    "So many men are what they do." Which mask is that?
Is doing loving? Or loving the mask of ritual ceremonies
    where we praise unity of opposing flesh,
bodies plunging through force of opposite destinies
    creating a universal vision of love's radiant embrace.

(5)

I am dreaming a mask that grows within me.
    This mask wants to reveal action in stomach and heart.
Do I feel depressed about things, am I pursuing happiness?
    A two-faced mask grows in my soul.

Sometimes at night I want to reach in with my hands
　　and tear out the mask as if sacrificing an animal.

(6)
The animal, love, is always the sacrificial offering.
　　My mask comes home, starts cleaning out the refrigerator
and drawers. I'm mad at her mask because she's painting
　　the kitchen wildly. Everything smells like lead.
The silence is like dark layers inside an oily bowl.
　　Masks imitate silent, mocking linguistic gestures.

(7)
Such marriages beckon divorce, how find another mask?
　　Perhaps I travel suddenly into an artificial landscape
with a supreme reality I have never seen before.
　　Immediately I sprout a face for the landscape
and it continues to grow like seeds or germs.
　　Transformed, I put on my black malignant mask.

(8)
Is this malignant mask my sense of death or love?
　　In duality, is there an American Liebestod?
At my age the masks of death burst around me,
　　even if malignant they shine with agony of wonder.
My dead friends wear earthmasks beyond Wagnerian ecstasy;
　　staring into natural beauty, they imagine immortality.

(9)
What good is a mask? To create a style.
　　Like Coyote I wish a mask for dawn celebrations.
A mask should glow with joy, masks are for dancing.
　　I will join ancestral festivals of masked dancers
where homage is always paid to flare of natural glory
　　and the mask enables deliverance to soar in the sun.

(10)
My mask dances beside her ancient feminine mask.
　　Aging, she becomes transparent with love.
In distant cities our children dance youthful masks.
　　I hardly recognize them in their difficult passages.
My wife is singing into the wind, her singing mask
　　vibrates sweeping golden leaves from fall trees.

288

(11)

I am moving into the sacrificial dance of old age.
    Master of rhythm, I dance the circle of fertile earth
back into childhood when I walked green fields to bless the sun.
    At night I lie dreaming infinite stars, my eyes glowing.
Tomorrow I will be invisible, my mask dancing
      in lucid magic of the communal world.

1990s

Toward the Millenium

Naked

(1)

Begin with naked
as water, beach, sand,
    elemental—
skin glowing naturally,
darkening flesh, sun,
    magical mirrors,
flesh and natural weather
uniting in fiery relaxation,
search of naked rhythms,
    naked burning.

(2)

Continue with naked
as bare, eternal question—
    naked truth, naked lie—
"Half-naked fakir,"
Churchill called Gandhi—
naked obsessions,
fantasies weaving
    a texture in time
    to curse or bless—
"Naked I shall sing
    stripped of all illusions."

(3)

I travel through space, naked country.
My watch points at naked time.
Machines force me into naked perspectives.
In heavy clothes I hear America
    searching through naked obsessions.

(4)

Walking this beach I see every grain of sand is naked.
Swinging through this snow storm every floating crystal
    shines different naked forms.
Languishing in this garden's color I grope for naked roots;

Feeling invisible wind lash through trees
     I am pierced by naked air.
Studying your naked body I see every tiny pore open
     like maps of invisible worlds.

          (5)
"Energy is the only life
and is from the body," wrote Blake.
     Naked Energy.

          (6)
Naked can be simple nothing
     or complex everything,
endless revelation of details,
natural precision making you laugh
     at slapstick scenes—
or sensuous exploration of space,
all that whiteness,
          blackness,
               brownness,
naked color, infinite shadows of light.

          (7)
At an exhibit of *Les Fauves,*
"Wild Beasts of Color,"
I see nudes colored red, green, purple.
Does it demand vision of Wild Beasts
to discover naked colors?

          (8)
Naked as restriction of color
     to emphasize color,
Naked as ritual source
     of Mayan "White Roads,"
white arrows of communication
     through dense jungle,
naked runners bringing to costumed priests
who cover every inch of their bodies,
     naked messages of invisible gods.

          (9)
Pause then for naked danger.
Naked as God.

Fall down on American evangelist knees,
pretend no longer in suburban churches.
America runs to seek God as naked force.
"Jesus was a Naked Hippie"
    reads a bumper sticker.

    (10)
Naked as Hard Rock, Acid Rock,
massive pounding sound above the pain level
inducing ancient trance rituals—Naked Sound.

    (11)
Aftr the invisible gods kill us
with earthquakes, disease, war,
we arise and continue "civilization,"
another spindrift word for naked search.

    (12)
Every sequence in poetry, art, film, life,
shows naked arm, eye, mouth,
now even sacred penis, sacred vagina,
    exposed, waiting for revelation;
      the daring sequence
    can never finish in perfection.
Every naked orgasm
    creates the next orgasm,
and the most naked dream
    is the dream of resurrection.

    (13)
At the Montreal Olympic Games
during the final ceremonies
as mass dancers whirled
in national costumes, flags,
a streaker streaked his nakedness
until arrested by police,
carried blanketed away from
the satirical, wavering television eye.
Comic nudity, Sir, is anti-social,
what if the Games once were naked?
International nudity is absurd.
Society is always formally clothed.

295

Costumes cover, creating formal equality.
Naked mystery must always be supreme.

(14)
I ask two women for their
instant reaction to *naked:*
One says, "Death!"
The other smiles, "Love."
Can this be what
Wagner means by "Love-Death"?

(15)
Goya's Naked and Clothed Majas
recline in seductive majesty,
        classic opposition:
naked to clothed as moon to sun;
as light strikes the senses
with legends of naked clothing
to make bright wearing of clothes
        glow with flesh-songs.

(16)
Why is nudity often pornography,
naked the source of art?
Naked is not merely the shining, stripped source,
but also fantasies hidden under surface reflections;
Naked is lavish expansion of elemental being,
night weather that strikes to cure or kill.

(17)
See the eternal traveler
displayed in his best clothes,
makeup by any anonymous mortician
who knows that the point of arrival is
the naked center this traveler will never reach.

(18)
Duchamp's "Nude Descending the Staircase" is
all geometrical staircase, Cubist abstraction.
True nakedness can never be abstract.
At the end of his life Duchamp spent twenty years
creating a secret assemblage he installed

296

at the Philadelphia Museum of Art:
   Etant Donnes:
   1) la chute d'eau
   2) le gaz d'eclairage
"Given: The Waterfall, the Illuminating Gas."
Entering a bare, empty institutional room
I see in the far wall only an old Spanish
splintery wooden barn door set in
a mortared arch made of red bricks.
Weathered silver grey, the door is studded with iron rivets,
a door without knob or handle that can never be opened.
A tourist in gold glasses walks past me and complains:
   "Who says an old naked door is art!"
She stalks out of the naked room in disgust.
I approach the door gingerly, perceive two small holes.
If I peer through these holes I may never recover.
   Old voyeur, go ahead, look . . .

   (19)
I am staring into the depth of obscenity. How mysterious, how trans-
forming it can be. Obscenity as landscape. Amidst a clutter of leaves and
twigs a nude woman opens her thighs to me. Face obscured by a mass of
blonde hair. Legs, feet cut off from sight to emphasize open thighs, wait-
ing vagina. A vacancy of pubic hair to underline the art of naked entrance.
But what enters? In her raised left hand she holds up a small gas lamp
that flickers its naked glow. In the distance beneath small, intensely white
clouds a miniature waterfall falls endlessly. What enters her through the
waterfall, the illuminating gas? "Eros c'est la vie," the Eros landscape,
light and water as the naked machines of flesh, and Peeping Tom with
his fantasies trapped by naked vision.

   (20)
"A painting that doesn't shock
isn't worth painting," says Duchamp.
Only naked mystery shocks
in an age when pornographic films
drain nudity of mystery.
Yet why should naked *Shock?*
(the censor blinks at his awesome fantasies)
Why can't naked peace transform?
   In the shock of vision
   rides transformation, redemption.
Naked vision teaches us compassion,

297

assent of tranquility,
naked as restless source of rest.

(21)
Naked is not alone, but together,
naked transforms with secret knowledge.
I come home to our nakedness.
I take off my clothes,
   my body rises from its roots,
      she takes off her clothes,
         her body as sea of my shore,
            floating source of birth,
               we open our naked vision
                  to the naked world.

Professional Lover

"Critics have accused me of coldness.
Yet I consider myself a professional lover."
ALEXIS WEISSENBERG

Is the professional lover
Cool whore or passionate savior?
Professional lovers are
"Almost always" in
Control of their nerves.
At the peak of tension,
Knowing how to relax,
Shines the performance wonder.

In the *Esultate* of Verdi's *Otello*,
The tenor soars in triumph
Over the raging storm,
Disaster if he misses.

If the fast, wide receiver
Drops one of his first
Two passes, he's a failure.

In bed, the two lovers
Stare at each other, dazed,

Beginning the terrifying
Struggle between passion and love.

To be a professional lover,
Sit on your nerves focusing passion,
Sensing your way to revelation.
A certain cool control of passion
Reveals the true professional lover.

Colleagues

Colleagues—I am haunted
By the communal Latin root,
Collega, one chosen
At the same time as another . . .
Suspicious, we may remain,
Yet we are attached one to another.
In institutional worlds, we condemn
Colleagues embittered by ambition,
But I would praise colleagues I've loved,
Who sought the true communal world
Without egos dancing over fallen coffins.
Speak the word, *colleagues,* as if it means
The tapestry of suffering woven with dancing
Figures or argument, knowledge suffused
Finally with communal joy's transforming power.

Song of Old Age in
the Driftwood Landscape

Flow, flow with the drift,
    sings the driftwood landscape,
    do not impose your thrift
    on the art of change.
        Flow, flow.

Flow, flow with the change,
    sings the driftwood landscape.
    Choice springs at you
    out of the deep black.
    You can never go back,
    sings the driftwood landscape.
        Flow, flow.

Flow, flow with the art of drifting,
    sings the driftwood landscape,
    flow clear with each
    possible new form you must see.
        Flow, flow.

Ghost Translations

How to sleep well. I can't do it.
Sleep is a voyage through dreams
Beyond time into a time of renewal—
        with ghost translations.

Invisible Wrappings

It is not enough
to go forward
or back to find
what there is to find.
Where I stand,
what wraps me
around and around
are the invisible wrappings
of the many times
I have lost my life.

Iona Brown Rehearsing
Vivaldi's *Four Seasons*

 Rehearsal: The Druidic Priestess presides:
Long black dress split up one leg,
Bare feet arching on the wooden stage,
Blond hair flowing over her shoulders,
Violin singing joys of seasonal change.

Dancing in ecstasy, her bare feet
Challenge the players to more
Passionate rhythms: "Feel the pace!
The supreme emotional charge soars
Only from the right musical pulse!"

So we rehearse again in jubilant places
The possibility of perfect performance,
The shattering ideal shining in triumph
Revealing the impossible goal of perfection.

The Kitsch Market of Desperation

Before the long ferry trip
To the islands of escape,
The last stop is the wharf with
The Kitsch Market of Desperation,
Where everything is sold
With wild, unruly affection:
Gaudy purple earrings droop
With hammered, ugly teardrops,
Hideously painted balloons,
Miserable dolls, repulsive doormats,
T-shirts worn by gargoyles—
All sold by friendly, imploring faces
Crying: "If I can't make something
Glow with magical structure,
I will show you the terror of futility
In my fridge magnets, rattlesnake eggs,
Ceramic owls with movie-star eyes;
Bitter inventions for the swamplands of dream!

301

The Test-Pilot Speaks
of Pushing the Envelope

"If you want to grow old as a pilot, you've got to
know when to push it, when to back off."
CHUCK YEAGER

Examining the envelope
I didn't want to live trapped,
Sealed tight in security's wasteland,
So I started to push the edges.

Chaos threatened as I soared
Into a vision of black holes.
If I wanted to grow old, back off!
I grounded myself back into security,
But the dream haunted—*pushing the envelope!*

Old, I'm resigned to the way I live,
But I'll never forget pushing the envelope,
The edges shining miracles or mirages!

The Horror and Joy of
American Saturated Life

American raw images,
guns, car crashes, drug busts, attack my television eyes
like volcanic lava.

My senses reel
with outlaw fever; the eyelid must never shut
on the violent eye.

I begin
to perceive the horror and joy of American
saturated life.

Creating a Beautiful Place

Build like a demon
Corridors of grace,
Final master of property.
Work with monstrous energy
Creating perfect decorative
Details in tantalizing forms.

At last, a beautiful home,
You've sacrificed your life to it—
Structure of rooms fluid
In the blessed mix
Of family and privacy.

At last, you expect
The rippling of beauty,
Dawns unveiling quiet days,
Evenings of dark peace
Settling with soothing cadence
On redwood shadows.

Yet as darkness descends,
Nothing is stationary.
Beauty, too, is something—
The invisibility of change—
That does not belong to you.

Old Aging

Body relaxes,
uncovers in sun.

What can it do now?
Change into death.

But mind hums inside
more experienced than youth.

Memories of time so exact
they hum with love's coupling;

with scent of remembered roses
and language of foreign places.

Nothing can kill memory
except memory itself

which washes out and in
on tides of resurrection.

The HIV Positive Dancer

To the Bill T. Jones/Arnie Zane Dance Company

Where does the final dance lead
If not to love and the expression of loss?
You gotta dance the opposites together
Because time is short and waiting
With luring love, bitter hating.

And if you're HIV Positive
You gotta dance with crazy passion
Because death dances with you
In a final frenzy; you're trying to freeze
Time because you've got the disease.

How does a man flirt with a man?
Live with him all of his life?
I got myself a white messenger of fire
Who broke the black-white boundary
And challenged me to be free.

He felt he was too short
And funny-looking to dance,
So we danced boldly together,
Funny bear and sleek panther
Breaking the animal and gender barrier.

When he thinned and disintegrated
Into full-blown AIDS and slowly died,

I put his ashes in a Hopi urn
And started a Survival Workshop
For cancer-ripped kids who need to hop.

Everyone is tormented by time
But that don't mean we have to go easy.
Even if a death-storm's finally out there
I aim to be resilient, not live in a trance,
Because every dance may be my last dance.

Turn AIDS from spectre to spook, choreograph
Every aching move into a positive high,
Because a dancer thrusts into time
Beyond abstraction the way a black cat in fun
Stretches to find a special place in the sun.

When I dance now, I dance bald,
Cut off my two hundred dreadlocks,
Naming each, sent them downtown
To a tapestry artist weaving hair
Into the timeless, invisible dancing air.

In the World of Sunsets

Our college room hovers on a high balcony
With a view of incredible sunsets.
Every evening our neighbor would
Perch out there, watching for the way
Light hung filtering through clouds,
Changing colors no painter could match.
He'd stare until campus buildings darkened.
A physics major, struggling to fit
Into a practical scientific future,
Music was what he really liked.

At night we'd hear him playing violin.
He saw the country narrowing down on music;
In every state, schools facing desperate budgets
Were dropping music classes to cut expenses,
Musical grace vanishing beneath computer hum.

A closed-up, pleasant person, he never talked
About himself, only computers and sunsets.

The only person he talked to was a girl.
Even though she lived a flight of stairs away,
They communicated mostly by E mail.
I wish I'd been able to talk to him about music,
Not computers; never seeing him express emotions,
I never gave much thought to his feelings
Until he finally jumped off into the sunset
Feeling a desire for eternity, word of thunder.

Last Urban Cowboy

Hat, topmost dangler of defiance,
Rooster bedecked with a red ribbon,
Broad brim drooping down like a mask
Hiding the thick-bearded gambler of misfortune
Who peers out belligerently from this hunk of cloth
                    passing for hat;

Next comes dirty, spinich-green sweater
Embroidered with flowing, liquid logo:
Feeling Is All. Tight, worn jeans
Features prominent outline of penis
Promising practical, natural service
                    never mind love;

Swagger of boots emphasizes urban cowboy,
Anti-historical memories of frontier myth,
Movie freedom still open to worship
Despite worn image of difficult survival,
Bravado dope-dealing in the frenzied city,
                    last message of lost time.

The Actor of Covert Action

"By their very nature covert actions are a lie."
OLIVER NORTH

When the secret order reads, *Go To Black*,
The President must divorce his shadow.

I hunker down in the designated city,
My face coiled in its new identity.

My solitude is tense, extreme like a monk
Trained to the lonely passion of his cell.

From my well-trained actions flow true lies
That my President requests and denies.

Worms must crawl underground in the Black
Before the soil breaks with fertility.

In the Culture of Cruelty

The endless pressure is from ignorance,
A buoyant surface life bland with affluence,
No visionary leaps into the enticing blue.
You hardly even notice a culture of cruelty.

Suburban values may build walls of isolation
When bored children ride off to the city
And malls may loom like an improbable blessing
As leisure extends a thorny, benevolent hand.

But foreign exiles crowd into the luring culture,
Seeking a peaceful refuge from lost memories;
They find strange offerings prick with enticing claws,
Frozen and packaged for easy wholesale consumption.

When night comes, the frozen culture is released.
Television's immune system switches on
Warding off the attack of virus dreams, where
Sparks of the visionary world flicker like fireflies.

307

The Creator of Corporation Culture

Aim your mind at the glamorous edge of things,
Not central compromise, or fat commercialism.
Why should any yearning person buy or sell
Unless glamour attracts, some bright, hunting mystery?
A great entertainment company looks everywhere,
Jumps over every fence, or you're just a silly specialist.

I began with the mortuary business, expanded to
Parking lots and rental cars. Start with cars and death,
You're deep into the restless flow of American life.
You learn to deal with the bony reality of shadow money.
You have to pay the Mafia, corrupt cops, union officials,
But position yourself above the dark color of business blood.

You're a top persuader, an artist of conviction for whom
Convincing people opens high the lucid ladder to power.
Your executive presence sets the right office tone.
You motivate your executives by giving them almost
Complete power, pay extravagant salaries fostering illusions.
You create an atmosphere of pleasure in the office,
Employ a jester to keep employees laughing, expensive pictures
On the walls, photographs of stars whom you control.

Every flash reveals you meeting with Number One personalities,
Their beauty and strength adorn your quiet, guiding presence.
Behold, I am there with every singing and dancing star,
With every television idol performing your dreams,
But you cannot see beneath the calm, influential masks I wear.

Modestly concealed, a hidden honesty is my strength,
But sometimes it gets in the way; you learn
To step ahead, leave it behind, continue on
Persuading one by one, the way I like to operate.

Board meetings, committees, are only acts of compromise.
The country is vast, lonely, eager for friendship,
Avid for love; when the barber comes to my office
Every morning to trim, blow, and style my hair,
It's the mask I live, the social mask of authority
Behind which I shape the new corporation culture.

A Woman Cutting
on the Killing Floor

I cut like an athlete, gesturing big,
Slashing, carving, keeping the rhythm
So we get some order on the killing floor.

At one end of the plant, cattle-jam!
Huge beasts waiting to be smashed on the head,
Hung up on hooks dangling from chains
That carry the carcasses past us workers
Who carve the meat into designated cuts.

Sometimes I cut a thousand times an hour,
Maybe a hundred thousand times a week.
Bloody nights, I cut more hours
Dreaming I'm in a secret army
Providing meat for hungry customers,
Our sharp knives and power saws
Deep in grease and blood reddening
The slippery floor, men and women
So tight together we hardly know
Which sex we are—the stench from
Open bladders and stomachs gags us,
And I want to slap a clothespin on my nose.

One day, working in the bacon slicer,
The damn blade jammed. I turned off the power,
Opened the bastard machine, started
Clearing out thick, sticky chunks of bacon
Like cleaning gunk out of your cellar—
No safety lock to keep the power off—
The company didn't bother installing one.
Another stupidass worker doesn't see me,
Thinks I'm done cleaning, off for a smoke,
Hits the switch to turn the power on . . .
The blade says hello, goodbye to my hand,
Shears off four of my fingers, leaving a stub.

My life was built around the packing house;
I made enough money to buy a home and lose
A lot of weight, begin looking for a man.

I wanted out of that stinking hole into
A feminine world to find who I am.
When my fingers flew off, I started hiding
In my home on the insurance money.

Sometimes I sit on the porch summer evenings
And think about cutting on the killing floor.
Maybe I should become a man, go back
Into the killing time . . . If I can't make it
On the floor, I'll go to bars after work,
Travel free like a man, signal customers:
"Look! My hand sacrificed for your meat!"
I've earned the right to walk in a man's world,
No more thinking about the killing floor,
How five fingers point to a woman's marriage.

Homeless in the Gourmet Ghetto

"The section of the city nicknamed "the Gourmet Ghetto" illustrates
the increasing national gap between the wealthy and the poor, where
gourmet restaurants exist with customers riding up in stretch limousines
while homeless panhandlers beg in the street outside."
NEWSPAPER COLUMNIST

Life of a Panhandler

You know panhandling's going good
If you find you're able to repeat.
All you need is a shelter bed
And a good place on the street,
Then you just repeat, repeat, repeat.

Miss a night at the shelter, you're out.
You take your plastic sheet and sleeping bag
Out of your grocery cart and hunker down
On a cold sidewalk where you dream of heat
And a room you can repeat, repeat, repeat.

Sometimes I collect some old cardboard
And walk way out to the railroad tracks
To sleep. I count too many lonely stars out there,
But it's better than being hurt on the street
So I let lonely repeat, repeat, repeat.

I can't blame cities for pushing us out,
But where do they expect us to go?
Their handouts are just band-aid and blindfold,
And the stink of a shelter and toilet seat
Is what we get to repeat, repeat, repeat.

I suppose America's homeless from the start.
The Indians were mostly wanderers;

People landing on Plymouth Rock
Were homeless looking for a place.
Maybe that's why we end up on the street
Where we just repeat, repeat, repeat.

Stork Lady Confronting
the Demon of Dignity

That lady, in white sailor hat,
Standing motionless on one leg
In the crosswalk, confronting
The slow jerk of smoking traffic,
Thinks she's a stork. Back
Straight as a flagpole, neck
Bird-alert, her one-legged stance
A defiant ultimatum to solitary space,
She sits waiting for a still pond
Mirroring a day of eternal quiet.
Homeless, brain wired to infinity,
Her stork confronts the demon of dignity.

Death of the Plastic Man

Wrapped in a coat
of garbage bags,
the "Plastic Man,"
his newspaper name,
never spoke
or panhandled;
he spent hours
collecting
paper scraps,
pushing them
through sewer grates
under the university
garage where he slept.
When he died

the garage was
covered with
graffiti praise,
soon painted over.

Singular Museum Woman

Singular museum lady,
who are you,
well-dressed,
perfect makeup,
neat pile of
wrapped possessions,
day after day
in front of the
anthropology museum,
talking to yourself
with invincible pride
in your special
museum site
like an unknown,
precious artifact,
subject to questions
without answers,
and without
museum entrance.

Street Corner Counterpoint
of Homeless Voices

1
Before dawn
every day
I think of how
to live
the after-life.

313

2
Homeless age is
not more difficult
than rebellious youth;
each contains
a disbelief
on the edge
of a cliff.

3
After I say
hello or goodbye,
nothing
begins again
and repeats.

4
At night
I think of how
the noise of things
turns into
the silence of nothing.

Sitting in a Bar in Election Time

"You can't not *almost* vote.
50% of the people don't vote anymore!"
A loud, defiant voice
batters us evening barhangers:
"*Almost* is only good for
suckers and for horseshoes!
Almost is the failure
of the whole damn country!"
I *almost* drop my beer.
In the climate of ethnic wars,
grating economic struggles,
desperate pursuit of goods,
the American word, *almost*,
struggles to repeat
old democratic victories,

as if *almost* will result
some impossible day in
Finders' keepers, made it,
Done deal! Almost!

Master of the Colloquial

In memoriam: William Stafford 1914–1993

If the necessity of
colloquial language
nags at the poet,
how does the
relevant word—
(Mr. Relevant, Bill!)—
pierce through the
channels of confusion
and create the right tone?
How can the commonplace
confront the sacred mystery?

A huge country
with gaping mouth
seeking to absorb
many languages
into one American tongue—
how can a floodtorn
midwestern corn field
speak the syllables of
an urban skyscraper?

To be "the slow guest
of the world," to connect
things with patient
gesture, to listen
and not just be, to find,
the infinitive is the world,
to listen is to see.

The Distance of AIDS

Across the Russian River
where I spend summer time
lives a man dying of AIDS.
He sits in his chair on the dock,
absorbing the sun with quiet intent.

From a distance I watch him,
unknown to the core,
and he watches me,
abstract figure on my high deck
against the river's flooding,

and we watch the river's
current like a waiting crime—
while two white and black
butterflies flash over the
wild grass, disappearing
clash in summer's dying time.

The Spirit of Mark Twain in 1993
Thinking about the Mississippi Flood

(1)
Sandbag it! Save the sinking town!
Married to rain, my river flows wildly
With chaotic joy as if to prove
Sensuous water the composition of the world.
"Mad world! Mad kings! Mad composition!"
Wrote Shakespeare in *King John*.
Mad floodwater seeps, ascends, inevitably,
Ambiguous destiny masking the eye of chaos.

(2)
"Nature's wretched excess!"
Cries a newspaper dramatist,
But an old scientist
Protests with hope:

316

"The river re-arranges itself,
The sediment moves, scours out,
Helping nature promote new growth.
Shore birds love fresh arrangements,
Fly in ecstasy seeking
A Smorgasbord of stranded fish
In this greatest of all river-floods!"

(3)
Every new flood I've seen they call the greatest,
But back in time the river flowed the same,
Dividing the country with enormous power,
An awful solitude, interrupted only
By huge barges, keelboats, broadhorns,
Carrying cargoes downriver to New Orleans;
Warped and poled back upriver by hand,
A tedious voyage by rough and hardy men,
Sometimes occupying nine months;
Every man fond of barbaric finery,
Prodigious braggarts, yet in the main
Honest, trustworthy, picturesquely magnanimous.

(4)
Thrust suddenly into the next layer of history
The way a painter layers paint on canvas,
The steamboat chugged downriver absorbing
The entire commerce. Keelboating died
A permanent death though river characters
Remained blazing with grotesque color
Like the Child of Calamity, a true Confidence Man
Claiming anyone who drank Mississippi water
Could grow tall corn in his stomach.
I can still hear his storyteller's voice:
"You gotta look in a graveyard for tall corngrowers.
In a Cincinnati graveyard, trees won't grow
Worth shucks, but in a St. Louis graveyard
They grow eight hundred feet high, all on
Account of the river water people drunk before
They laid up. Downriver drinkers grow like crazy!"

(5)
Beyond and above the river characters
Loomed the Pilots, the only Masters

317

Who could pierce the Mississippi chutes.
Every kid dreamed of becoming a Pilot.
The Pilot was like a great athlete
Able to relax, watch the current's force
Gather in slow motion, the smooth water-flow
Grow slowly in power as the big river
Stretches out its fingers; from that relaxed
Observation flows the true nature of kingship.
A Pilot was the only unfettered
Entirely independent person on earth.
At docks, along riverbanks, people
Gaped at him as if he were the
Novelty of a king without a keeper,
An absolute monarch in sober truth.
When a Pilot spoke, language became belief,
Words arrowing from his mouth like lightning,
A King of Nature speaking. When I became
A Pilot, I assumed command of myself,
No more Samuel Clemens, but Mark Twain.

          (6)
Water dazzles with each reflecting mirage.
Shapes of the surface
Deceive shapes of the bottom.

Clarity, the momentary surface illusion,
Fades slowly as the depths
Create their dark, visionary pressure.

The clarity we vainly seek in language is
Like a river, river-language diffusing in
Complexity as we speak, resent, and praise.

River-language measures our measured days.

          (7)
After the flood, the stinking aftermath of mud.
"Mississippi gumbo, the dark, oozy,
Slimy, greasy topsoil mixed with sand that's
Washed our way from Minnesota, Illinois, and Iowa,"
Says the Mayor of Hannibal, Missouri,
"First, you have to scrape it, and it's oozy
Below. But it dries and cracks, so you

Wash it down. You have to clean and keep
Washing it down."
                    Mud, the stench and stick of it,
Dark brother of shit, leaving a slime trail,
An open sewer of natural slop to which
Flock mosquitoes, flies, and rats.

In the end, people always come back,
Settlers always settle again.
The river attracts as it repels.
You can't fight the river by diverting it
With dams, levees, and dikes.
Where duck ponds used to be,
Ghost marshes surge into the farmer's fields.
Always the river takes back its lost places.

        (8)
After a flood, you can't define a river.
It keeps changing the way molten language
Sparks a new way of existence and never rests.
Riverbanks cave in and change constantly,
The river's snags always hunt new quarters;
Its mercurial sand bars never rest.
Out of solitude, the river always seeks renewal,
Floating into eternity with mythical mischief.

T.S. Eliot, born in St. Louis, called the river
"A great brown god." More than a god, it's the
Summoning of gods, the Indian heritage we grabbed
Only to find it living ghostly before our eyes.
As a Pilot, I learned to read the face of water
As one learns to read the tone of a newspaper.

I saw how the merciless sun hides,
The merciless rain falls in punishment,
The merciless waters rise calmly, slowly,
Ignoring human pinprick calls for pity;
We river kings learned the gods of merciless water.

No matter how deeply we studied twists and bends,
The old current flowed into strange channels,
Every summer saw a mocking, different shore.
That's the way life's movement goes, I figure,

Water or words, you can't contain a pounding heart
No more than you can contain a river like Old Miss.

Arguments in the Coffee House

(1)
If illusions
rarely illuminate,
mere facts
often
contaminate.

(2)
The horizon's
testing line is
only an early point
for visionary eyes.

(3)
On television
the fantasy of fame
based on personality
is a laughing,
eager, sudden wipeout.

(4)
Time refuses
to acknowledge you,
but loves to
condition you.

Listening in a Raging Rain

Raging, blocking,
quickening
my senses alert,

the rain cautions me
look, listen,
learn how the senses
unify all meaning:
Speak or I will be unspoken,
Read or I will be unread,
Write or I will have no signature.

Sanctuary of the Blue Heron

That great sentinel
the Blue Heron,
alert, watches me
from his river bank perch.

Through binoculars I admire
his silent beauty,
bird and man
dreaming space visions.

Space glows for me as galactic marvel
or furtive missile lust;
this graceful heron only regards space
as hunting sanctuary.

High redwood trees hide his roost
from which he sails
up river with caution
proudly hunting his hidden prey.

In endless pursuit like me, he wishes
infinite clarity;
sudden still points
in the day's constant violence—

when vision opens to sanctuary's wonder,
and we discover
sanctuary is how
we shape the solitude of others.

321

The Song that Floats

The gentle song may not triumph
Amidst the day's brutal news,
But those soft sounds float better
Than the driven, violent story.
Silence and softness
Frequently endure beyond
The loud, popular sound,
As at revealing midnight
A sweet, distant bell
Convinces lovers of eternity,
While the shock of sun
And the day's clocked time
Only end things,
And the night memory
of a small, singular bell
May be the lost music
That always continues,
The invisible, weightless sound
Of floating salvation.

The Fragrant White Blossoms of Spring

The fragrant white blossoms of spring
Tell a narrative that falls unfinished.
Floating with sudden color, the air
Radiates with quick, shining appearances
Washed away suddenly by wind and rain.

Disguised as eager observer, I watch
Sensing the resurrected narrative springs
Alive again from unseen roots,
Invisible clash of arterial plant threads.

Through changing time the narrative
Climbs into vines beyond our vision,
Telling us strongly that every story is
Always unfinished, fragmented,
Unless the natural veins of wonder
Transform the magic eyes of reality.

322

A Final Fantasy at 75

The Fantasies dissolve, splintered in time and space,
But they are not ended; they have no power of end.
Word-cracks in the Fantasies continue their drift
Forcing new-born dreamers to respond, dreamers
Searching for the supreme goal of flowering myth
In a troubled country without deep mystical vision,
Only an uneasy pragmatic stance filtering Fantasies.

Perhaps death, the final fantasy, is the real dreamer;
There we come to the heart of American Fantasy—
Death as tapdancing bogeyman in the country of youth,
Submitting slyly "pass away" as euphemism for endgame,
Yet we can begin joyfully only if we feel the end
And do not sentimentalize that subtle, approaching shadow
Radiating a final peace beyond the instant appetite quest.

If finally the Fantasies are fragments of being,
Grotesque sparks bursting from pressure of personalities,
They deny the darkness, flashing in dawnlight,
Flickering the need of compassionate vision
Frozen in a time of skeptical search, ironic gesture.
The Fantasies remain as bright, tattered flags of endeavor
Probing the slick surfaces of commercial conquest.

A final Fantasy should celebrate democracy's dream—
Without the Fantasies projected by curious imaginations,
Electric promise would vanish from the country's vision,
No proud names would accept invisible transformations,
No questions would be asked by courageous, eccentric doubters,
As the Fantasies continue their churning, laughing search
For enduring truth in a century of obscene wars.

Acknowledgments

Many of the poems in this sequence, some in different versions, appeared first in the following magazines and anthologies: *Poetry Now, The New Republic, Saturday Review, The Nation, Poetry* (Chicago), *Western Humanities Review, Counter/Measures, Blue Unicorn, Mill Mountain Review, Pembroke Magazine, The Humanist, The American Scholar, The Michigan Quarterly, Portfolio and Arts News Annual, The Southern Review, Antaeus, Hearse, Prairie Schooner, The Midwest Quarterly, New Letters, Jeopardy, Voyages, Three Rivers Poetry Journal, The Chowder Review, Choomia, Hellcoal Annual, Exile, Contact, The Reporter, Ramparts, Coastlines, The San Francisco Review, The Colorado Review, The Paris Review, The Arizona Quarterly, Whetstone, Yankee, The Yorkshire Post, Release: Hellcoal Press, The New Orleans Poetry Journal, Imagi, Interim, Poems and Pictures, The Sparrow, Galley Sail Review, Variegation, Poetry and Audience* (Leeds), *Approach, Sun, Metamorphosis, Diana's Bi-Monthly, Eight American Poets* edited by James Boyer May, *53 American Poets of Today* edited by Ruth Witt-Diamant and Rikutaro Fukuda, *Fifteen Modern American Poets* edited by George P. Elliott, *Poems from the Pacific Northwest Poetry Conference at Reed College* edited and written out by Lloyd J. Reynolds, *The New Modern Poetry* edited by M.L. Rosenthal, *A First Reader of Contemporary Poetry* edited by Patrick Gleeson, *Traveling America with Today's Poets* edited by David Kherdian, *The Treasury of American Poetry* edited by Nancy Sullivan, *Images, WIP, Poet Lore,* and the *Minnesota Review.*

"The Glorious Devil at the Dovecot" was the Phi Beta Kappa poem at Brown University in 1971.

I am grateful to the Ford Foundation, the Guggenheim Foundation, and to the American Academy of Arts and Letters for grants and literary awards that gave me free time to work on this sequence.

I would like to express my gratitude to Edwin Honig and M.L. Rosenthal for reading and commenting on this MSS; to Peter Davison for help with information about his father, Edward Davison, in the section, "The Saga of Walter Schoenstedt," and to Hugo Leckey, David Cloutier, and Bill Broder for their helpful comments about various stages of this sequence.

Several of these poems are dedicated to friends, colleagues, relatives and children: Josephine Miles, George P. Elliott, Edwin Honig, Alan Swallow, Barton St. Armand, Keith and Rosmarie Waldrop, Jeremy Ingalls, Wright Morris, Kay Boyle, Herbert Wilner, Rudolph Schevill, Margaret Schevill, Deborah Schevill, Susie Schevill Sinai and Robert Sinai, Paul and Nathalie Blum, Sherifa Zuhur, Bonnie and Jacques Fabert, George W. Taylor, Mark Linenthal, Catherine Bauer Wurster, T.J. and Mary Kent, Robert and Pilar Coover, John Hawkes, Ferol Egan, Harold Witt, Stanley Noyes, Richard Diebenkorn, Nathan Oliveira, Hyatt Waggoner, Rosalie Moore, Karl Shapiro, Robert Francis, Robert Peters, Michael Anania, Horst Höhne, Ray B. West, Jerome and Sylvia Rosen, and M.L. Rosenthal.

Index of Titles

A dream of high school, 53
A drip poem for Jackson Pollock, 125
A fame for Marilyn Monroe, 162
A fantasia for Harvard, 64
A final fantasy at 75, 323
A funeral for Hinky Dink, 29
A game against age, 255
A guilty father to his daughter, 113
All day driving across Kansas, 129
Alone, in Another Lost Room, 196
Always we walk through unknown people, xxi
American Gigantism: Gutzon Borglum at Mt. Rushmore, 32
An astonished listener hears the radio announcer bat out
   the long balls of verbs, nouns and adjectives, 124
AND: a funeral hymn for Ernest Hemingway, 169
Apple, the family love and asshole, 212
Arguments in the Coffee House, 320
A screamer discusses methods of screaming, 216
At Frank Lloyd Wright's Taliesin, Wisconsin, 195
A Tongan in a tree in Utah, 134
At Frost's farm in Derry, New Hampshire, 254
At Packer Lake, 196
At Plymouth Rock, 71
At the Mexican border, 133
At the White House, Washington, D.C. 1973, 207
At the Sin and Flesh pond, 231
At Whitman's house in Camden, 221
At writer's end: for William Goyen, 285
A woman cutting on the Killing Floor, 309
A woman staring through a telescope at Alcatraz, 157

Bashir was my name, 145
Berkeley wildfire, 3
Bird, 31
Blues from a thunderhead, 128

327

Bouncing vision of the commuter, 258
Boy watching a light-bulb death in a country town, 44
Buffalo man, 135

Chaotic changes, 184
City funeral, 117
Clown at crafts fair, 130
Colleagues, 299
Confessions of an American viewer of the large screen, 121
Confidential data on the loyalty investigation of Herbert Ashenfoot, 137
Co-pilot to God, 132
Creating a beautitul place, 303

Death of a cat, 115
Death of a teacher, 237
Death of my brother, 52
Death of the plastic man, 312
Dog-pack, 221
Donkey at the door, 272
Driving through Clyde, Ohio, 1985, 264
Dumb love, 215

Edmund Wilson in the 1920s, 10
Emily Dickinson in the asylum of poetry, 82

Fabulous debris, 244
First London press conference in the American campaign to bring the
    yo-yo to England, 120
Fantasies of Europe, 56
Flesh of the fawn, 114
Fra Elbertus or the Inspector General, 16
Frank Lloyd Wright desperately designing a chair, 47
Frontier photographer: Sumner W. Matteson, 46

Gambling in Las Vegas, 216
Ghost translations, 300
Girl covered with pigeons, 116
Graveyard aesthetics, 127
Green frog at Roadstead, Wisconsin, 195

Hank Snow, the evangelist, prays for the President, 28
Hats and ears for Charles Ives, 17
Hershey's chocolate kiss, 25

High school football coach, 55
Hog's elegy to the butchers, 244
Home life of the circus dancers, 14
Horatio Greenough writes of reason, 79
How language spells us: a sequence for Josephine Miles, 274
How to create music by William Billings, 71
Huck Finn at ninety, dying in a Chicago boarding house room, 154

If God does not see you, 220
Illumination: Martha Graham, 211
In a bar at Las Vegas, New Mexico, 274
Indian dawn in Gallup, 271
Indian summer, 36
In 1970 in Madrid, President Nixon presents General Franco with a red, white and blue golf bag, clubs, and twelve autographed balls, 206
In nervous motion: Charles Willson Peale, 80
In praise of a Diane Arbus photograph: "A Jewish Giant at home with his parents in the Bronx, 1970," 210
In the arena of ants: German prisoners of war, 92
In the blind years, 137
In the culture of cruelty, 307
In the Ginsberg supermarket, 182
In the peaceable kingdom a man sings of love, 73
In the theater of the absurd, 206
In the world of sunsets, 305
Invisible wrappings, 300
Iona Brown rehearsing Vivaldi's *Four Seasons,* 301
Island time of animal sensibilities, 268

James Gates Percival pleads for a unity of vision, 80
Jazz-drift, 12
Jazz-drift II, 31
Jazz-drift 1950s, 127
Jefferson dreaming about the Declaration of Independence, 73
Joyrider, 155

Kristallnacht, 189

Last words for Count No 'count, 170
Last urban cowboy, 306
Learning to read, 9
Life of a panhandler, 311
Limited service, 1942, 88

Listening in a Greenwich Village bar, Joe Gould scribbles notes for his
    "Oral History," 13
Listening in a raging rain, 320
Living in a boxcar in San Francisco, 223
Lookin' for gas at the youth guidance center, 260
Looking at old tombstones in a New England graveyard, 285
Looking at wealth in Newport, 220
Love as a cubist landscape, 286
Love, do not shun the dark gargoyle, 196
Love song in summer's furnace heat, 286

Madness, 271
Ma Rainey's boilin' rhythm, 21
Marriage in wartime, 91
Marsden Hartley: from Maine to Europe and back again, 10
Masks in 1980 for age 60, 287
Master of the colloquial, 315
Meditation on the new space language, 175
Mississippi sheriff at the Klan initiation, 180
Mr. Castle's Vacation Drive, 41
Mr. and Mrs. Herman Melville at home, isolated in their rooms, 78
Mr. Martin in his advertising ageney, 123
My father, the scholar, 49
My wife's dream in the midst of war, 97

Naked, 293
Neighbors in a coastal town, 43
New York subway rush hour, 122

Obsessive American sight, 239
Off the sea into the merchant's life or the search for quality, 35
Oklahoma farming song, 130
Old Aging, 303
Old Barry, the balloon seller, 147
Old salesman planning the fit of his death, 39
One-eye and the German prisoners of war in Colorado, 95
On the beach watched by a seagull, 245
On the burning of Mingus's bass, 175
On the photographs of torture in Vietnam, 203
Out of the city into Miracle Valley, 266

Parade at the livestock show, 40

Pasadena Museum, 272
Passion and divorce, 187
Perhaps a prayer, 63
Place, 190
Postmodern Mixed Media, 283
Professional lover, 298
Purchasing new bicentennial stamps, 1975, 209

Ralph Waldo Emerson receives a visit from the sane man and rejects
    him, 76
Reading Creeley's Collected Poems, 272
Remedial, 256
Report to the moving company, 230
Ronald Reagan and the American soul, 280

Sanctuary of the blue heron, 321
Shanghai stories, 98
Singing madly, 267
Singular museum woman, 313
Sitting in a bar in election time, 314
Sitting on the porch at dawn, 256
Song of Aeterna 27 over Los Angeles, 224
Song of misgiving—officers' candidate school, 91
Song of old age in the driftwood landscape, 299
Song of the little official of maybe, 209
Specialty barber in beast-heads, 164
Stork lady confronting the demon of dignity, 312
Street corner counterpoint of homeless voices, 313
Street corner signals, 261

The abstract expressionist searching for the angel track, 126
The actor of covert action, 307
The alcoholic's imaginary dinner, 131
The American dream on Superbowl Sunday, 263
The artist of escape: Houdini, 26
Theatre in Providence and Washington, 232
The big room, 48
The boilerman, 241
The broken-field runner through age, 213
The Buddhist car, 147
The city planner: Catherine Bauer Wurster, 178
The columnist listening to "you know" in the park, 226
The commuter in car tunnels, 211

The confidence man as soap opera salesman, 131
The connoisseur's history of the bathroom, 37
The corn palace in Mitchell, South Dakota, 33
The corporation lady in Bughouse Square, Chicago, 122
The country fair of childhood, 14
The creator of corporation culture, 308
The dance of Theodore Roethke, 182
The distance of AIDS, 316
The dream of fathers, 119
The duck watcher, 246
The dynamite artist, 282
The Elizabethan fool applies for a corporate executive position, 258
The executive and the giveaway list, 146
The exterminator, 36
The flower-washer in New York, 219
The forgotten wall, 242
The fragrant white blossoms of spring, 322
The fury of a midwestern thunderstorm, 129
The game-master explains the rules of the game for bombings, 204
The gold salvation of Oral Roberts in Tulsa, Oklahoma, 265
The glorious devil at the dovecot: Edgar Allan Poe and
    Sarah Helen Whitman, 83
The graffiti fingers of the theology student, 161
The great rock quarry of youth, 8
The hippie shack under the redwood tree, 278
The hiv positive dancer, 304
The horror and joy of American saturated life, 302
The images of execution, 156
The immigrant tailor stitches the singer's concert dress, 132
The island handyman, 281
The Japanese tea garden in San Francisco, 118
The jovial mortician, 212
The kitsch market of desperation, 301
The last New England transcendentalist, 239
The listener to rock above the pain level, 261
The maestro pickpockets in New York, 273
The mailman and *das ewig Weibliche*, 223
The mathematician thinking of ghost numbers, 222
The momentary glimpses of women through windows, 113
The money man, 208
The moon and the beautiful woman, 257
The motorcycle gang honors the newsboy's seventieth birthday, 215
The muscle memories of ancestral houses, 269

The New England island handyman, 281
The newsboy enters the bar, 135
The no-name woman in San Francisco, 214
The old woman and the cat, 45
Theory of American grotesque, 251
The painter studying trees without leaves, 125
The peaceable kingdom of Edward Hicks, 72
The quiet man of simplicity: Robert Francis, 218
The real parader, 259
The refugee and his library, 63
The refugee Jewish grocer and the vegetable forest, 284
The risk of improvising, 31
The saga of Walter Schoenstedt and the re-education of German
  prisoners of war, 101
The scientist surveys the protozoa, 171
The search and discovery of Rodin's nude, 257
The search for a subject, 262
The shape of the poem, 114
The shapes our searching arms, 194
The shining dust of scholarship, 6
The strange names of America, 262
The song that floats, 322
The sound magician, 277
The spirit of Mark Twain in 1993 thinking about the Mississippi
  flood, 316
The suicide runner, 228
The terrorist, 205
The test-pilot speaks of pushing the envelope, 302
The traveler of lavishness, 136
The t-shirt phenomenon in Minnesota on the Fourth of July, 217
The violence and glory of the American spirit, 164
The "Vulgarians," 181
The washing machine cycle, 118
The watch of the live oaks, 116
The white writing of Mark Tobey, 124
They call me "Football," 280
Trailer dweller in Miracle Valley, 34

Uncertain messages across the country, 263

Wallace Stevens at ease with Marble Cake, 25
Wander, 267
What are the most unusual things you find in garbage cans?, 172

Where we were, 197
White woman with the Navajos, 4
Whitman stock-taking, cataloguing, 77
Willa Cather in Red Cloud, Nebraska, 19
William Carlos Williams and T.S. Eliot dancing over London Bridge in
    the Arizona desert at Lake Havasu, 227
Windowshade Vision, 15
Winter peace, 269
Wrecking for the freeway, 138
Youth and the Abyss, 120

GARDENS OF MYSTIC SEAPORT
BOOK OF DAYS

THE MYSTIC SEAPORT MUSEUM®

JANUARY

1

2

3

4

5

6

7

Geranium
Buckingham House
Photo: Gene Myers

JANUARY

8

9

10

11

12

13

14

15

JANUARY

16

17

18

19

20

21

22

23

JANUARY

24

25

26

27

28

29

30

31

NOTES

January Gardening Tip:
Call the local Extension Service office to determine the last frost date
for your area; make up your seed-starting calendar and count back from the last
frost date to determine when each variety you plan to grow should be started.

FEBRUARY

1

2

3

4

5

6

7

Roses
Fence outside the G.W. Blunt White Library
Photo: Mary Anne Stets

FEBRUARY

8

9

10

11

12

13

14

FEBRUARY

15

16

17

18

19

20

21

FEBRUARY

22

23

24

25

26

27

28

29

NOTES

February Gardening Tips:
Call the local Extension Service office and order latest bulletin
on organic controls; inquire if gardening workshops are being offered.
Get lawnmower tuned up; clean up tools and equipment; have blades sharpened.

MARCH

1

2

3

4

5

6

7

Magnolia
Arch detail of the Thomas Greenman House
Photo: Mary Anne Stets

MARCH

8

9

10

11

12

13

14

15

MARCH

16

17

18

19

20

21

22

23

MARCH

24

25

26

27

28

29

30

31

NOTES

March Gardening Tips:
Most annual seeds need to be started this month; check your calendar.
Pull back mulch from bulb foliage starting to poke through
the ground; late frost will not hurt exposed foliage.

APRIL

1

2

3

4

5

6

7

Tulips
The North Boat Shed
Photo: Claire White-Peterson

APRIL

8

9

10

11

12

13

14

15

APRIL

16

17

18

19

20

21

22

23

APRIL

24

25

26

27

28

29

30

NOTES

April Gardening Tips:
Make lawn repairs this month as soon as soil is settled. Rake up winter debris
and apply slow release fertilizer. Fertilize shrubs, bulbs and perennial beds.
Apply oil for dormant scale before weather gets too warm.

MAY

1

2

3

4

5

6

7

'Ballerina' Roses
Wrought iron fence of the Bartram Building
Photo: Mary Anne Stets

MAY

8

9

10

11

12

13

14

15

MAY

16

17

18

19

20

21

22

23

MAY

24

25

26

27

28

29

30

31

NOTES

May Gardening Tips:
Divide perennials which need it now; share with a new
gardener in your neighborhood. Put stakes or chicken wire corsets in
for those perennials which will be flopping over by July.

JUNE

1

2

3

4

5

6

7

'General Jacqueminot' Roses
Trellis at Burrows House
Photo: Judy Beisler

JUNE

8

9

10

11

12

13

14

15

JUNE

16

17

18

19

20

21

22

23

JUNE

24

25

26

27

28

29

30

NOTES

June Gardening Tips:
Inspect for insect problems now, while they are most active. Hand picking is often
sufficient to control; aim for a least toxic approach. Get leaf mulch into flower beds before
plants get much larger; you will be rewarded in August for the effort made now.

JULY

1

2

3

4

5

6

7

Perennials and Annuals
River Garden with the New York Yacht Club in background
Photo: Judy Beisler

JULY

8

9

10

11

12

13

14

15

JULY

16

17

18

19

20

21

22

23

JULY

24

25

26

27

28

29

30

31

NOTES

July Gardening Tips:
Monitor rainfall now, and water deeply rather than frequently. Watering is best
done early in the morning before the sun is high. Side dress flower beds and vegetables
with fertilizer if needed, but not after this month. Replenish mulch where necessary.

AUGUST

1

2

3

4

5

6

7

Cone Flowers
Burrows House Garden
Photo: Judy Beisler

AUGUST

8

9

10

11

12

13

14

15

AUGUST

16

17

18

19

20

21

22

23

AUGUST

24

25

26

27

28

29

30

31

NOTES

August Gardening Tips:
Beat the heat; arise early to tend to garden chores. Enjoy the special
quality gardens have in the early hours. Deadhead annuals and perennials
regularly to keep them blooming. Stay ahead of weeds.

SEPTEMBER

1

2

3

4

5

6

7

Tiger Lillies
Burrows House Garden
Photo: Judy Beisler

SEPTEMBER

8

9

10

11

12

13

14

15

SEPTEMBER

16

17

18

19

20

21

22

23

SEPTEMBER

24

25

26

27

28

29

30

NOTES

September Gardening Tips:
Perennials can be divided this month. Continue watering if weather is dry.
Prune any shrubs which have bloomed since you pruned the spring-bloomers in June.
Prune and repot houseplants; bring them in the house before the weather starts to cool.

OCTOBER

1

2

3

4

5

6

7

'Angelique' Tulips
Memorial Garden
Photo: Katherine Cowles

OCTOBER

8

9

10

11

12

13

14

15

OCTOBER

16

17

18

19

20

21

22

23

OCTOBER

24

25

26

27

28

29

30

31

NOTES

October Gardening Tips:
Clean up garden as frost starts to take its toll; keep deadheading late
blooming plants. Install netting or wire to protect against winter foraging by deer.
Empty hoses and put them away. Bring garden notes up to date.

NOVEMBER

1

2

3

4

5

6

7

Ornamental Cabbages
Sailors' Reading Room
Photo: Judy Beisler

NOVEMBER

8

9

10

11

12

13

14

15

NOVEMBER

16

17

18

19

20

21

22

23

NOVEMBER

24

25

26

27

28

29

30

NOTES

November Gardening Tips:
Continue mowing lawn in areas mild enough to sustain growth.
Go through seed packets; store "keepers" in a plastic bag in the refrigerator.
Clean up garden tools and equipment. Paint and store outdoor furniture.

DECEMBER

1

2

3

4

5

6

7

Tulips and Daffodils
View overlooking Mystic village
Photo: Claire White-Peterson

DECEMBER

8

9

10

11

12

13

14

15

DECEMBER

16

17

18

19

20

21

22

23

DECEMBER

24

25

26

27

28

29

30

31

NOTES

December Gardening Tips:
Clean leaves out of gutters and give lawn a final raking. Add a layer of winter
mulch to perennials and roses. Prune evergreens judiciously for holiday decorations;
save extra branches to cover tender perennials after ground is frozen.